# BRITISH TANKS IN NORMANDY

Ludovic FORTIN

Translated from the French by Ludovic FORTIN and Alan McKAY

Profiles by Nicolas GOHIN
Drawings by Antoine POGGIOLI, Yann Erwin ROBERT.

*HISTOIRE & COLLECTIONS*

*To Adeline and Hazel*

# CONTENTS

(IWM 4836/A6)

# INTRODUCTION

In 2004, the ceremonies for the 60th Anniversary of the Normandy Landings were spoiled in France by political considerations about the French-American relationship, which had nothing to do with the event. These questions, which mainly interested the journalists, focused the attention of the Media on the American veterans, often keeping in the dark the role of the British and Canadian combatants.

Once again, the Invasion has been shown as an essentially American operation. But although the material and military participation of the USA in the liberation of France was fundamental, we should remember that between the 6 and 16 June 1944, the British put ashore in Normandy as many men as the Americans (279.000 and 278.000 respectively), and more vehicles (46.000 against 35.000)*, not even to mention the predominance of the Royal Navy at sea.

The American and Anglo-Canadian forces were thus balanced up to mid-July.

In order to redress this injustice, which is too often repeated, it was necessary to pay the British combatants the tribute they deserve for their major part in the battle of Normandy. Moreover, the study of the British armoured units in Normandy is particularly interesting, for the diversity of the equipment they used as well as for their constant confrontation with the "elite" Panzer-Divisionen.

This book is intended to provide the military history enthusiast, and the military modeller, with a general view of all the historical, technical, tactical and human information in order to understand the Normandy campaign as experienced on the British side, and especially within the armoured forces. The first part is dedicated to the history of each of the British armoured units during the summer of 1944, and to their participation in the limited operations or large-scale offensives. Precise and complete technical notices, supplemented with about thirty colour profiles, enable every type of tank or specialized armour used in Normandy to be identified. Finally, the last part deals with themes that were less often considered in previous historical works: the tactics and organization of the British armoured units, and the daily life of the tank crewmen.

The latter chapter is too often neglected, although it is in my opinion essential to gain a good impression of the real Normandy campaign. The memoirs of the veterans who published their story are the main sources of information, and the enthusiast is encouraged to read these books, several of which are mentioned in the bibliography.

*Ludovic FORTIN*

* *Figures from "Victory in the West" by L.F. Ellis.*

**NB :** *considering the wide scope of the topic, I have decided to limit my work to the tanks and specialized armour. It may seem strange that the armoured cars are excluded from this study, but they are absent for two main reasons: their equipment and even their way of functioning were different from those of the armoured regiments, and above all they were assigned to the Army corps and not to the armoured divisions in Normandy, and were sometimes so up to September Ÿ1944.*

# 7th ARMOURED DIVISION
## the Desert Rats

The white circle on red square background adopted in 1940 was adorned with the Desert Rats' black jerboa in 1941.

THE 7TH WAS THE SENIOR ARMOURED DIVISION COMMITTED IN NORMANDY: **regular mobile division in 1938, then armoured division in September 1939 in Egypt, it took part in every great battle in North Africa (Sidi-Barrani, Bardia, Tobruk, Gazala, Alam el Alfa, El Alamein, Tunisia), and in the early campaign in Italy (Sicily, Naples, Volturno River).**

Most of the armoured regiments sent to these fronts belonged, at one moment or another, to 7th Arm.Div., which was reduced to a single armoured brigade (22nd Arm.Brig.) in August 1942. When the forward party embarked from Italy to England in November 1943, the 22nd Arm.Brig. was composed of 1st and 5th RTR, and 4th County of London Yeomanry. In early January 1944, the last units joined the bulk of the division in Norfolk. Then began a short but intensive period of reorganization of all services, for young recruits had to be integrated into the ranks of veterans. Some units, such as 11th Hussars (Cherry Pickers) and their armoured cars, or 8th (King's Royal Irish) Hussars, left the division to be attached to 30th Corps. Officers were also transferred to other divisions to share their combat experience.

Old hands from North Africa and Italy as well as raw recruits had to familiarize themselves with new equipment and new tactics, since 7th Arm.Div. was reequipped with the new Cromwell tank, which was very different both from its forerunners like the Crusader, and from the Sherman. It was a reliable and fast tank, seemingly suitable for great armoured rides, but the old campaigners regretted their roomier Shermans. They all deplored the too thin armour, and the main armament restricted to a 75-mm gun at best. The issue in April and May of 36 Sherman Vc Fireflies, armed with the formidable 17 pounder gun, increased the anti-

tank ability and allowed to form Troops of three Cromwells and one Firefly each. The 22nd Arm.Brig. embarked on 4 June to Normandy, followed by the rest of the division.

### Landing and first combats

The 7th Arm.Div. began to land upon arrival on 7 June: preceded by forward parties, the armoured elements were put ashore in the Gold sector, and gathered to the north-east of just recently liberated Bayeux. 5th RTR were the first to see action on 8 June against the German 352.ID and the formidable 12.SSPz-Div. Hitlerjugend: A Squadron supported 56th Inf.Brig. for the mopping-up of the Sully and Port-en-Bessin pockets, whilst B Squadron was fighting with the 47th RMC Commandos. Soon after, 1st RTR intervened with 69th Inf.Brig. (50th Inf.Div.) In the evening of 7 June, the division had lost two tanks, an officer and five other ranks. From the beginning, the Desert and Italy veterans were surprised by the hedged-off and horizon-less bocage country, where the fighting was taking place.

On 10 June, 22nd Arm.Brig. and 56th Inf.Brig. attacked towards Tilly-sur-Seulles, south of Bayeux. 4th CLY (the *Sharpshooters*) made progress towards Juvigny while 5th RTR followed the parallel axis towards Verrières, with 1st RTR remaining in reserve. The infantry was reinforced by 1st Battalion Rifle Brigade (R.B), the divisional Motor Battalion. In the hamlet of Jerusalem, 4th CLY were probably the first in the division to destroy an enemy tank. The regiment took Bucéels, which was unfortunately regained by the Germans at night-Top.

**A column of 7th Arm.Div. vehicles at the Normandy beaches exit, on 7 June 1944: six Stuart Vs are preceded by a Crusader III AA Mk III, bearing the double name of "*The Princess*" and "*Skyraker*", the latter seeming more appropriate... Every tank is still fitted out with its "*deep wading equipment*". (RR)**

*Above.* **A Crusader III AA Mk III from 22nd Arm.Brig. HQ is going ashore from LCT n°3506. Division and brigade insignias as well as tactical number can be seen on the tank front. Strangely, it bears a nickname, "*Allahkeefik*", similar to the one painted on a 4th CLY Firefly Vc, which was destroyed at Villers-Bocage: "*Allakeefek*", probably the transcription of an Arabian expression.** *(IWM B5129)*

fall. 5th RTR led by A Squadron ran into violent opposition during the advance towards Verrières, they had to move back in order to leaguer with 2nd Battalion Essex Regiment (56th Inf.Brig.)

They lost five Cromwells and Stuarts, and even a Firefly, against the position that was defended by Panzer IVs and Panthers of Panzer-Regiment 130 of the Panzer-Lehr, a crack division recently arrived on the Invasion front.

Because the troop carrying vehicles had not landed in due course, the armoured regiments sorely lacked their accompanying infantry. On 11 June, these regiments successfully supported 2nd Essex and 2nd Gloucester, but 1st RTR and 131st Inf.Brig. (7th Arm.Div.) made only slight progress on the following day.

## Bloody nose at Villers-Bocage

Although they were attached to 30th Corps, 8th Hussars frequently fought alongside the 7th Arm.Div.: on 12 June, followed by 4th CLY, *Below.*

**A Firefly is getting ashore, coming out of the same LCT, whose number is inscribed on the tank mudguard. As Desert "*old hands*", the tank crews of 7th Arm.Div. already knew how to bring along all the equipment that was needed (barrels, jerrycans), and even a ladder is fastened to the tank side.**
*(IWM B5130)*

*Above.*
**According to the wartime caption, this column of Cromwells and Shermans has just come ashore at Arromanches on 7 June. These vehicles necessarily belong to 7th Arm.Div., which was the only Cromwell-equipped unit to land so early. The stowage box besides the machine-gunner's post bears the inscription "Chez Célibataire": the man has laid his cards on the table!** *(IWM B5251)*

*Right.*
**One of the Sharpshooters A Squadron's Fireflies that was knocked-out in Villers-Bocage on 13 June: this just-disembarked tank still retains most of its mudguards, which were usually quickly lost in combat. The number 4 on the turret stowage box could identify the vehicle or the Troop.** *(RR)*

*Next page, bottom.*
**A Stuart V from 7th Arm.Div. (the insignia of which can be seen on the left of the glacis plate) is speeding along a Norman road on 15 June. At this early stage of the campaign, the LCT number was still present on the left mudguard, as well as the shipping stencils on the right.** *(IWM B5608)*

1st Rifle Brigade and 5th RTR, they had to lead a breakthrough attempt towards Villers-Bocage, 15 miles to the south-west of Caen. The movement starting in the afternoon developed without difficulty up to Livry, where the Germans put up strong resistance. By-passing the village from the east was stopped by antitank guns, which knocked out the two leading tanks. The advance resumed on the next day, often slowed by French civilians offering drinks to their liberators. An Order Group at the rear was gathering most of the officers in command at the same time when A Squadron, 4th CLY and A Company, 1st Rifle Brigade cautiously led the column through Briquessard and Amaye-sur-Seulles, and entered Villers-Bocage, where they stopped. Without knowing it, they just by-passed the German positions. Suddenly, the last two tanks in the column were knocked out, and Tigers were reported in the vicinity.

The event is well known now: Obersturmbannführer Michael Wittmann, from schwere SS Panzer Abteilung 101, had been informed about the British coming. In a hurry, he climbed up on the first available Tiger, ordered the other crews to support him, and started to speed along the column, playing havoc as he went. Assaulted from the rear, the British, without most of their officers, were slow in reacting and Wittmann was able to destroy three Stuarts, eight Cromwells and two Fireflies on his first attack, in addition to many Carriers and half-tracks. The Cromwells scattered in the surrounding country, but one after the other was knocked-out or scuttled on order by their crews. The German tank was

shot at by a 6 pounder gun while returning, but the support of three other Tigers easily overcame British resistance.

Despite the presence of nine Tigers and the arrival of Panzer-Lehr troops, the situation was more balanced at 13.00, when fighting resumed. Reinforcements eventually caught up on the British side, with several antitank guns from 1/7 Queen's and infantry PIATs. Above all, the fighting now took place within the town centre, where the German tanks were in an awkward position. Four Panzer IVs and Tigers were quickly knocked-out. However, the Cromwell's 75-mm shots kept bouncing off the latter's armour, and only the Fireflies' 17 pounder gun succeeded in punching holes through their carapace, as did 6 pounder guns firing at the rear or running gear.

The British fought with gallantry, Lieutenant Cotton being awarded a Military Cross for his achievements. With his four Cromwell Troop, his own tank armed with a 95-mm howitzer ineffective against the Panzers, he played hide-and-seek with the enemy armour and managed to destroy a Panzer IV and a Tiger. With the arrival of enemy tanks and infantry reinforcements later in the day, 7th Arm.Div. was forced to fall back under cover of a thick smoke screen. About 15 destroyed or heavily damaged Panzer IVs and Tigers were left on the battle ground, a respectable score. But with the destruction of 20 Cromwells, 4 Fireflies, 3 Stuarts, 14 Bren Carriers and 14 half-tracks, and above all the loss of a hundred men killed,

wounded or missing (including 15 officers), the Desert Rats had got a bloody nose.

The surviving troops withdrew towards Amaye-sur-Seulles, and their forward positions were only held with artillery support. Several counterattacks by Panzer-Lehr and 2.Pz-Div. made an alignment of the front on the Americans positions necessary, on a Briquessard – Torteval line. The failure at Villers-Bocage was a heavy blow for the division: it made the veterans and recruits doubt, for they had had to move back despite initial gains and heavy human losses. Intervening just a week after the invasion, this event caused a crisis in the high command: Major General Erskine commanding 7th Arm.Div., and Lieutenant General Bucknall of 30th Corps were questioned about their incapacity to support the assault with infantry in sufficient numbers. Nevertheless, the material losses

*Above.* **From the cap badge of the soldier standing in the foreground, "Satan's Chariot" is a Cromwell from 1st or 5th RTR, 7th Arm.Div. This bogged-down tank, seen on 14 June, is going to be recovered by a bulldozer. Note the metal sheet extensions for the turret hatches, a necessary part of the Cromwell's "*Deep Wading Equipment*" since this tank was lower than a Sherman or a Churchill.** *(IWM B5580)*

inflicted on the Germans were numerous and much more difficult to make good than the British ones. But the Allies were not yet accustomed to the balance of power and the fighting conditions that they were to be confronted with during two months in the Norman bocage…

After the severe punishment at Villers-Bocage, 7th Arm.Div. was limited to a defensive role until 30 June. 22nd Arm.Brig. was in reserve at Ste-Honorine-de-Ducy, and activity was restricted to patrols, mainly

*Above.* **After a limited commitment during Goodwood, 7th Arm.Div. was again in action for Operation Swing: 1st or 5th RTR Cromwells (see tank commander's cap badge) are passing by a column from 3rd MG Company, Royal Northumberland Fusiliers, as indicated by the tactical sign (64 on a black square) seen on the Lloyd Carrier in the background.** *(Tank Museum 4799/D2).*

by infantry. Some harsh combats did take place, like that on 17 June at Briquessard, where C Squadron, 8th Hussars lost five tanks. But the crews especially got used to the stonks from mortars and Nebelwerfers, depriving them of any long-lasting rest or relaxation. On 26 June, 4th CLY, severely weakened by the losses endured at Villers-Bocage, learned that they were to be amalgamated with their parent regiment, 3rd CLY, within 4th Arm.Brig., to be replaced by the fresh but untried 5th Inniskilling Dragoon Guards. The division left its positions on 30 June, and was at rest near the hamlet of Jerusalem, between Bayeux and Tilly-sur-Seulles, until 17 July. In a three week period, 7th Arm.Div. had lost a total of 1149 men (mainly infantrymen), and the refitting of the unit went with many changes of officers commanding infantry battalions.

## Operation *Goodwood*

In order to push towards Falaise, Montgomery gathered the three "standard" armoured divisions (11th, Guards and 7th) within 8th Corps for *Goodwood*: they had to follow the same attack axis in succession, and break through the line of villages that had been fortified on Rommel's orders. The 7th Arm.Div., last in the column, gathered on 17 July with the other divisions in the narrow start area north-east of Caen. On the next day, the attack went off rather badly: traffic jams delayed forming-up, and in spite of 11th Arm.Div.'s initial successes taking advantage of the effective preliminary air bombardment, the offensive came to a standstill and Guards Arm.Div. found it difficult to come back out. The *Desert Rats* could hardly make any progress on the attack axis, congested with all the other units' vehicles. But Brigadier Hinde commanding 22nd Arm.Brig. was also questioned for having not pushed his troops far enough. The sight of dozens of destroyed tanks from other divisions did not encourage one to make a mad charge... Furthermore, the units became intricate in the minefields laid by their fellow countrymen a few weeks ago, when the beachhead was settling down.

The division entered the fray at 17.00, and only 5th RTR were committed near Cuverville, where they knocked out two Panzer IVs at the cost of four tanks and twelve men. The attack resumed on the morning of the 19th with the clearing of Grentheville. Because of huge losses in other divisions (nearly 150 tanks), 7th Arm.Div. now took the leading

role. 5th RTR had to capture Soliers, then 1st RTR had to take Four, these regiments heading next towards the Bourguébus ridge. These objectives were reached on 20 July with panache, 5th RTR claiming four destroyed or captured Panthers, and three brewed-up Tigers: the latter were probably two tanks belonging to sPzAbt. 503 which were knocked-out by a single Firefly, and another one that sPzAbt. (SS) 101 registered as lost. 5th RTR took the lead anew for the offensive towards Bourguébus, but heavy rains starting in the afternoon stopped the attack, and Operation *Goodwood* was interrupted. The 7th Arm.Div. was set back for five days to reorganize, very close to the front line: the area was pounded by the German artillery, which compensated for the small number of shells with deadly precise fire. The German counterstrokes launched during the following days were driven off by the intervention of the artillery alone.

## Operation *Spring*

The 7th Arm.Div. was transferred to 2nd Canadian Corps for the next operation, and was in support of 2nd and 3rd Canadian Inf.Div. east of River Orne, with Verrières and Tilly-la-Campagne as objectives. On the evening of 24 July, the usual air and ground-bombardments preceded the attack, which started at dawn on the 25th: 4th CLY supported 2nd Canadian Inf.Div. towards May-sur-Orne and Verrières, and immediately came up against vigorous enemy counterattacks. With the help of 1st RTR, Verrières was reached and barely held, under the threat of Panzers, three of which were knocked-out by 4th CLY Fireflies. The scene was similar in Tilly, where 5th RTR with 3rd Canadian Inf.Div. only seized the village at nightfall, in spite of support from 2nd Tactical Air Force Typhoons. The opponent, 1. SS Pz-Div. "*Leibstandarte*", was formidable, and was soon reinforced with elements from other Panzer divisions. Operation *Spring* could not succeed any more, but had

8

# REGIMENTS ACCORDING TO THE ORDER OF PRECEDENCE

## 5th Royal Inniskilling Dragoon Guards

- **Origins:** Regiment raised by the Earl of Shrewsbury in 1685. Committed in Flanders in 1694-95, in Holland in 1702, fought at Ramillies and Lille in 1706. Known as *"2nd Irish Horse"* in 1746, then *"5th Dragoon Guards"* in 1788, it was notably committed against the rebellion in Ireland in 1796, and became "5th (The Princess Charlotte of Wales's) Dragoon Guards" in 1804. After having fought the French at Salamanca in 1812, returned to England and Ireland. Committed in the Crimea at Balaclava in 1854, took part in 1884 in the Gordon Relief Expedition. A Squadron fought in South Africa in 1899, the others remaining in India. In 1914-18, the regiment was assigned to 1st Cavalry Brigade, which was transferred to Egypt and then to Palestine. Became "5th Inniskilling Dragoon Guards" in 1927, after amalgam with "6th Dragoons", then "5th Royal Inniskilling Dragoon Guards" in 1935, converted into light mechanised regiment in 1937.

- **1939-44:** Sent to France in 1939 within 2nd Arm. Reconnaissance Brigade, and evacuated to England via Dunkirk in 1940 after having acted as armoured rearguard. Part of 28th Arm.Brig. in England from June 1940 to July 1944, replacing then 4th County of London Yeomanry within 22nd Arm.Brig. (7th Arm.Div.)
Nicknamed *"The Skins"*.

## 8th King's Royal Irish Hussars

– **Origins:** Regiment raised in Ireland by Colonel Henry Cunningham in 1693, under the name of "Conyngham's Regiment of Irish Dragoons". Fought against the Spaniards at Almenara in 1710, then returned to Ireland. Disbanded in 1714, but restored in 1715, sent to Ireland. Became "8th Regiment of Dragoons" in 1751, then "8th (The King's Royal Irish) Regiment of (Light) Dragoons" in 1777. In action in Flanders in 1794, was posted to the Cape of Good Hope in 1796 then to Egypt (1801) and to India (1803). Served in the Crimea in 1854, with the Light Brigade at Balaclava, then fought the Mutiny in India in 1857, and became "8th (King's Royal Irish) Hussars" in 1861. Departure in 1914 for France with 1st Indian Cavalry Division. In India then in Iraq in 1919-20, in Egypt in 1921, then became "8th King's Royal Irish Hussars", and was part of the occupation army in Germany in 1926. Afterwards, served in Egypt and Palestine in 1934-36.

- **1939-44:** Became armoured reconnaissance regiment in 1939, from September in North Africa with 7th Arm.Brig., until April 1941 (Sidi Barrani and Sidi Rezegh). Served with 1st Arm.Brig. from May to July 1941, and with 4th Arm.Brig. from August 1941 to May 1942 (Tobruk, Gazala, Mersa Matruh). This unit was restored as 4th Light Armoured Brigade in July 1942, 8th Hussars serving there associated with 4th Hussars from July to November 1942, notably at El Alamein. Under direct command of GHQ, Middle East Forces from December 1942 to July 1943, the regiment was committed in North Africa and in Italy, and then incorporated into 7th Arm.Div. from December 1943 to August 1945, for the campaign in North-West Europe, 8th Hussars remaining one of the three armoured regiments.
Sometimes nicknamed *"The Twenty Five"*.

## 4th County of London Yeomanry

- **Origins:** In common with "3rd County of London Yeomanry". Regiment formed in 1900 for the war in South Africa, by the Earl of Dunraven. The "4th County of London Yeomanry" was recruited among overseas residents in the United Kingdom. Became "The King's Colonial Imperial Yeomanry" in 1901, then "King Edward's Horses".

- **1939-44:** Absorbed by the 3rd Regiment during First Word War, reconstituted in September 1939 as duplicate of the latter, served within 22nd Arm.Brig. (1st Arm.Div.) In Egypt and South Africa in 1941 (with 7th Arm. Div. from January 1942), then fought in Sicily and Italy in 1943. 4th CLY landed in Normandy in June 1944, but in July, they were amalgamated with their parent regiment, 3rd County of London Yeomanry, because of heavy casualties.
Nicknamed *"The Sharpshooters"*.

## 1st Battalion, Royal Tank Regiment

- **Origins:** In common with the whole Royal Tank Regiment. Battalion derived from the "Armoured Car Section, Machine Gun Corps" (more exactly from A Company, Heavy Section) created in 1916, then from the Tank Corps of 1917. The latter became "Royal Tank Corps" in 1923, then "Royal Tank Regiment RAC" in 1939. 1st Battalion, Royal Tank Regiment was part of Regular Army.

- **1939-44:** Fought with 4th Arm.Brig. from September 1939 to March 1940 (and again in June 1942) in North Africa. From April 1940 to April 1941 within 7th Arm.Brig. (Bir Enba, Bardia), then from May 1941 to January 1942 with 3rd Arm.Brig., absorbed by 32nd Tank Brigade in September 1941 (this unit was formed for the defence of Tobruk). In January 1942 with 1st Arm.Brig. (El Alamein), from October 1942 incorporated until the end of the war into 22nd Arm.Brig. (7th Arm.Div.) for the last combats in North Africa (Tunisia) and the campaign in North-West Europe.
Members of the Royal Tank Regiment were nicknamed *"Sprockets"* by the Cavalry.

## 5th Battalion Royal Tank Regiment

- **Origins:** In common with the whole Royal Tank Regiment, see 1st RTR. This battalion (the battalion being the size of a regiment within the RTR) was derived from E Company, Heavy section of the Machine Gun Corps in 1916.

- **1939-44:** Established in England in September 1939 with 3rd Arm.Brig.; fought in France in 1940, and after coming back then left for North Africa where they remained until February 1941. From May 1941 to June 1942, incorporated into 4th Arm.Brig., still in Libya (Sidi Rezeigh, Bir-Hakeim, and Alam El Halfa). From October 1942 onwards, fought in North Africa (El Alamein, Tunisia), in Sicily and in Italy with 22nd Arm.Brig. (7th Arm.Div.). Served with the Desert Rats for the whole campaign in North-West Europe.

---

allowed important forces to be distracted from another spot of the front line: in the Cotentin, Operation Cobra had been launched by the Americans, and had broken through the German positions, opening the gates of Brittany.

From 26 to 28 July, the division limited its activities to defensive missions, even if 8th Hussars advanced with 6th Queen's towards Rocquancourt. 5th RTR supported 4th Canadian Inf.Brig. in Verrières, 4th CLY moved up along the Falaise road for their last mission, and 1st RTR remained in reserve. On 28 July, 7th Arm.Div. came under the control of 30th Corps, and 4th CLY sadly departed, their place being taken by 5th Inniskilling Dragoon Guards (*the Skins*). The latter unit had not been committed since 1940, and was dispatched from England-based 9th Arm.Div. The *Skins* benefited from a full complement in men and tanks, an advantage that no other unit in the division could enjoy.

## Operation *Bluecoat*

To support the Americans dashing southwards, Montgomery decided to launch a new operation from Caumont towards Le Bény-Bocage, Vire and Condé-sur-Noireau. For *Bluecoat*, 8th and 30th Corps were involved with support from 12th Corps on the eastern flank. 30th Corps, composed of 43rd Inf., 50th Inf. and 7th Arm. Divisions, was to carry out an encircling movement from the east via Villers-Bocage, towards Aunay-sur-Odon and then Mont Pinçon. On 30 July, 43rd Inf.Div. led a preliminary assault on Cahagnes, while 7th Arm.Div. was concentrating 5 miles north-east of Caumont. On the following day the real offensive began in a very closed-in bocage country, where it met a multitude of German but also American and British minefields, the location of which were not marked on the maps. Under grey and misty skies, aerial support was restricted, and 50th Inf.Div. made only slight progress towards Orbois. This day was also marked by the *Cherry Pickers*, the 11th Hussars Regiment that had been attached to 30th Corps so far, returning with the *Desert Rats*.

The action began on 1 August for 7th Arm.Div., in still foggy weather, and among the inevitable traffic jams caused by the narrowness of the start-line. The Queen's Brigade took the lead with support from 1st RTR and a 8th Hussars Squadron, but stiff opposition from German 326.ID made it necessary to reinforce these troops with the *Skins*, for a slight progression towards Aunay. On the next day, 8th Hussars and the Inniskilling Dragoons resumed the attack, but still slowly and with negligible progress, even if 1st RTR made a better advance on their side towards Sauques, at the cost of six tanks. On 3 August,

*Right.*
**This Sexton of 3rd Rgt, Royal Horse Artillery bears the tactical insignia (76 on a red and blue square) coupled with the 7th Arm.Div. jerboa, as frequently seen within the latter unit. Two road signs in the background show that the bridge was built by the 51st Highland Division.**
*(Tank Museum 4796/C6)*

*Bottom.*
**This Firefly Ic Hybrid passing by the crossroad at Canteloup on 31 July, is heading for Aunay-sur-Odon and probably belongs to 7th Arm.Div.,**
**for both towns were within the unit boundaries at that time. A large stowage box, normally fitted to the rear of Fireflies Vc, has been added at the front. Once again, the RTR cap badge can be seen on the tank commander's beret.**
*(IWM B8370)*

the Queen's Brigade made a successful night-attack between Sauques and Aunay. At dawn, A Squadron, 5th RTR covered a distance of 1 1/2 miles only before the fog lifted, enabling the German defence to stop further advance. B Squadron tried in vain to take over from 5th RTR, but lost four tanks for two Panzers destroyed.

A fierce counterattack was barely stopped at 14.00, but it resumed moments later and cut off two 5th RTR Squadrons together with the Norfolk Yeomanry antitank guns. Only the intervening 8th Hussars made it possible to stem the enemy advance, and the encircled 5th RTR had to break through at night, losing three tanks in the process, for a total of seven knocked-out tanks since the morning. The offensive phase of *Bluecoat* was coming to an end, and 7th Arm.Div. was stopped 5 miles from its objective, Aunay-sur-Odon.

## Montgomery's purge

The third failure of the *Desert Rats* made Montgomery angry, and he started to look for who was responsible at every level of the hierarchy: *Bucknall* (30th Corps) and *Erskine* (7th Arm.Div.), already accused at the time of *Goodwood*, were transferred and replaced on 4 August by Lieutenant-General Horrocks and Major-General Verney respectively. But other senior officers were also concerned: Brigadiers Hinde (22nd Arm.Brig.) and Mews (Royal Artillery) had to give up their jobs in favour of Mackeson and Lyon-Smith. A hundred men and officers among the veterans of North Africa and Italy, who had the longest fighting experience, were also posted to other units or sent back to England. Some were satisfied to leave the front, but most were not very pleased with being scape-

Above.

**Infantry from 7th Arm.Div. is advancing towards Caumont-l'Eventé in early August, with support from a Cromwell Mk IV of the same unit (see the insignia on the left of the hull). The tank serial number is very interesting for it is followed by a capital W, sometimes seen on Churchills: this could indicate that it is a rare chassis with welded-hull.** *(Tank Museum 3579/D4)*

*Below.*
**On 1 August, a Firefly Vc with its turret in 6 o'clock position is travelling in a dust cloud along the road between Villers-Bocage and Caumont-l'Eventé. The long 17 pounder barrel is camouflaged with hessian tape. The triangle of an A Squadron can be seen on the rear hull, maybe yellow for the Second Regiment (5th RTR)?** *(IWM B8384)*

goats for the errors of the high command. Major-General G.L. Verney, who was commanding 6th Guards Tk.Brig. until then, gave a portrait of the division without any concessions on his arrival: 1st and 5th RTR were exhausted; infantry units, Queen's Brigade as much as Motor Battalion, were sparse and rather unmotivated; only the newly-arrived *Skins* seemed ready to fight. It must be said that during the first week which Verney was in command, there were 120 desertions within 7th Arm.Div., a very rare phenomenon in the British Army, and revealing a lot about the low morale of the troops.

## The battle south-east of Caen

With the confirmation of the encirclement of the German forces, 7th Arm.Div. was now in control of the pocket's north-eastern flank, and carried out several limited actions on 4 August. 11th Hussars, in recce towards Vire and moving up with Flails from the Westminster Dragoons, reached the suburbs of the city. For their part, the Skins were splendidly leading 22nd Arm.Brig. on 5 August, reaching then going beyond Bonnemaison by the evening. 1st RTR took part in this beautiful 14 miles advance, which stopped just in front of the German defences set up on Mont Pinçon, overlooking the valley. In Villers-Bocage, so many ruins filled the streets that 11th Hussars could not pass through the city and had to by-pass it to reach Aunay, where the destruction was even greater. Verney decided to by-pass the village from the east, towards La Vallée, to reach Mont Pinçon. 6 August was a busy day around La Vallée: from north and west, 6th and 7th Queen's attacked through the woods towards Mont Pinçon, losing many Carriers. But 3rd Royal Horse Artillery found excellent observation posts from which to deliver effective counter-battery stonks. In Bonnemaison, in spite of 1st RTR's help, the Cherry Pickers were unable to find a passable road.

In the night of 6 to 7 August, 7th Queen's resumed the attack against the woods around Mont Pinçon, which were defended by about forty guns, but this time it met success thanks to the support of the Norfolk Yeomanry SP antitank guns. The German counterstroke was driven off at 7.00, with help from artillery and 1st RTR. Operation Lüttich was launched by the Germans on 7 August to cut off the American forces at Avranches, and 30th Corps was then directed towards Condé-sur-Noireau to separate the enemy from its rear elements. 7th Arm.Div. advanced in two columns: one with 1st RTR and 7th Queen's from the Aunay – Condé road, the other from the just-conquered positions at La Vallée. On 8 and 9 August, territorial gains were insignificant but costly: the area was not suitable for the deployment of tanks, for the "*Suisse normande*" is a very hilly country, cut by many rocky escarpments. Infantry was moreover not available in sufficient number, and hand-to-hand fighting between tanks

and Panzerschrecks or Panzerfausts was becoming more and more frequent. In the evening of 9 August, the advance was stopped for lack of accompanying infantry.

The division had lost about a thousand men since *Goodwood*. For three weeks, it had been in almost constant contact with the enemy, even if not taking part in any large-scale operation. On 10 August, the main part of 7th Arm.Div. moved a few kilometres back, around Aunay-sur-Odon. The Skins with the divisional artillery were left at 43rd Inf.Div.'s disposal, while 11th Hussars came under command of 30th Corps. Still under German fire, the men could nevertheless enjoy baths and showers, clean uniforms, and entertainment. Reinforcements began to arrive from 59th Inf.Div. (officially disbanded in October), but not enough to bring all units up to full strength.

## From the Falaise pocket to the River Seine

The rest period was brief: on 15 August, 7th Arm.Div. had to join up in a hurry with Lieutenant-General Crerar's 1st Canadian Army. Under command of Crocker's 1st Corps, it was to lead the thrust towards the River Seine, and thus had to reach its concentration area east of the Caen – Falaise road. The tank men were happy to leave the bocage and the Caen plain for a more open and living country, which seemed more appropriate for the deployment of their Cromwells. Their drive was to take them along 100 km from Caen to the River Seine, across many rivers, whence the importance of the Royal Engineers

*The end of August and the pursuit of the Germans gave the Cromwell a chance to show its speed and manoeuvrability: a Close Support Cromwell Mk VI from 7th Arm.Div., camouflaged with foliage, is speeding along a road in Normandy during the Allied race to the River Seine. (Tank Museum 4834/A6)*

*Bottom,left.* **Back at Villers-Bocage on 5 August 1944, the 7th Arm.Div. found the wrecks of the tanks that had been destroyed on 13 June again in the devastated village: here, a Sherman Artillery OP from 3rd Rgt Royal Horse Artillery, which has lost its dummy gun. The letter X identifies a battery commander.** *(IWM B8632)*

to repair or build bridges. Fortunately, there was no longer any continuous enemy front, the Germans only carrying out a series of delaying actions. The 7th Arm.Div. reached Saint-Pierre-sur-Dives on 16 August, and crossed the river on a bridge that 51st Inf.Div. had taken control of. It went on towards Livarot and Lisieux from the 17th onwards, the Queen's Brigade and 8th Hussars taking the lead whilst three 11th Hussars Squadrons were undertaking recces, and whilst Norfolk Yeomanry self-propelled antitank guns were securing the southern flank. Then followed two days of poor and intermittent progression, for too many bridges had been blown up by the Germans in their retreat. The opposition still included seasoned elements from 12.SS and 21.Pz-Div., as well as dangerous paratroopers. As the advance was now moving steadily, information did not regularly reach the highest levels of command, causing serious mistakes: for instance, the forward elements of the division were often strafed and bombed by the RAF, notably 8th Hussars and Norfolk Yeomanry. 5th and 1st RTR for their part were hit by the Luftwaffe which intensified its night-attacks.

Sainte-Marguerite was reached on 18 August, and 11th Hussars cleared Jory, discovering a shaky but intact bridge on the River Vie, north of Livarot, on the 19th. Verney reacted immediately and changed the progression axis to set up a bridgehead there. 5th Queen's and 11th Hussars crossed and then reached Livarot where the main bridge had been blown, the village being regularly harassed by 88 fire, with Tigers from sSS-PzAbt.101 marauding around.

On the morning of the 20th, advance resumed on a cleared road, through almost untouched country where the British were warmly welcomed as liberators by the civilian population. FFIs and members of the Resistance offered precious help by guiding and informing them: the Cherry Pickers appreciated their services so much that they engaged civilians who helped them later to find crossing sites forgotten by the enemy.

C Squadron, 11th Hussars, with 5th RTR and 1st Rifle Brigade pushed towards Fervaques. Despite stiff opposition, three Troops made it to the River Touques: two bridges were blown, but the third one was intact, and these units settled in to defend it. The Lisieux road being cut

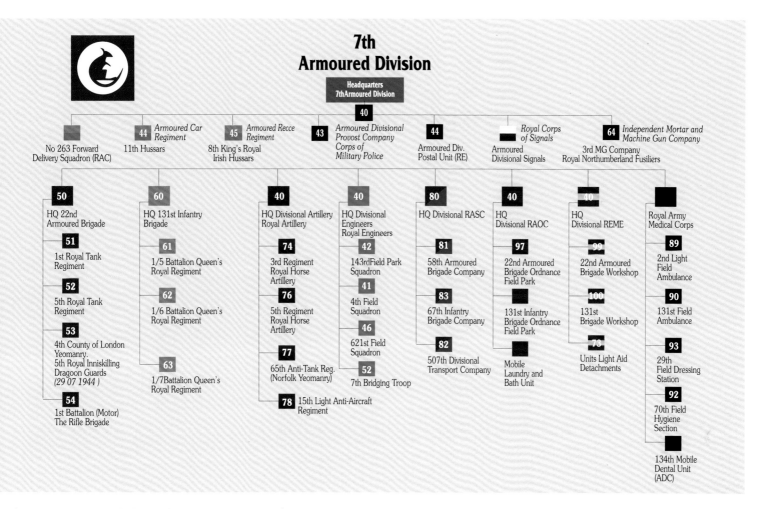

# 7th Armoured Division

**Headquarters 7th Armoured Division** — 40

| | |
|---|---|
| No 263 Forward Delivery Squadron (RAC) | |
| 44 — Armoured Car Regiment / 11th Hussars | |
| 45 — Armoured Recce Regiment / 8th King's Royal Irish Hussars | |
| 43 — Armoured Divisional Provost Company Corps of Military Police | |
| 44 — Armoured Div. Postal Unit (RE) | |
| Royal Corps of Signals / Armoured Divisional Signals | |
| 64 — Independent Mortar and Machine Gun Company / 3rd MG Company Royal Northumberland Fusiliers | |

**50 — HQ 22nd Armoured Brigade**
- 51 — 1st Royal Tank Regiment
- 52 — 5th Royal Tank Regiment
- 53 — 4th County of London Yeomanry. 5th Royal Inniskilling Dragoon Guards (29 07 1944 )
- 54 — 1st Battalion (Motor) The Rifle Brigade

**60 — HQ 131st Infantry Brigade**
- 61 — 1/5 Battalion Queen's Royal Regiment
- 62 — 1/6 Battalion Queen's Royal Regiment
- 63 — 1/7 Battalion Queen's Royal Regiment

**40 — HQ Divisional Artillery Royal Artillery**
- 74 — 3rd Regiment Royal Horse Artillery
- 76 — 5th Regiment Royal Horse Artillery
- 77 — 65th Anti-Tank Reg. (Norfolk Yeomanry)
- 78 — 15th Light Anti-Aircraft Regiment

**40 — HQ Divisional Engineers Royal Engineers**
- 42 — 143rd Field Park Squadron
- 41 — 4th Field Squadron
- 46 — 621st Field Squadron
- 52 — 7th Bridging Troop

**80 — HQ Divisional RASC**
- 81 — 58th Armoured Brigade Company
- 83 — 67th Infantry Brigade Company
- 82 — 507th Divisional Transport Company

**40 — HQ Divisional RAOC**
- 97 — 22nd Armoured Brigade Ordnance Field Park
- 131st Infantry Brigade Ordnance Field Park
- Mobile Laundry and Bath Unit

**40 — HQ Divisional REME**
- 99 — 22nd Armoured Brigade Workshop
- 100 — 131st Brigade Workshop
- Units Light Aid Detachments

**Royal Army Medical Corps**
- 89 — 2nd Light Field Ambulance
- 90 — 131st Field Ambulance
- 93 — 29th Field Dressing Station
- 92 — 70th Field Hygiene Section
- 134th Mobile Dental Unit (ADC)

---

by the British, many vehicles and their passengers in full retreat were captured by surprise. The rest of 22nd Arm.Brig. moved up with B Squadron, 11th Hussars, and 7th Queen's towards Lisieux to the north, and drove all night long. Three kilometres from the city, a second bridge was seized on the River Touques, after many skirmishes on the way. On 21 August, the division's columns were scattered several kilometres along. A counterstroke by the Hitlerjugend at Livarot, supported by Tigers, was repelled by 5th Inniskilling Dragoon Guards who destroyed several tanks, but 5th Queen's was temporarily cut off. At Fervaques too the enemy counterattacked, isolating 5th RTR and support troops for a time. The outskirts of Lisieux were strongly held by the Germans, and attempts to get into the centre failed; they were resumed on the next day with help from 51st Inf.Div. on the western flank. Recces were also undertaken along the River Orbec, but all the bridges blew up when 11th Hussars approached them. 5th RTR tried to break through at Fervaques, lost several tanks, but enabled C and D Squadrons, 11th Hussars, to go on and find other routes; in the evening, the regiment was relieved by the Canadians. On the same day, 1st RTR and 5th Queen's entered Lisieux at last. The fighting went on in the city on 23 August, but the *Skins* could not get through, for the shelling by British artillery the day before had piled up too much rubble in the streets. The regiment operated in support of 5th Queen's which were able to reach the town centre, despite the intervention of several Panthers.

The *Cherry Pickers* passed by Lisieux on 24 August, followed by 5th Inniskilling Dragoon Guards and the rest of 22nd Arm.Brig., with the River Risle at Pont-Authou as objective. Ten miles were covered without enemy intervention, by small roads in order to avoid the Germans' destructive delaying action. In the evening, another 25 miles record advance by 7th Arm.Div. allowed them to reach the River Risle, the access to which was well defended. On the 25th, 11th Hussars discovered that the bridge was still standing, but that the road was impassable because of the many RAF bomb craters, hence an important rebuilding work for the Engineers. Near Montfort, the *Skins* found a wooden bridge they crossed with a motorized company. This bridge was strong enough to withstand the whole regiment and most of the brigade. The division then spent three days mopping up the woods in the vicinity, at Bourneville, Routot, and up to the Brotonne forest, through numerous combats against infantry supported by antitank guns.

*The Desert Rats* were withdrawn on 28 August for a few days rest, waiting to cross the River Seine: one third of the tanks were missing in 22nd Arm.Brig. (which was at full strength in terms of crews), and every Queen's Brigade battalion was only at 50% strength.

**The closing of the Falaise pocket and the hastened German retreat allowed the Allies, at last, to liberate villages that had get out almost intact of the combats, and to enjoy the sincere welcome of the population. Here, civilians are gathering around a Cromwell from 8th Hussars, the typical parade headgear of which is worn by the soldier in the foreground.** *(Tank Museum 4546/C3)*

# 11th ARMOURED DIVISION

Charging black bull (red muzzle, feet and horns) on yellow background. The black bull was chosen by Major General Hobart, first unit commander, when it was formed in 1941.

**T**HE 11TH ARMOURED DIVISION WAS CREATED IN MARCH 1941 IN YORKSHIRE, under command of Major General Percy Hobart, who left in September 1943 to be replaced by Brigadier General "Pip" Roberts. If the latter had already commanded two armoured brigades in North Africa, Hobart was the main personality to leave his mark on the new armoured division.

After the departure of 30th Arm.Brig. in May 1942, only he 29th Arm.Brig. remained, under the command of Brigadier Harvey, another Desert veteran. It was originally composed of 23rd Hussars and 24th Lancers, joined by 2nd Fifeshire and Forfarshire Yeomanry (2nd FFY) in June 1941. 24th Lancers left for 8th Arm.Brig., and their place was taken by 3rd RTR in February 1944. This regiment's arrival was welcome, for 11th Arm.Div. was composed of only as yet untried and inexperienced units, even if some of their members had already seen action. Considering the importance of the battles fought at that time in North Africa and in Italy, it is hard to believe that an armoured division at full strength had remained in England for more than three years. That was however the case for the Guards Arm.Div. too.

After having cut its teeth on Valentines and Crusaders, 11th Arm.Div. was finally equipped with different types of Shermans (mainly Sherman Vs) in late 1943. The divisional reconnaissance regiment, 2nd Northamptonshire Yeomanry, was issued with Cromwells following the early Centaurs. The "old hands" were sceptical about the qualities of both these models of tanks, but the recruits who had remained in England had great confidence in their equipment: their confidence was to distinctly dwindle after their meeting with the first Tigers and Panthers in Normandy…

The long training period preceding the Invasion was exploited to develop a close cooperation between infantry from 159th Brigade, 8th Battalion The Rifle Brigade (divisional Motor Battalion), and armoured regiments. Unfortunately, this precious experience was not always used in combat. Major General Hobart had been encouraging the cooperation with artillery, the personal initiative of his officers and NCOs, as well as increased adaptability to unknown situations, ideas that were in contrast with the rigidity with which the British Army usually functioned.

## The landing

Since 11th Arm.Div. was not part of the initial assault, it landed principally on 13 and 14 June, even if forward elements went ashore on the 9th. The units were notably disembarked on Juno Beach, in front of Ouistreham, Courseulles-sur-Mer and Bernières. The division gathered together to the south of Creully, waiting for the last elements to join up: 23rd Hussars, for instance, only landed on 23 June. While 7th Arm.Div. was getting a thrashing at Villers-Bocage, 11th Arm.Div. was kept to the rear for more than ten days, mainly for lack of ammunition and fuel caused by the storm on 19-22 June. The crews had enough time thus to carry out the de-waterproofing operations. As 3rd RTR wanted to get rid of their cumbersome .50 turret AA machine-guns, they traded them with 8th Rifle Brigade who fitted them as added firepower on their Carriers and Scout Cars.

## Operation *Epsom*

The 11th Arm.Div. was first committed for Operation *Epsom* on 26 June: this was the third attempt to take Caen, an objective

*Top.*
**A Cromwell from 11th Arm.Div. HQ passing through Hérouvillette on 14 June. The division's charging bull is clearly visible, and the tactical sign white 40 on black background can be seen on the left. Although a Sherman-equipped unit, 11th Arm.Div. headquarters were issued with many Cromwells.**
*(IWM B5557)*

that should have been reached 15 days ago according to the plans of Overlord. For this offensive, 8th Corps (15th and 43rd Inf. Div., 4th Arm.Brig., 11th Arm.Div.) led with support from 1st and 30th Corps. From the start-line Rauray – Carpiquet, 15th Inf.Div. led the assault followed by 2nd Northamptonshire Yeomanry who had to get through Saint-Manvieu and Cheux to reach the Odon river bridges. 23rd Hussars was on the left, with 2nd FFY covering the right flank, and 3rd RTR remaining at the rear. Under intermittent rain, the tanks made slow progress: Cheux was blocked by ruins, and the Panzers from Hitlerjugend and sSS-PzAbt.101 overlooked the whole area. In support of 15th Inf.Div., 2nd Northamptonshire Yeomanry and 23rd Hussars had a bad time: the latter had to by-pass Cheux from the east, their C Squadron reaching La Bijude despite the loss of four tanks. At the end of the day, the units were in disorder, the River Odon was still out of sight, and the losses were heavy: 12 Shermans for Northamptonshire Yeomanry, and nine for the Fife and Forfar.

On the morning of 27 June, 2nd FFY led 15th Inf.Div. towards Grainville, where German defences stood firm. The supporting 119th Anti-Tank Battery knocked-out a Tiger and five Panthers for the loss of an M10. To the east, 23rd Hussars lost three Stuarts while pushing their B Squadron up to Mouen, the latter having

four Shermans destroyed by 88-mm guns. To the south-east, Mondrainville was occupied by Panzers and snipers hidden in the ruins. Thanks to a bridge captured on the River Odon at Tourmauville, C Squadron crossed in late afternoon, followed by a company from 8th Rifle Brigade and 23rd Hussars' other Squadrons. The regiment lost six more tanks to an enemy counterattack towards Mondrainville, while 2nd FFY were also crossing the River Odon in the evening. During the day, 4th King's Shropshire Light Infantry and 8th Rifle Brigade had taken Baron and dug in on the slopes of Hill 112. But the Germans from 1. and 12.SS-PzDiv. were holding the summit reinforced with half a dozen Tigers ambushed around Esquay, and they resisted every assault from 23rd Hussars and 8th Rifle Brigade on the 28th. 3rd RTR relieved 23rd Hussars for the night on the top of Hill 112, 2nd FFY remaining in a covering position. But under the pounding of mortars and Nebelwerfers, 8th Rifle Brigade, weakened by heavy human and equipment losses, had to give up their position during the night.

On 29 June, 3rd RTR were in action for the whole day with support from Typhoons and artillery to counter a German attack under a hail of Nebelwerfer rockets. 2nd FFY were confronted with Panzers in Mondrainville, and 23rd Hussars had to be committed too on the right flank. The advance was slow and restricted, but

all units made progress. 119th Anti-Tank Battery destroyed five more enemy tanks including a Tiger, M10s and Achilles proving more effective than Shermans in the antitank fighting. The arrival of 9. and 10.SS-PzDiv. from the south-west stopped the advance of 11th Arm.Div., especially since 1st and 30th Corps did not follow the progression, leaving the flanks unprotected. 2nd Northamptonshire Yeomanry who were holding on the western side thus lost many Cromwells from A and C Squadrons. The mission for the armour was now to hold the Odon bridgehead, while 8th Rifle Brigade were gathering at the rear to lick their wounds. The final situation was less than glorious: for meagre results, the division had lost more than 250 men killed.

Even though Operation *Epsom* was over, fighting went on from 30 June to 6 July: the units remaining on the spot (159th Inf. Brig., 2nd FFY, and 118th Anti-Tank Battery) could not prevent the Germans from re-taking Hill 112, but they repelled the attack launched on 30 June by 10.SS-PzDiv., with help from the artillery shooting 15000 shells. The division was at rest for 12 days afterwards, even if 2nd FFY were committed from 10 to 14 July

around Baron. The Sherman guns were tested against wrecked Panther hulls: it appeared that the latter's armour was impervious to 75-mm fire. Taking advantage of the lessons learnt during the last encounters, Major General Roberts changed the commanding officers of 159th Inf.Brig. and of two regiments.

## Goodwood: the charge of the Bull

On 18 July, Montgomery wanted to launch an almost all-armoured great offensive towards Falaise, to spare infantry units who had suffered a great deal. 11th Arm.Div. was chosen to lead the attack, but without 159th Inf.Brig. against Roberts' opinion. The objectives were the villages of Bras, Hubert-Folie, Verrières and Fontenay. The Guards Arm.Div. was to continue the advance, followed by 7th Arm.Div. The surprise was nil, as the Germans were keeping a close watch on this salient in their lines, and had fortified the villages in depth. The division's units gathered together with difficulty from 16 July onwards, for the concentration area did not have enough bridges, thus entailing huge traffic jams before

*Top.*
**On 30 June, a line of Sherman Vs is in hull down position behind a hedgerow, ready to attack an enemy post on the Eterville area. The 11th Arm.Div.'s insignia can be seen on the first tank's rear, which has kept part of its left front mudguard: the poor condition of the latter shows that it will not last, thus explaining why this item is so rarely seen on tanks in combat.**
*(RR)*

*Left.*
**A Sherman belonging to 29th Arm.Brig. HQ (see tactical sign 50 on red background) is passing a Carrier on a Normandy lane with some difficulty: from the road sign on the left, the scene took place south-east of Caen, probably along the then-called N175 road. Oddly, the left track includes a back-to-front link.**
*(IWM B6980)*

the operation could begin. 3rd RTR and G Company, 8th Rifle Brigade, led the assault, followed by 2nd FFY, and 23rd Hussars who were to turn left. 2nd Northamptonshire Yeomanry were in support on the right towards Cuverville and Démouville. The Corps artillery was set up too far away and could only provide efficient support at the early stages, the 13th RHA having to take over very soon. Opposite them, 12.SS and 21.PzDiv. were the main adversaries.

The attack launched on 18 July started well with the Inns of Court's armoured cars scouting ahead, the 3rd RTR Recce Troop advanced but soon met more and more resistance. In reaching the Caen – Troarn railway line at 10.00, the column was slowed down and then shelled when it tried to climb the high embankment. About ten tanks were knocked-out or damaged by the fire from 88 guns, Tigers, and Panthers. 2nd FFY met the same problem on the Caen – Vimont line, but managed to cross the obstacle and to destroy three Panzers, to be stopped just in front of Hubert-Folie. 23rd Hussars watched 3rd RTR charging against Bras and Hubert-Folie suddenly stopped by enemy fire in front of Bourguébus and being then unable to resume despite the help of 2nd Northamptonshire Yeomanry, the tanks of which were brewed up one by one.

Their B Squadron then gave assistance to 2nd FFY and disabled three Panzers, under enemy tank fire coming from Cagny. C Squadron moving up towards Four were also stopped by SPG and 88 fire. 29th Arm.Brig. was in great difficulty, spearheading the advance and threatened on three sides. 7th Arm.Div. took a long time coming, and only arrived at 17.00 to resume the attack timidly. In the meantime, the different units were seriously depleted: there were only 16 tanks left in 2nd FFY, and 23rd Hussars which had been assaulted by Tigers from sPzAbt.503 and then

by Panthers, had lost 20 Shermans. A counterattack by Panthers from Four and Frénouville in the early afternoon was driven back by 2nd FFY which destroyed six tanks but again with losses. Early in the evening, 3rd RTR were marking time in front of Hubert-Folie, 2nd Northamptonshire Yeomanry were west of the Caen –

On 14 August, Major General Roberts in shirt sleeves talking with the officer in command of 29th Arm. Brig., Brigadier Harvey, in front of the latter's Sherman. As on many 11th Arm. Div. tanks, the regulation-position of the markings is reversed. The wooden box on the mudguard is an ammunition box for the Panzerschreck! *(IWM B9184)*

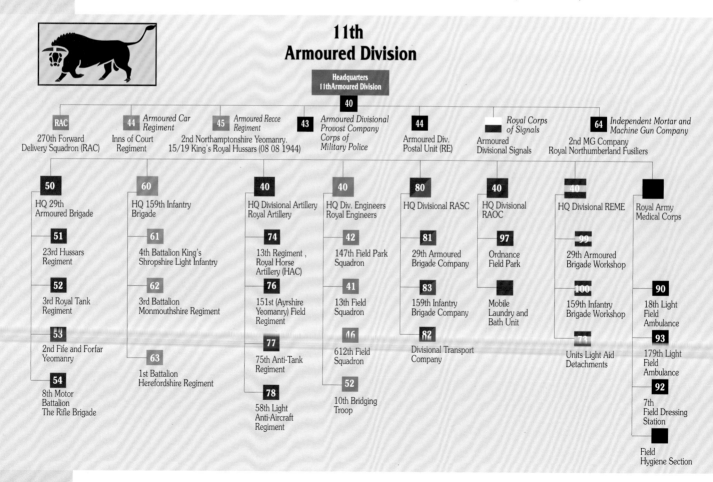

# 11th Armoured Division

**Headquarters 11th Armoured Division** `40`

| | |
|---|---|
| **RAC** | 270th Forward Delivery Squadron (RAC) |
| `44` Armoured Car Regiment | Inns of Court Regiment |
| `45` Armoured Recce Regiment | 2nd Northamptonshire Yeomanry. 15/19 King's Royal Hussars (08 08 1944) |
| `43` Armoured Divisional Provost Company Corps of Military Police | |
| `44` | Armoured Div. Postal Unit (RE) |
| Royal Corps of Signals | Armoured Divisional Signals |
| `64` Independent Mortar and Machine Gun Company | 2nd MG Company Royal Northumberland Fusiliers |

| `50` HQ 29th Armoured Brigade | `60` HQ 159th Infantry Brigade | `40` HQ Divisional Artillery Royal Artillery | `40` HQ Div. Engineers Royal Engineers | `80` HQ Divisional RASC | `40` HQ Divisional RAOC | `40` HQ Divisional REME | Royal Army Medical Corps |
|---|---|---|---|---|---|---|---|
| `51` 23rd Hussars Regiment | `61` 4th Battalion King's Shropshire Light Infantry | `74` 13th Regiment, Royal Horse Artillery (HAC) | `42` 147th Field Park Squadron | `81` 29th Armoured Brigade Company | `97` Ordnance Field Park | `99` 29th Armoured Brigade Workshop | `90` 18th Light Field Ambulance |
| `52` 3rd Royal Tank Regiment | `62` 3rd Battalion Monmouthshire Regiment | `76` 151st (Ayrshire Yeomanry) Field Regiment | `41` 13th Field Squadron | `83` 159th Infantry Brigade Company | Mobile Laundry and Bath Unit | `100` 159th Infantry Brigade Workshop | `93` 179th Light Field Ambulance |
| `53` 2nd Fife and Forfar Yeomanry | `63` 1st Battalion Herefordshire Regiment | `77` 75th Anti-Tank Regiment | `46` 612th Field Squadron | `82` Divisional Transport Company | | `73` Units Light Aid Detachments | `92` 7th Field Dressing Station |
| `54` 8th Motor Battalion The Rifle Brigade | | `78` 58th Light Anti-Aircraft Regiment | `52` 10th Bridging Troop | | | | Field Hygiene Section |

18

Troarn railway line, when 23rd Hussars entered Grentheville then Four, while 2nd FFY were in reserve to reorganize: they had only 9 tanks left out of the usual issue of 60! A heavy toll had also been taken from the infantry of 159th Inf.Brig. during the first day.

On the following day, 3rd RTR could muster 30 tanks thanks to the night's reinforcements, and resumed the assault at dawn, destroying a Panther and two SPGs at Bras, but being soon stopped by antitank guns just as on the day before: in a matter of minutes, only 17 Shermans were left unscathed, and the situation was similar in the whole brigade. The objective was consequently limited to the seizing of Bras and Hubert-Folie. With 2nd FFY in reserve and 23rd Hussars at rest, the fresher 2nd Northamptonshire Yeomanry led the attack with 8th Rifle Brigade towards Bras. Bearing to the west by mistake, they ran into an 88 barrage and lost five tanks. 3rd RTR came to resume the assault, and Bras was captured despite fierce enemy opposition, the Germans losing 70 killed and 300 prisoners. 2nd Northamptonshire Yeomanry went on towards Hubert-Folie and knocked-out two captured Shermans for the loss of five tanks. 2nd FFY were then brought in a hurry to conclude the attack, and Hubert-Folie was finally taken with the help of 23rd Hussars and 3rd Monmouthshire. The objective

was reached at last, but 65 more tanks had been lost.

On 20 July, heavy rains put an end to Operation *Goodwood*; the division was relieved by the Canadians and then pulled back to the north of Caen. The 29th Arm.Brig. regimental commanders were obliged to choose: either their units would be reorganized to absorb massive reinforcements as fast as possible, or they would be withdrawn from the front for six weeks to be entirely reequipped. The Colonels preferred the former solution, despite the troops' lowering moral. The first decision was to disband the antiaircraft armoured regiments, now of limited use since the Allies enjoyed air supremacy. Their crews were rapidly trained to be issued with new Shermans. Most of the damaged tanks that had not burnt during the attack were recovered and overhauled by the divisional and 8th Corps workshops. However, the loss of 735 men and 191 tanks was not easily overcome, even with the ensuing rest period which lasted until 29 July.

## Operation *Bluecoat*

For the next offensive, the thrust was to be delivered east of Caen by 8th and 30th Corps, southwards from Caumont-l'Eventé.

8th Corps (15th Inf.Div., 11th and Guards Arm.Div.) was in charge of attacking towards St-Martin-des-Besaces, Le Bény-Bocage and Vire, on the 5th ID US boundary, while 30th Corps was to approach Mont Pinçon. The first assault was to be led by 15th Inf.Div. with 6th Guards Tk.Brig. Churchills in support. Major General Roberts at last had the opportunity to arrange his units at will, and he re-created the infantry/armour mixed groups that had been often put in practice during training: 23rd Hussars/ 3rd Monmouthshire on the left, 2nd FFY/4th KSLI on the right, 3rd RTR/1st Herefordshire Rgt and 2nd Northamptonshire Yeomanry/8th Rifle Brigade in the centre. The structure was not to be so rigid in combat, but would allow the high degree of the division's combined cooperation to develop. The combatants had their first encounter with real Bocage country, close and divided, but these hard conditions were at least interesting in restricting the German advantage in tank gun range.

At 7.00 on 30 July, the attack began after artillery preparation and aerial bombardment. Progress was satisfying, despite human losses mainly caused by American minefields and German mortars. The tanks often made it with a cut track or a torn-out bogie. Sept-Vents was reached by the 23rd Hussars/3rd Mons group, who also took St-Ouen-des-Besaces, then Cussy was seized by 14.00 (3rd RTR/1st Hereford), as well as La Basselière (2nd FFY/4th

KSLI). In the evening, success was undeniable, as the division entered St-Martin-des-Besaces and had lost only a few tanks to Panzerfausts or Panzerschrecks. St-Martin was attacked on the next morning by 4th KSLI supported by a 2nd FFY Squadron, while 8th Rifle Brigade, 3rd RTR and 2nd Northamptonshire Yeomanry by-passed the village and went on advancing. At the boundary between 3. Fallschirmjäger-Div. and 326. ID, an intact bridge on the River Souleuvre was discovered: 4th KSLI and 2nd Northamptonshire Yeomanry being the nearest units, they combined to cross it and hold it until 23rd Hussars and 3rd Mons could arrive and take possession of the heights. The day ended successfully again.

23rd Hussars and 3rd Mons spearheaded the attack on 1 August to take the heights overlooking Le Bény-Bocage, with support from 8th Rifle Brigade, 3rd RTR and 4th KSLI: the village was quickly reached and the population spared by the fighting put up a triumphal welcome to its liberators. That was the first almost intact village to be captured by 11th Arm.Div. Relaxing his initial combined-arms structure, Roberts sent 3rd RTR and 4th KSLI along the River Souleuvre towards Cathéolles, which was taken in the morning. A 3rd RTR Squadron continued to advance with 8th Rifle Brigade and 75th Anti-Tank Rgt, and came in sight of St-Charles-de-Percy on the Caen – Vire road. In the afternoon,

23rd Hussars and 8th Rifle Brigade, with 2nd FFY securing on the right, pushed on towards Le Désert and Presles up to Chênedollé, but the Vassy – Vire road could not be reached by the evening. Tank losses were kept to a minimum for no tanks and few antitank guns were met.

On 2 August, 2nd Northamptonshire Yeomanry resumed the attack via Etouvy, north of Vire, and reached the town located within the American sector boundaries. While 23rd Hussars and 8th Rifle Brigade were going beyond Le Bas Perrier, 2nd FFY and 3rd Mons moved along the Caen – Vire road. Whilst advancing towards St-Charles-de-Percy, 3rd RTR and 4th KSLI were slowed down by Panzer-supported enemy infantry. Three Panthers were destroyed in the evening, including one with a PIAT. 2nd FFY and 3rd Mons had taken Burcy then Pavée in spite of friendly fire from American P47s… 23rd Hussars were driven back by attacking Panthers and SPGs, their A Squadron was wiped out, and they withdrew to Le Bas Perrier. 2nd Northamptonshire Yeomanry laagered north of Vire for the night; 11th Arm.Div. had again made a good 11 km progression, but opposition was stiffening. On 3 August, the division had to hold its positions with support from 185th Inf.Brig. (3rd Inf.Div.) against counterstrokes launched by 21., 9.SS and 10.SS Pz-Div. with Tigers from sSS-PzAbt. 102. Presles was recaptured by the Germans, 23rd Hussars and 8th Rifle Brigade were cut off for 24 hours: the nine available Fireflies managed to keep the Panthers away, but four tanks were lost. 3rd RTR helped 4th KSLI to hold Le Grand Bonfait, losing several tanks to Panthers, and the attack was finally repelled thanks to the artillery. 2nd Northamptonshire Yeomanry reached the Paris – Granville railway line whilst patrolling on the right, but four Tigers attacked in the early afternoon and knocked-out three tanks. Eight more were lost during the night, through raids carried on by Hohenstaufen Panzergrenadieren assaulting the laager with Panzerfausts.

A Sherman from 11th Arm.Div. crossing the River Orne at Putanges, on 20 August. Close examination of the photograph reveals that this is the tank of Brigadier Harvey, seen on a previous view taken on 14 August: one can recognize the markings, the cover on the glacis plate, and above all the still present Panzerschreck ammo box on the mudguard! Steps welded on the transmission housing to allow older officers to climb in, confirm that it is a command tank. (RR)

*Bottom.* **On 20 August, a Sherman Ic of 11th Arm.Div. (see divisional insignia on the left rear) is parked on the central square at Putanges. The rear cut-out in the hull and the angular armour on the front confirm that it is a Firefly on M4 chassis. A pair of socks is drying on the gun tube: what a funny way to use a 17 pounder!** (IWM B9477)

On the following days, progress was limited but combats were frequent. The morning of 4 August was marked by a new attack by American P47s, and by the break-up of the 23rd Hussars and 8th Rifle Brigade encirclement in Presles by 2nd Royal Warwickshire (3rd Inf. Div.) The Germans supported with four Tigers resumed the assault at 15.00 against Le Bas Perrier, and once more temporarily cut off 23rd Hussars. On the next day, several concentric attacks from 9.SS-PzDiv. were repelled thanks to the artillery, but Guards Arm.Div. on the left and the Americans on the right made too slow progress to protect the 11th Arm. Div.'s flanks. On 6 August, 10.SS-PzDiv. was transferred from Aunay-sur-Odon to attack Pavée and Le Bas Perrier with sSS-PzAbt.102 and strong Nebelwerfer and mortar support, but the frontal assault against 23rd Hussars and 2nd Warwicks was stopped by the barrage of tank guns, and of the divisional and 8th Corps artillery, disrupting the enemy lines. Only a few infantrymen managed to infiltrate, and the renewed attacks were not more successful:

# REGIMENTS ACCORDING TO THE ORDER OF PRECEDENCE

### 15/19th King's Royal Hussars

- **Origins:** Resulting from the amalgamation in 1922 between "15th The King's Hussars" (from the "Newton's Dragoons" raised in 1715, later known as "15th Light Dragoons"), and "19th (Queen Alexandra's Own Royal) Hussars" (derived from "19th Light Dragoons" formed in 1715). 15/19th Hussars was transferred to Egypt in 1924, then to India in 1929. Became "15/19thThe King's Royal Hussars" in 1935, and then converted to light tank regiment in 1937.

- **1939-44:** Sent to France in 1939, as part of 28th Arm.Brig. from April 1940, retreated on the River Escaut. Formed a composite regiment with 5th Dragoon Guards, evacuated via Dunkirk. Remained in England with the same brigade until July 1944. On 17 August 1944, replaced 2nd Northamptonshire Yeomanry in Normandy within 11th Arm.Div., as reconnaissance armoured regiment.

### 23rd Hussars

- **Origins:** Regiment raised in 1716 in Ireland by Brigadier Ferrer, disbanded and reformed several times between 1781 and 1794. "26th Light Dragoons" raised in 1794 by Lieutenant Colonel Manners took the name of "23rd Light Dragoons" in 1803, and served in India. Return to England in 1808, fought in the Peninsula in 1809 (Talavera), then in Belgium in 1815 (Waterloo). Became "23rd Lancers" in 1816, disbanded the following year.

- **1939-44:** The 23rd Hussars was re-created in 1940 with officers and NCOs from 10th Royal Hussars and 15/19thKing's Royal Hussars, and was incorporated in January 1941 into 29th Arm.Brig. (11th Arm.Div.) with which it landed in Normandy in June 1944.

### 2nd Northamptonshire Yeomanry

- **Origins:** "The Northamptonshire Yeomanry Cavalry" was raised by the Earl Spencer in 1794. After disbanding in 1828, reformed in 1902 under the name of "The Northamptonshire Imperial Yeomanry". Became "The Northamptonshire Yeomanry" in 1908, divided into 1st, 2nd then 3rd regiments in 1914-18, for the fighting in France (regiments were distributed between cavalry, infantry then Tank Corps). Fought at Ypres and Arras, then in Italy. Reconstituted in 1920, became armoured car regiment, Royal Tank Corps in 1922.

- **1939-44:** Converted into armoured regiment in 1939 ("1st Northamptonshire Yeomanry"); 2nd Regiment was formed as duplicate and became reconnaissance armoured regiment, Royal Armoured Corps in 1943. From September 1939 to March 1943, 2nd Northamptonshire Yeomanry was part of 20th Arm.Brig. in England. Attached in March 1943 to 11th Arm.Div. as reconnaissance armoured regiment. Disbanded in August 1944 after the heavy losses endured in Normandy, to be replaced with 15/19thKing's Royal Hussars.

### 2nd Fifeshire and Forfarshire Yeomanry

- **Origins:** Two-regiment cavalry troop created in 1797 (Fifeshire, and Forfarshire), intermittently raised and disbanded until 1860. Became "The Fifeshire Mounted Rifle Volunteers", disbanded in 1862, reconstituted as "The 1st Fifeshire Light Horse Volunteers" in 1870, and then "The Forfarshire Light Horse Volunteer Corps" in 1876. In 1900, departed

for South Africa, and was amalgamated when back in England: became "The Fifeshire and Forfarshire Yeomanry TF (Dragoons)" in 1908. Several regiments formed in 1914-18, fighting at Gallipoli, in Egypt, in Palestine. Reconstituted in 1920 as "20th (Fife and Forfar) Armoured Car Company Royal Tank Corps TF". Became "The Fife and Forfar Yeomanry RTC Territorial Army" in 1938, again divided in 1st and 2nd Regiments in 1939.

- **1939-44:** 2nd Fife and Forfar Yeomanry was integrated into 29th Arm.Brig. (11th Arm. Div.) in June 1941, and landed with this unit in Normandy.

### 3rd Battalion, Royal Tank Regiment

- **Origins:** In common with the whole Royal Tank Regiment, see 1st RTR. Previously C Battalion "The Armoured Car Section, Machine Gun Corps" in 1916, fighting at Cambrai, Ypres, Arras. Became 3rd Battalion, Tank Corps, in 1918 (battles of the River Somme, St Quentin, Bapaume…). Left for Ireland in 1920, returned to England in 1922. In 1924, "The Royal Tank Corps" notably included 3rd Battalion as part of the Experimental Mechanised Force. In 1939, battalions became regiments, keeping their number, within Royal Tank Regiment RAC.

- **1939-44:** The 3rd Battalion RTR was one of the three regiments in 3rd Arm. Brig. in September 1939, for the fighting in France, until June 1940; then intermittently in 1940-41. Sometimes attached to 1st Arm. Brig. from February to July 1940, and fought in North Africa with 4th Arm.Brig. from August 1941 to June 1942 (operation Crusader, Sidi Rezegh), then with 8th Arm.Brig. from July 1942 to January 1944 (El Alamein, Medenine, Tripoli, Mareth Line). Joined the 29th Arm. Brig. of 11th Arm.Div. in February 1944, for the whole campaign in North-West Europe.

---

they just increased losses on both sides. 2nd FFY were with 3rd Mons on the frontline of the sector that was attacked at Pavée: they lost four Shermans against two Panzers destroyed during a fierce battle. P47s were always a plague and strafed the infantry during the relief by 1st Royal Norfolk (3rd Inf.Div.) Tigers once more creeped through the British positions but had to move back because the grenadiers did not follow. Fighting ceased at nightfall, after heavy losses again.

From 7 to 12 August, the division only held the frontline and carried out a few patrols, since the heavy losses had to be made up for, and the infantry had not even enough troops carrying vehicles. 2nd FFY were shelled at Le Bas Perrier by Tigers, but succeeded in disabling several enemy AFVs. There were only 5 tanks left per Squadron instead of 19. A gradual relief by the Guards made it possible for 11th Arm. Div. to withdraw and assimilate new reinforcements, including previous members of the recently-disbanded 24th Lancers. Infantry and artillery were again lent to other units. The division, having lost 200 men during *Bluecoat*, came under control of 30th Corps on 12 August.

## The breakout

The encirclement of 7th and 5th German Armies was confirmed

in early August: 30th Corps was ordered to exploit the Panzer-Divisionen's withdrawal ahead of the British frontline. Followed by 50th and 43rd Inf.Div., 11th Arm.Div. took the lead on the front's right, in contact with the US forces, to advance towards Vassy, Flers, and even Briouze.

On 14 August, on the Lassy – Estry starting line, three combined groups were formed: 23rd Hussars/8th Rifle Brigade, 2nd FFY/3rd Mons, and 3rd RTR/1st Hereford. Preceded by the Inns of Court's armoured cars, the infantry travelled on the tanks. The advance beginning on the 15th was slow but regular, the 3rd RTR group taking La Rocque and Le Theil, with 4th KSLI being then substituted for 1st Hereford. The 23rd Hussars group captured Canteloup at night, and 2nd FFY with 3rd Mons made progress towards La Rocque and Gacé to reach St-Germain-du-Crioult, not without enduring heavy infantry casualties. On the same day the sad news arrived that the 2nd Northamptonshire Yeomanry, the reconnaissance regiment, was to be disbanded because of heavy losses, and replaced with 15/19th King's Royal Hussars. Two hundred men were incorporated into the Cromwell-equipped 7th Arm. Div., the others joined the parent regiment (1st Northamptonshire Yeomanry).

On the morning of 16 August, the 3rd RTR group was leading

and it received artillery support against the very hard defence put up by 3.FJ-Div. and 363.ID. 4th KSLI crossed the River Noireau, followed by 1st Hereford with 3rd RTR heading to Flers, after they had seized Cerisy-Belle-Etoile. The group was then in charge of taking the Vère river bridge, under a hail of German artillery and mortars, and it was finally captured late in the evening, on the Flers – Condé road. For their last action, 2nd Northamptonshire Yeomanry took part in the mopping-up of the area north of Flers deserted by the Germans. 2nd FFY and 3rd Mons, west of Condé-sur-Noireau, were slowed down by mines and antitank guns but managed to cross the river on a Scissors bridge. The objective for 17 August was Briouze via Flers, 3rd RTR leading 159th Inf. Brig. and 29th Arm.Brig. towards Aubusson and Putanges. 2nd FFY seized a bridge on the River Rouvre at the cost of two destroyed tanks.

Prisoners crowded around 23rd Hussars and 8th Rifle Brigade whilst they were leading the main thrust: the river was reached and forded at Taillebois. 159th Inf.Brig., with 3rd RTR and 1st Hereford in spearhead, moved on towards Briouze.

23rd Hussars and 8th Rifle Brigade advanced towards Putanges on 18 August, but the Orne River bridge was blown up: no other way was found northwards or southwards, so 3rd Mons had to cross on rafts at night. Briouze was freed by 3rd RTR and 4th KSLI, against the will of 3rd US ID: high command however confirmed that the town was within the British sector boundaries.

Units were so intermingled that when the 3rd RTR group arrived at Ecouché at night, it found the place occupied by the 2nd French Arm.Div.! While 2nd FFY were capturing Putanges, the Americans let the British use the bridge they had taken in Argentan so that the advance could go on. 15/19th Hussars entered the fray on 18 August at Moulins-sur-Orne, to protect the division's right flank. C and B Squadrons shot at enemy columns in the distance, and lost a tank to a Panther. 4th KSLI, 3rd RTR and 1st Hereford advanced via Montgaroult and Sentilly, and despite the delay caused by the meeting with American and French units, 29th Arm.Brig.

led by 2nd FFY and 3rd Mons passed through Putanges, 23rd Hussars and 8th Rifle Brigade then taking over towards Courteilles and destroying two SPGs for one Sherman lost.

## The pursuit to the Seine

Without any coherent enemy front, 11th Arm.Div. now carried out rapid advances punctuated by skirmishes, sometimes very tough ones. From 20 August, increasing numbers of prisoners were made and the roads were littered with equipment abandoned by the fugitives. 8th Rifle Brigade by-passed Ocagnes and penetrated the forest of Gouffern with help from 23rd Hussars followed by 2nd FFY. The next objective was Laigle, to be reached by 159th Inf.Brig. via Avenelle and Omméel: 29th Arm.Brig. got through Exmes and Croisilles, both units having to meet in Gacé. Omméel and St-Pierre-La-Rivière were liberated on 21 August by 3rd RTR, 4th KSLI and 1st Hereford while 2nd FFY and 15/19th Hussars were stopped before Gacé. In the afternoon, 3rd RTR sent a Squadron in support of 4th KSLI to take the village. 2nd FFY lost several tanks whilst taking the Touques river bridge, while 23rd Hussars and 8th Rifle Brigade seized Authieux-du-Puits. Still pushing on towards Laigle on the next day, the division freed villages one after the other, without any other difficulty than mines, craters, blown bridges, ruins… and the madly rejoicing population! Early in the evening, 23rd Hussars entered Laigle at last. 23 August was a day off, the division leaguering around Aube-sur-Risle and building up its forces again after two days of cavalcade and combat.

The pursuit was handed over to fresher units. On 28 August began the long trip towards the River Seine, 29th Arm.Brig. spearheading 11th Arm.Div. via Chambray and Evreux, with 3rd RTR, 8th Rifle Brigade, 2nd FFY and 23rd Hussars in the lead. Combats were over on this road, and the River Seine could be crossed without difficulty at Vernon on 30 August.

A Sexton 25 pounder SPG named "Hyperides" crossing the River Seine on a Bailey bridge, on 30 August. The divisional insignia can be clearly seen, but the tactical sign is hidden by a cover, and it is not known to which Field Regiment the vehicle belonged.
(RR)

# 79th ARMOURED DIVISION

**F**ORMED IN OCTOBER 1942, the 79th Arm.Div. was a standard armoured division under command of Major General P.C.S. Hobart, including 27th Arm.Brig. and 185th Inf.Brig. Its task was radically modified in April 1943, when it was appointed to gather all the engineers or armoured specialised vehicles, existing or to be developed, in order to prepare the landings in Europe.

It became the only British fully-armoured division when 185th Inf. Brig. left to join 3rd Inf.Div. and was replaced with 35th Tk.Brig. (June 1943) and 30th Arm.Brig. (October 1943). 27th Arm.Brig. became independent in November 1943, but was to keep close relationship with the division since it took part in the development of the Duplex Drive tanks, with which its three regiments were equipped. Seven other regiments issued with DD tanks were trained by 79th Arm.Div.: two Canadian, three American, Nottinghamshire Yeomanry from 33rd Arm.Brig. and 15th/19th Hussars (the latter did not take part in D-Day). Each brigade in the division was to be issued with special equipment: 1st Assault Brigade, Royal Engineers was created in November 1943 and was issued with special armoured engineer vehicles (AVRE), 30th Arm.Brig. was equipped with anti-mine flail tanks (Crab), and 35th Tk.Brig. was to develop a very secret piece of equipment codified CDL (for Canal Defence Light), in fact a tank fitted out with a powerful searchlight projector. It was replaced in the same role by 1st Tk.Brig. in March 1944. 43rd RTR was also attached to the division, but this regiment was intended

Black and white bull head on a yellow triangle outlined in black, pointing downwards. As for 11th Arm.Div., the black bull was chosen by Major General Hobart since it was part of his family's coat of arms.

for carrying out tests with the various machines, and did not land in Normandy.

For several months, 79th Arm.Div. was scattered all over Great-Britain, depending on suitable terrain for the development of the various specialised vehicles, nicknamed "*Funnies*": DD amphibious tank; AVRE (Armoured Vehicle, Royal Engineers); Churchill Ark, SBG and Scissors (bridges); Sherman Crab; Churchill Crocodile (flamethrower tank); Fascine (crossing means); Grant CDL... Many tests and studies were undertaken, and some were only completed a few days just before D-Day. For instance, during the weeks prior to 6 June, it was discovered that the beaches chosen for the landings included large patches of blue clay where the armour were likely to bog down: the AVRE Bobbin fitted with a roll reeling off carpet was designed in a hurry to allow these areas to be crossed. All units were not however committed on D-Day (see distribution table), only 22nd Dragoons and Westminster Dragoons (Crab), together with 5th and 6th Assault Regiments (AVRE) were part of the assault force, others remained in reserve or were not even concerned, such as 1st Tk.Brig. and its CDL tanks.

*Top.* **Although taken during training before the Invasion, this photograph is a perfect illustration of the transport conditions of 79th Arm.Div.'s specialised armour for D-Day. Behind an early production Sherman can be seen in this landing craft a Crab and two AVRE Bobbins. The tactical sign 40, usually on black background, identifies the divisional HQ.**
*(Tank Museum 444/C5)*

*Above.*

**Carriers from the 2nd Battalion Middlesex Rgt pass in front of a Churchill AVRE named "Bulldog" from 5th Assault Rgt, probably in Hermanville-sur-Mer in the afternoon of 6 June. The device seen at the front of the tank is probably the fastening system of an SBG bridge, as confirmed by the winch on the engine deck.** *(RR)*

*Bottom.*

**A Small Box Girder bridge, seemingly painted in white, has been placed on the beach above a large bomb crater. The 25-ton capacity is indicated on a board at the bridge entrance. A track made of wire mesh strengthened with metal rods is already established in parallel, indicating that the photograph was taken some days after 6 June.** *(Tank Museum 2834/A6)*

## Gold Beach

On 6 June at dawn, Westminster Dragoons' B Squadron and 82nd Assault Squadron (6th Assault Rgt) landed in front of Le Hamel in support of 231st Inf.Brig. (50th Inf.Div.) The tanks were put ashore too far east, a prematurely-launched AVRE was drowned and the other vehicles waited until the tide was higher to land and open the planned breaches. On the right, two Crabs cleared the mines towards Le Hamel, but the first one was quickly knocked out. The second one blew up on a mine soon after, as did an AVRE, and the mines had to be cleared by hand. Progression was easier on the left, a single Flail was destroyed, but another Crab and two AVREs got bogged down. Once passages were cleared of mines, the task was mainly to suppress machine-gun nests and artillery, pending the arrival of the DD tanks that were delayed by the sea conditions. Crabs and AVREs helped to clear Le Hamel, where the enemy held until late in the morning.

In La Rivière, C Squadron, Westminster Dragoons opened the way for 69th Inf.Brig. (50th Inf.Div.) The efficient preliminary bombardment had weakened the opposition, and the first Crab opened up a track towards Ver-sur-Mer. It was stopped by a crater that was soon crossed thanks to an SBG bridge brought up by an AVRE. Another Crab widened the passage for the DD tanks from 4/7th Dragoons (27th Arm.Brig.) Another exit had to be abandoned, for although the mines had been cleared, two bogged-down Crabs were blocking the passage which furthermore was under 88 fire. Three AVREs cleared the Pillboxes with their Petards, and laid down an explosive charge to breach the seawall. A single AVRE was lost on the beach when rammed by an LCT, but further west two others were hit by a German antitank gun. Crabs completed the cleaning work, but finally bogged-down: this exit was also abandoned, as well as the third one where two Crabs had got stuck in the mud and an AVRE had been destroyed. On the 30th Corps front, seven exits were secured out of the twelve that had been planned.

## Juno Beach

Four Troops from B Squadron, 22nd Dragoons and 26th Ass. Sq. preceded 7th Inf.Brig. (3rd Canadian Inf.Div.) before Courseulles-sur-Mer, but with a 30 minutes delay: six Canadian DDs from 1st Hussars were already on the spot and had suppressed most of the opposition. If the clearing of mines was simple on the left, things got worse on the right: two Crabs began to open a passage but lost their tracks on mines. A third Flail almost completed their task when it fell in a crater: an AVRE Fascine came to help but bogged down, and it fell to a bulldozer to bring up another fascine and an SBG bridge so that the passage was set up over

the AVRE itself. East of the River Seulles, the landed teams only met minor opposition, Crabs and AVREs did their job and two roads were opened at 9.00. Six AVREs then took part in the clearing of wreckage and beach obstacles, while three others supported infantry in mopping up Courseulles.

In front of Bernières, the other part of B Squadron, 22nd Dragoons was operating with 80th Ass.Sq. in support of 8th Inf.Brig. (3rd Canadian Inf.Div.) A Crab opened the road, followed by an AVRE which blew up on a mine and blocked the passage. It was pushed aside by a bulldozer, and the mine clearing was resumed by hand. Two other Crabs cleared away another path towards a breach in the pier, and passed over the latter up to a ditch which had to be filled up with two fascines. Infantry had already cleared a fair part of the area, without waiting the late DD tanks. Another team was less fortunate: two of its AVREs were hit, the Flails cleared a passage in the antitank wall but the latter was too strong for the Petards. Only infantrymen were able to get through a corridor where C elements were destroyed with accurate shooting of Dust-

bins. As for the vehicles, another group had launched an SBG bridge on the pier without difficulty, with the supporting fire of Crabs and AVREs. Within the last team, an AVRE was damaged by a landing craft, and then a Bobbin carpet was laid down on a very soft passage arranged by Crabs. Twelve exits were opened on Juno beach, and the Crabs went on flailing the surroundings and the beach.

## Sword Beach

22nd Dragoons' A and C Squadrons, half of A Squadron, Westminster Dragoons, and 5th Assault Rgt supported 3rd Inf.Div. which landed before Lion-sur-Mer and Ouistreham. The firing was very dense, the defences still strong, and although the Crabs managed to open a track on the right, the following AVRE sank in a water hole. Three other AVREs pushed up to Lion-sur-Mer with 41 Royal Marine Commando but they were hit by antitank guns: the attack was cancelled on this side. Further on the left, the second team's Flails carried out their mission, lost a tank, and the AVREs

advanced towards Lion-sur-Mer after having launched a Bobbin and an SBG bridge over the open passages. Another AVRE Bobbin blew up on a mine and was finished off by an enemy antitank gun. The third team landed a Crab but the second one was hit in the middle of the LCT exit and blocked all other vehicles. A single Crab from 22nd Dragoons thus continued its task, even when its flail was destroyed and it only had its 75-mm gun. A Squadron, 22nd Dragoons later landed to clear up the beach, while 80th Ass.Sq. were helping to seize Lion-sur-Mer.

In front of La Brèche and Ouistreham, a wide smoke screen was set above Roger Beach, the most difficult to seize since it was under the fire from long-range guns on Le Havre promontory. Two Crabs were put ashore at La Brèche, one being quickly knocked out, then a badly-launched SBG bridge blocked the exit; another way out was fortunately found. The second team lost its two leading Crabs, the AVRE SBG launched its bridge too early, and the mines in the dunes had to be cleared by hand: every other AVRE was drowned by the tide, only a bulldozer survived. The situation was not better for the third team, which lost one Crab disabled and another one destroyed. The SBG bridge was blocked by a tipped-up DD tank, and the ground was once again cleared of mines by hand so that a bulldozer could open up another lane through the dunes. Four exits were opened, but late, and the price was high. The tide prevented the beach from being cleared of mines, and 79th Ass.Sq. provided support to mop up the fortified villas on the seaside. Three Troops from 22nd and Westminster Dragoons joined 27th Arm.Brig. for an unsuccessful breakout attempt towards

Caen. 4 Commando called for 79th Ass.Sq. to help them in seizing the Ouistreham flood gates and bridge. Ten AVREs supported the Commandos from 15.30 onwards, the flood gates were taken intact but the bridge had been blown. Four AVREs then supported 2nd Royal Ulster Rifles in Bénouville, whilst part of 22nd Dragoons and of 5th Assault Rgt were doing the same with 51st Inf.Div. in a failed attempt to seize the radar of Douvres-la-Délivrande: they lost four AVREs in the process.

The D-Day achievements were positive for 79th Arm.Div.: all specialised equipment had worked, even if not on every occasion, with a particular distinction for the Crab and Petard. The losses were generally fairly light (seven men only for the Westminster Dragoons), but reached a peak of 117 killed or wounded in the 5th Assault Rgt. Twelve Crabs out of 50, 22 AVREs out of 120 were totally destroyed, and many others were damaged. As planned, the units settled near the exit of their respective beach in the evening of 6 June, and remained in reserve during the following days to undertake the needed repairs, although they took part in the clearing of the beaches and villages in the vicinity. However, following their great success on D-Day, high command was going to have recourse to the *Funnies* much sooner than expected.

*Above.*

**A Sherman Crab from 30th Arm.Brig. with its flail still wrapped in a protective cover is passing through a hedgerow in a dust cloud on 11 June. Quite oddly, it is fitted with two stowage bins, including one on the engine deck, of the type normally used on Fireflies. The tactical sign 53 shows that it belongs to the Westminster Dragoons.** *(RR)*

*Below.*

**Although 141st RAC from 31st Arm.Brig. was the only unit equipped with flame-thrower tanks, and although only a handful of them landed on 6 June, the Crocodiles were to see more and more widespread use in Normandy because of their formidable effectiveness on enemy equipment as well as on his morale.** *(RR)*

### Distribution of units for *D-Day*

● **8th Inf.Brig. (3rd Inf. Div.)** A Squadron, 22nd Dragoons; 77th and 79th Ass.Sq. (5th Assault Rgt).

● **7th and 8th Inf.Brig. (3rd Canadian Inf. Div.)** B Squadron 22nd Dragoons; 12 Crab from A Squadron Westminster Dragoons; 26th and 80th Ass.Sq. (5th Assault Rgt).

● **69th and 231st Inf.Brig. (50th Inf. Div.)** B and C Sqn Westminster Dragoons ; 81st and 82nd Ass.Sq. (6th Assault Rgt).

### Distribution of units for *Totalize*

● **51st Inf.Div.**

22nd Dragoons ; 80th Ass.Sq. (5th Assault Rgt)

● **2nd Canadian Inf.Div.**

1st Lothian & Border Horse Yeomanry ; 79th Ass.Sq. (5th Assault Rgt)

● **Army Corps reserve :**

A and B Squadron 141st RAC ; 87th Ass.Sq. (6th Assault Rgt).

## The beachhead

As early as 7 June, 82nd Ass.Sq. AVREs were required to help the progression of 50th Inf.Div. towards Bayeux, but without real fighting. C Squadron, Westminster Dragoons were in Crépon to drive off an enemy attack, and were reinforced with two Crocodiles from the just-landed 141st RAC (The Buffs): although belonging to 31st Tk.Brig., the latter regiment was put under control of 79th Arm.Div. for the whole Normandy campaign. The British counterstroke allowed the capture of five antitank guns and 100 prisoners. On the same day, five AVREs were lost during an attack towards Cambes by 3rd Inf.Div., 79th Ass.Sq. and A Squadron, Westminster Dragoons. The attack resumed on the two following days against 716.ID and 22.PzRgt. and was also supported by 26th Ass.Sq. On 15 and 16 June, 82nd Ass.Sq. moved up with 4/7th Dragoons (27th Arm.Div.) towards Lingèvres and Verrières but failed before Hottot on the 19th. After the assaults against the radar installations at Douvres-la-Délivrande had failed, a bigger operation was launched on 17 June by 46 Commando, with support from B and C Squadrons, 22nd Dragoons and 17 AVREs from 26th Ass.Sq. After an ineffective RAF bombardment, the assault was launched against the position heavily fortified with minefields, bunkers and trenches: success came fast, despite the loss of five Crabs and four AVREs. At the same time, Westminster Dragoons opened a road towards La Senaudière for 1st Hampshire (50th Inf.Div.) and lost two out of its six leading Crabs.

During the days following D-Day, the elements of 79th Arm.Div. were used piecemeal for various small-scale operations. Unfortunately, the vehicles were often used in too small number, under control of

officers who did not know their characteristics: their development had been too secret! For example, the AVREs were often used to breach the high Norman hedgerows with their Petard. Losses became too high, wear on the specialised vehicles was too great, and the crews were exhausted through incessant running from a point of the front to another. Moreover, the division was still incomplete, some elements were only to arrive in mid-July (Lothian and Border Horse, and the remainder of Westminster Dragoons), or even late July for 1st Tk.Brig. It was necessary to wait until the end of June to see these problems partly solved.

## Operations *Epsom, Martlet* and *Mitten*

*Epsom* was the first major operation since D-Day in which the 79th Arm.Div. took part. Launched on 25 June, it saw initially the commitment of 15th and 43rd Inf.Div. by-passing Caen from the west. Cheux was reached thanks to the support of Flails from B Squadron, 22nd Dragoons, while C Squadron, Westminster Dragoons were operating around

Flails. The Buffs' B Squadron then achieved a superb action: taking the lead in front of 7th Canadian Inf.Brig., the Crocodiles flamed out and suppressed the bunkers and hangars one after the other, and lost a single tank in spite of a ferocious defence.

Operation *Charnwood* began on 7 July, and was to drive the Hitlerjugend out of the suburbs of Caen. 22nd Dragoons, as well as 27th Arm.Brig., were mainly dispatched between 185th Inf. Brig. (3rd Inf.Div.), 197.Inf.Brig. (59th Inf.Div.) and 176th Inf.Brig. A Squadron was moving up with 9th Canadian Inf.Brig. and the Sherbrooke Fusiliers. Only two Crabs were lost during the assault, but 141st RAC's A and B Squadrons, which were scattered along the attack line, did not get out of it unscathed: two Crocodiles ended up in flames, two others were knocked out, and casualties, mainly officers, were heavy because of mines. Two Troops of A Squadron, The Buffs took part in the final seizure of Le Bon Repos on 15 July, with 53rd Inf.Div. For their part, C Squadron were cooperating at best with 59th Inf.Div. For Operation *Goodwood*, 8th Corps had its disposal the 22nd Dragoons, who moved up in the lead with 11th Arm.Div.: a single Flail was lost at Le Mesnil-Frémentel. 1st Lothian and Border Horse Yeomanry, who had just landed, were immediately committed around Esquay and Evrecy, where their C Squadron suffered their first loss of three Crabs. B Squadron were with 3rd Inf.Div. near Escoville and lost a tank whilst supporting infantry. The AVREs, although less in demand, nevertheless provided regular support to the infantry: 82nd Ass.Sq. operated with 50th Inf.Div. in Grainville and Hottot on 10 and 12 July, and later supported 43rd Inf.Div. around Le Bon Repos. On 30 July, C Squadron, 141st RAC flamed out machine-gun nests in St-Germain-d'Ectot, and a tank commander led the attack of the infantry who were not too familiar with the use of flame-thrower tanks.

## August 1944, the breakout

The remnants of 6th Assault Rgt (87th and 284th Ass.Sq.) arrived on 31 July with the headquarters of 1st Assault Brig., and were installed in St-Gabriel. On the same day Operation *Bluecoat* was launched: in the course of this offensive starting from Caumont-l'Eventé, 141st RAC's C Squadron moved up with infantry without major fighting. On the other hand, 22nd Dragoons who had to clear the road up to Villers-Bocage on 3 August, lost five

St-Manvieu without meeting any minefields, and then continued with the Churchills from 9th RTR (31st Tk.Brig.) towards Carpiquet airfield. Crocodiles from A and B Squadron, 141st RAC also took part in the seizing of Cheux on 27 June. On 26 June Operation *Martlet* was launched which was to enable 49th Inf.Div. and 8th Arm.Brig. to take Rauray and Fontenay-le-Pesnel. 82nd Ass.Sq. brought effective support with its AVRE Petards and Besas.

For Operation *Mitten* starting on 27 June, Crocodiles from 141st RAC's B Squadron and AVREs from 79th Ass.Sq. supported 3rd Inf.Div. and Staffordshire Yeomanry (27th Arm.Brig.) for the seizure of the chateau de La Londe and Le Landel. Opposition was stronger than expected and was mainly made up of SPGs and tanks, of which 14 were around the chateau. The Crocodiles outran their infantry from the beginning of the attack. 8th Troop in the lead lost a Croc hit by a Panzer IV, another was disabled, and only one could continue the assault. One of the AVREs shelling the chateau was destroyed, others ran into Tigers in the Combes wood and hastily retreated. The attack resumed the following day, with C Squadron, 22nd Dragoons, but even help from the Crocodiles did not prevent it from failing. In late June, 81st Ass.Sq. supported 56th Inf.Brig. in Tilly-sur-Seulles against a Panzer-Lehr attack, and lost the first intact AVRE to the enemy, so their commanding officer was very angry.

## From *Charnwood* to *Goodwood*

During July, there was less demand for AVREs. On the other hand, Crabs and Crocodiles were constantly sought after, and Hobart succeeded in obtaining from Montgomery a certain amount of control upon the way his scattered units were used. The 79th Arm.Div. provided advisers for every major operation, and they took part in the planning with senior officers of the other units. But many local support was still given without enough coordination. For the assault on 4 July, which was to bring 3rd Canadian Inf.Div. from Bretteville-l'Orgueilleuse up to Carpiquet airfield, 15 Crabs from A Squadron, 22nd Dragoons, plus B Squadron 141st RAC and 80th Ass.Sq. were available. The village was taken, but the airfield was held by tanks of 12.SS-PzDiv., and the reinforcing Sherbrooke Fusiliers Rgt were also stopped while 22nd Dragoons lost two

Flails on a heavily mined and hard surface. On the next day, their C Squadron lost two more tanks, and clearing the mines up had to be continued by hand: out of the 21 Crabs at the beginning, there were only 9 left in running order 48 hours later! A Crab from C Squadron, Westminster Dragoons was destroyed while supporting 7th Arm. Div. in St-Germain-d'Ectot. From 5 to 7 August, B Squadron worked with 43rd Inf.Div. and 13th/18th Royal Hussars, then 6th Guards Tk.Brig., on Mont Pinçon. The Lothian & Border Horse preceded the infantry from 15th Inf.Div. in Sept-Vents, and lost two Crabs on mines.

Operation *Totalize* starting on 7 August was an attempt by 2nd Canadian Corps to break through towards Falaise. The armoured troop carrier Kangaroo made then its first apparition, and was soon to be part of the 79th Arm.Div. circus, which was greatly involved into Totalize (see distribution tables). Four columns were formed, where specialised armour was interspersed with tanks and troop car-

*Above.*
**In early August, a Westminster Dragoons Sherman Crab is crossing the Winston Bridge in Vaucelles. Almost all crew members are wearing a scarf around their neck, to protect their nose and mouth when the flail is in action: August in Normandy was very dry in 1944, and the dust cloud thrown up by a flailing Crab was impressive.** *(IWM B8778)*

*Below.*
**Empty Kangaroos are coming back into the 51st Inf.Div. sector after the 7 August night march. These specialised AFVs, gathered in two regiments and converted by the Canadian Engineers from 105-mm M7 Priest SPGs, were to be attached to 79th Arm.Div. in December 1944, but they sometimes worked from as early as August under control of this unit.**
*(Tank Museum 2292/E2)*

riers. The night march was hectic through smoke and dust: despite guiding and directional devices, vehicles got lost, crashed into each other, fell into bomb craters. Fortunately, the off-road progression enabled them to avoid most of the mined areas, and the armour of 79th Arm.Div. had not much to do during the first successful phase of the battle. For instance, 79th Ass.Sq. opened the road for the Canadians close behind the tanks of 2nd Canadian Arm.Brig., while the Crabs destroyed several antitank guns. Fighting got tough on 8 August, and 22nd Dragoons moved back in the evening with 14 damaged Flails, whilst two other destroyed ones were abandoned. On the following days, the regiment supported the 1st Polish Arm.

Operation Totalize was not the only opportunity to use the Crabs for 79th Arm.Div. in August: on the 8th, this column of Flails is stopped on a road south of Aunay-sur-Odon, waiting to advance towards Le Plessis-Grimoult as part of operation *Bluecoat*. (RR)

Div. (A Squadron with 2nd Armoured Regiment, B Squadron with 1st Armoured Regiment and C Squadron with 24th Lancers). The AVREs were not widely used, so their crews took part in the mine clearing and marking-out job. B Squadron, The *Buffs* moved up with the Gordon Highlanders in Secqueville-la-Campagne on the 8th, and then mopped up the surrounding woods with 148th

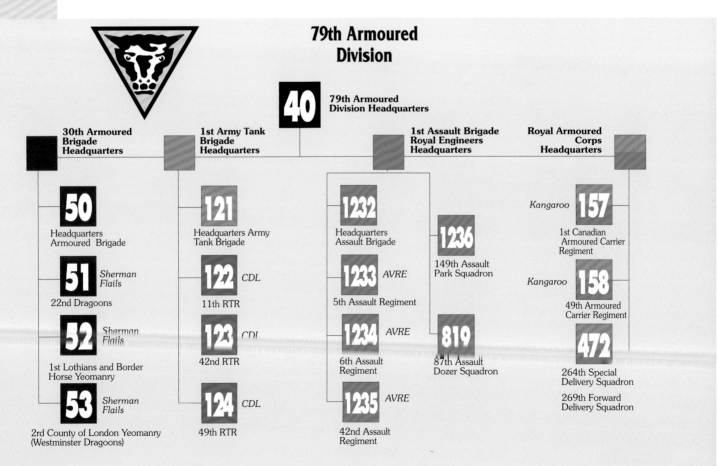

# REGIMENTS ACCORDING TO THE ORDER OF PRECEDENCE

## 22nd Dragoons

- **Origins:** Regiment raised in 1716 by Viscount Mountjoy, named "22nd Light Dragoons", disbanded in 1718. Reformed in 1760, but disbanded three years later. Recreated by Viscount Fielding in 1794, served in Ireland and in India in 1798, in Egypt in 1801. Disbanded in 1802, the name was given to "25th Light Dragoons" raised in 1794 in India. Sent to Java (1811) then to India (1817), disbanded in 1820.

- **1939-44:** The "22nd Dragoons" was reconstituted by Lieutenant Colonel Craig in 1940, with cadres from 4/7th and 5th Dragoon Guards. Joined 30th Arm. Brig. in January 1941, assigned to 79th Arm.Div. in October 1943. First commitment with this unit in Normandy, then fought up to Germany.

## 1st Regiment, Lothian and Border Horse Yeomanry

- **Origins:** Regiment raised in 1797 in five distinct corps, including "East Lothian Yeomanry Cavalry" and "Berwickshire Yeomanry". After many disbandments and reconstitutions of the various corps, "The East Lothian and Berwickshire Yeomanry Cavalry" was formed in 1880, and became "The East Lothian and Berwickshire Imperial Yeomanry" in 1900, to serve in South Africa. Became "The Lothians and Border Horse TF (Dragoons)" in 1908, three battalions formed in 1914 were dispatched in various Squadrons within 22nd, 25th and 26th Divisions, notably taking part in the battles of Bapaume, Flanders, Macedonia, the Somme. Joined the Territorial Army in 1922, and became "19th (Lothians and Border Horse) Armoured Car Company RTC TA". Converted into armoured regiment in 1936 under the name of "Lothians and Border Horse RAC TA"; a second regiment was raised in 1939.

- **1939-44:** The first regiment fought in France in 1940, at the side of 51st Highland Division in Saint-Valéry-en-Caux. Joined 30th Arm.Brig. in March 1941, attached to 79th Arm.Div. in October 1943. Fought from Normandy to Germany with this division.

## 2nd County of London Yeomanry (Westminster Dragoons)

- **Origins:** Raised in 1779 as "London and Westminster Light Horse", disbanded in 1783. Recreated in 1794 in several corps, all disbanded in 1829. The "24th Battalion Metropolitan Mounted Rifles" formed in 1901 took the name of "2nd County of London Imperial Yeomanry", and became "2nd County of London Yeomanry (Westminster Dragoons) TF" in 1908, after having served in South Africa. Two regiments formed in 1914 fought separately in Egypt, at Gallipoli, in Palestine. Reformed as a single regiment in 1917, converted into Infantry Regiment then "104th Machine Gun Battalion"in 1918. "The 2nd County of London Yeomanry (Westminster Dragoons) TF" was reconstituted in 1920, then joined the Territorial Army in 1922 and became armoured car regiment.

- **1939-44:** Converted in 1940 into Armoured Regiment, "2nd County of London Yeomanry (Westminster Dragoons) TA", then attached to 30th Arm.Brig. in March 1941. First committed with 79th Arm.Div. in Normandy in June 1944.

## 11th Battalion, Royal Tank Regiment

- **Origins:** In common with the whole Royal Tank Regiment., see 1st RTR (7th Arm.Div.).

- **1939-44:** Regiment raised in November 1940 and incorporated into 25th Army Tk.Brig. until April 1941. Joined 1st Army Tk.Brig. from November 1942 in Palestine, then returned to England in early 1944. Landed with this brigade in Normandy, as "Canal Defence Light"regiment.

## 42nd Battalion, Royal Tank Regiment

- **Origins:** In common with the whole Royal Tank Regiment. Regiment derived in 1938 from the conversion of "7th TA Battalion (23rd London Regiment) The East Surrey Regiment", an infantry unit with origins dating back to "7th Southwark Regiment" of the Rifle Volunteer Corps, created in 1859.

- **1939-44:** Integrated into 21st Army Tk.Brig. from its formation in September 1940 onwards, then joined 1st Army Tk.Brig. in July 1941 in North Africa then in Palestine. Took part with this unit in the North-West Europe campaign.

## 49th Battalion, Royal Tank Regiment

- **Origins:** In common with the whole Royal Tank Regiment.

- **1939-44:** Regiment formed in 1939 as duplicate of 46th RTR, itself raised in 1938 from the "Liverpool Welsh Regiment TA" as duplicate of 40th RTR. Integrated into 25th Army Tk.Brig. from its formation in September 1939 onwards, in England. Attached to 1st Army Tk.Brig. from January to March 1941, then joined again 25th Army Tk.Brig. from May 1941 to July 1942. With 35th Army Tk.Brig. from August 1942 to April 1944. Often assigned to 1st Army Tk.Brig. under direct control of 79th Arm.Div., landed with this unit in Normandy.

## 5th, 6th et 42nd Assault Regiments, Royal Engineers

- **Origins:** Created by conversion respectively of 5th and 6th Chemical Warfare Group Regiments, Royal Engineers, and of a composite regiment raised when 42nd Arm.Div. was disbanded in November 1943.

- **1939-44:** Formed the 1st Armoured Engineers Brigade in December 1943, which soon after became 1st Assault Brigade. Among the first units to land with this brigade in Normandy.

---

RAC (33rd Arm.Brig.) A Squadron's Crocodiles supported the Fusiliers Mont-Royal in May-sur-Orne, and attacked with nine tanks in a front row: using flame-throwers, 75-mm guns and Besas, they wiped out the enemy defence and prevented any loss for the infantry. In support of the Sherbrooke Fusiliers and 14th Canadian Hussars, and with no mines to clear, the Flails from Lothian & Border Horse operated as standard tanks in Fontenay-le-Marmion and Rocquancourt.

While 6th Assault Rgt were already training near Courseulles to river crossing, Operation *Tractable* was launched on 14 August by 2nd Canadian Corps, in order to seize Falaise at last. The AVREs from 80th Ass.Sq. led with fascines to cross the River Laison, and they were joined by Scissors bridges. C Squadron, Lothian & Border Horse supported South Alberta Rgt and lost three Flails to antitank guns. A and B Squadrons made progress towards Rouvres, eliminating two mortars and two 88s. 22nd Dragoons' A and C Squadrons were supporting Fort Garry Horse and 1st Canadian Hussars towards Estrée-la-Campagne, then the regiment was withdrawn on the following day for ten days. The clearing of Rouvres was carried out by the Régiment de la Chaudière and B Squadron, 141st RAC, while A Squadron of the latter had a hard time supporting 9th Canadian Inf.Brig.: five *Crocs* were lost to fire from 88s, 75s and Tigers. The Squadron was placed in reserve for

five days in Lion-sur-Mer. C Squadron, *The Buffs* did not take part in *Tractable*, since they were still fighting on Mont Pinçon. AVREs from 26th, 80th and 87th Ass.Sq. were likewise under control of 30th Corps from 5 to 14 August, helping by "*Petarding*" to clear strong points and machine-gun nests in Chênedollé and Viessoix, and launching fascines and Scissors bridges for the 7th Arm.Div.

The 1st Tk.Brig. had arrived on 8 August but was not engaged in *Totalize* despite the real advantages of CDL tanks for a night attack; it continued training. 42nd Assault Rgt (1st Assault Brig.) only arrived on 17 August with the 16th, 222nd et 617th Ass.Sq.; these took no part in the fighting and trained instead for river crossing, since the last stage was the River Seine. For the pursuit eastwards, specialised armour of the division provided support for 51st Inf.Div. and 7th Arm.Div., but was of little use because too slow.

Furthermore, the obstacles for which they had been designed (minefields, craters, unbridged waterways) were scarce. A Squadron, *The Buffs* followed the route of these units, while B Squadron stayed near Vimoutiers. The Westminster Dragoons were with 30th Corps in Gacé, Laigle then Rugles, while the Lothian & Border Horse remained in Louvigny for a week: they were to be one of the first 79th Arm.Div. units to cross the River Seine on 28 August.

# GUARDS ARMOURED DIVISION

**F**EARING AN IMMINENT INVASION BY THE GERMAN ARMY, Great-Britain discovered in the late spring 1941 that there were not enough armoured divisions in the country to counter the Panzer-Divisionen that had been so successful during the Battle of France.

In addition to the creation of several new units, it was also decided to convert elements of the Guards Brigade, who had however a long infantry tradition, into armoured regiments, and to form an armoured division. The Guards Brigade was a prestige and elite unit, the members of which had thorough knowledge in multiple domains, and most of whose officers were enthusiastic and volunteered for the armour. The Guards Armoured Division was created in June 1941, under command of Major General Sir Oliver Leese, and the first theoretical instruction was dispensed by the Royal Armoured Corps in Lullworth and Bovington. According to the organization tables of the time, the division included two armoured brigades (5th and 6th Guards Arm.Brig.) formed in September 1941, and one infantry brigade (32nd Guards Brig.) constituted in May 1942. Other units progressively joined this nucleus, although most of them did not belong to the Guards: Royal Artillery, Royal Engineers…

The insignia chosen for the division was directly inspired from that of the Guards Division during the Great War, an ever opened eye, but was redesigned by a Welsh guardsman and artist, Rex Whistler. For three

years, the Guards Arm.Div. trained on more or less muddy terrains, in often summary encampments. It took part in many exercises, first in the expectation of a possible invasion to be repelled, then for real offensive fighting. Unfortunately, there was not enough emphasis on the close cooperation between infantry and armour, which was to be detrimental for the future campaign. Brigadier Adair was appointed in September 1942 to command the division, which lost the 6th Guards Arm.Brig. a month later to match with the new structure of the armoured division. A single armoured brigade, the 5th Guards, thus remained including 2nd Armoured Battalion, Grenadier Guards; 1st Armoured Battalion, Coldstream Guards; and 2nd Armoured Battalion, Irish Guards. At the same period, the 2nd Household Cavalry became Corps Troop, and were replaced with the 2nd Welsh Guards converted to Armoured Reconnaissance Regiment and equipped with Centaur and later Cromwell tanks. In spring 1943, the armoured regiments substituted Sherman Vs for

*Top.* **On 30 March 1944, a few weeks before D-Day, Winston Churchill paid a visit to 2nd Welsh Guards and is seen inspecting one of their Cromwells: he seems to be interested in a device on the turret looking like some kind of sights or maybe a night vision system. Textbook markings are applied: tactical sign 45 on green and blue background of a recce armoured regiment; bridge classification disc; letter A (1st Troop?) in the square of a B Squadron; divisional insignia.** *(IWM H37169)*

*Left.*
**On 18 July, first day of Operation Goodwood, Carriers from 21st Anti-Tank Rgt are followed by an OP Sherman from 55th Field Rgt, both units belonging to the Guards Arm.Div. Such a column in exposed country and during daytime was only made possible by the aerial superiority the Allies enjoyed in Normandy.**
*(IWM B7654)*

*Bottom.*
**A 2nd Welsh Guards tank is crossing the River Orne on a Bailey bridge on 18 July, heading for the assembling area before the attack. The divisional insignia can be seen besides the C Squadron circle, surrounding the number 14. The Guards Arm.Div. Cromwells were modified by the fitting of two U-shaped sheet-metal protections above the exhaust, in order to prevent the combustion gas from being sucked in by the ventilation fans and entering the fighting compartment. An official device, named Normandy Cowl, was later fitted on every Cromwell.** *(IWM B7656)*

their Covenanters, and the division prepared intensively for the landings in France.

## Invasion and Operation *Goodwood*

Under command of 8th Corps, the Guards Arm.Div. was to go ashore in Normandy on 16 June, but the violent storm that devastated then the Channel coast delayed its landing until the 22nd. At that date, only the forward parties disembarked, soon followed by 32nd Guards Brig. and most of the artillery, which settled for a week on defensive positions near Bretteville-l'Orgueilleuse. The division suffered here its first losses to the fire of German field guns and mortars. These units provided casual support to other British or Canadian divisions during Operations *Epsom* and Windsor, and then they joined the rest of the division on 11 July.

From 14 July onwards, the Guards Arm.Div. prepared for Operation *Goodwood*, an attempt to break out towards Falaise through the fortified villages east of Caen. During this offensive beginning on 18 July, it was to follow the 11th Arm.Div. on the left flank.

For the first action of the division on its whole, the assault units gathered at night after having passed through the ruined city of Caen, in the dust and confusion of traffic jams. Waiting for information

from 11th Arm.Div., the progress of which dictated their own advance, the members of the Guards Arm.Div. had the opportunity to contemplate the huge air bombardment which was pounding the enemy lines. They were blocked in the drop zone of the 6th Airborne gliders on 6 June, and started soon after 8.00, initially meeting light opposition. The flank cover was provided by the 2nd Welsh Guards, and three groups were formed from the armoured regiments, with in departing order: Grenadier Guards on the one hand; 2nd Irish Guards and HQ Squadron of 5th Arm.Brig. on the other hand; and finally 1st Coldstream Guards.

These groups each included a company of motorized infantry from the 1st Grenadier Guards. They headed towards Cagny that 11th Arm.Div. had not been able to seize. N°2 Squadron, Grenadier Guards were engaged by antitank guns 1 1/2 miles from the village, they were stopped there and lost three tanks. Two Troops of N°1 Squadron were sent to by-pass the locality on the left, and reached the village in the afternoon for the loss of one Sherman. Whilst N°3 Squadron remained there in cover, an artillery barrage allowed the infantry to seize Cagny and to capture three 88 guns abandoned by the Germans.

The 2nd Irish Guards slowly advanced in the wake of this first group, gradually passing the many tank wrecks of 11th Arm.Div. and also of the Grenadier Guards who had lost nine in all. After several skirmishes, the regiment (or Battalion, in the Guards) almost came to a standstill at noon, and received the order to pass beyond Cagny to make for Vimont. But it was stopped dead by antitank guns and Panzers, including two Tigers from schwere Panzer-Abteilung 503, which were in ambush in the woods eastwards. On that occasion, Lieutenant Gorman commanding Troop 2 in N°2 Squadron, tried to reach the British lines with two Shermans, having left his own tank completely bogged-down in a stream. At the bend of a track, he ran

On 30 July, a Stuart VI from the 2nd Irish Guards (see tactical sign 53 and divisional insignia above the right light) is leading a column of Shermans and half-tracks during the attack south of Caumont. The Guards Arm.Div. was one of the rare British units to be issued with the more recent M5A1 version of the Stuart. (IWM B8275)

into four Panzers (a Tiger I, a Tiger II, a Panther and a Panzer IV), their guns aiming by chance in the other direction. Gorman ordered to fire, but the gun jammed! Seeing the Tiger II turret slowly rotating towards him, he ordered the driver to step on the accelerator, and with his Sherman rammed the Panzer before it could open fire. After having managed to avoid capture with his crew (alas, the second Sherman was destroyed by three shots), he went back to take command of the Troop Firefly which was without a commander, and came back to finish his prey: he was later awarded the Military Cross for this feat of arms. The 2nd Irish Guards reached the Caen – Lisieux road (N13), but the edge of the woods was harshly defended by enemy self-propelled or towed antitank guns, which knocked out two tanks right away: it proved impossible to advance farther. This left little room for the progression of the *Coldstreamers* who were following: N°1 Squadron entered the wood where the fire was coming from, and they destroyed the first Panther in the division.

The 32nd Guards Brig. was at the rear of the column, advancing by fits and starts, and it only caught up to relieve the armour in the evening. An attack towards Frénouville by the 3rd Irish Guards supported by the 2nd Irish Guards was launched indeed by night, but the village was too strongly held and the troops had to withdraw on 19 July at dawn.

Most of that day was spent on defensive positions, and only at 17.00 did the infantry (2nd Welsh Guards and 5th Coldstream Guards) attack Frénouville successfully, although without tank support: the latter had tried to go along the N13 but had been driven back towards Cagny by the 12.SS-Panzer-Division. The torrential rains falling from 20 July onwards interrupted Operation *Goodwood*, and for three days Guards Arm.Div. held its positions under the harassing air and ground bombardments: the Luftwaffe carried out a lot of day and night raids, in spite of the effective defence of 94th Light Anti-Aircraft Regiment which shot down three aircraft at least.

## A break in the fighting

The Guards Arm.Div. withdrawal was delayed by the rain, but 51st Highland Division finally came to relieve it on 22 July. The officers already assessed the situation after *Goodwood*: the results of the division's first commitment were mitigated, mainly because of an ill-conceived general plan, but also because of poor cooperation between infantry and armour, which were separated for the assault, in contradiction with the tactics developed while training. The ground considered as "*Tank Country*" and looking like Salisbury Plain had turned out to be fatal for the Shermans surpassed by the enemy guns' long range and large calibre.

Billeted for a week in the devastated suburbs of Caen, still within the range of German guns, the division suffered further occasional casualties although it was there to reorganize, take up reinforcements and be issued with 60 replacement tanks to make up the losses of *Goodwood*. On 28 July, after the failure of Operation *Spring*, the information about the American success of Operation *Cobra* caused the division to be transferred westwards of Bayeux and then to Caumont-l'Eventé; the units started to move on the 30th to come under control of 8th Corps and take part in the new British offensive.

On that occasion, a new and more balanced style of organization was adopted, combining an infantry regiment with an armour counterpart, in order to improve their cooperation: each brigade included two groups, 2nd (Armoured) Grenadier Guards/1st (Motor) Grenadier Guards and 2nd (Armoured) Irish Guards/5th Coldstream Guards in 5th Guards Arm. Brig.; 2nd (Recce) Welsh Guards/1st Welsh Guards and 1st (Armoured) Coldstream Guards/3rd Irish Guards in 32nd Guards Brig.

*Above.*
In Cagny on 20 July, two Sherman ARVs probably belonging to the Guards Arm.Div. are heading for the village church, in front of which a Sherman has fallen into a large bomb crater. Sappers are already working near the tank for its imminent recovery. *(RR)*

*Below.*
A Sherman V named "Vengeance" is passing by the church of Caumont-l'Eventé on 30 July, during operation Bluecoat. This tank may belong to the Guards Arm.Div., which was to attack on the following day in this sector, for other stills of vehicles from this unit can be found a bit further on the same photographic report.
*(IWM B8187)*

# Guards
# Armoured Division

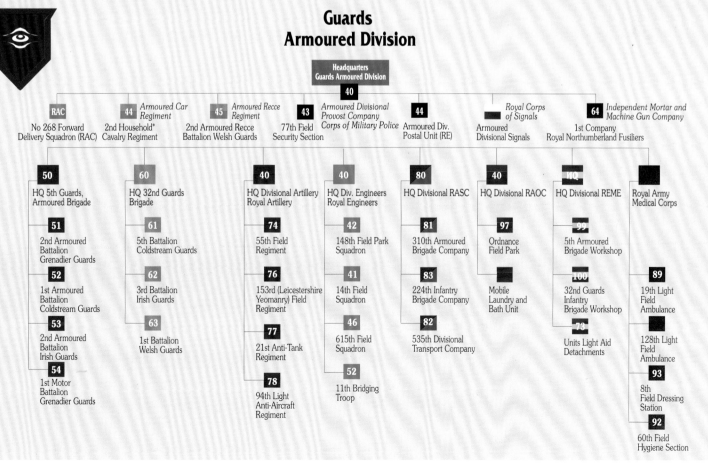

**Headquarters
Guards Armoured Division**
**40**

| RAC | | *Armoured Car Regiment* **44** | *Armoured Recce Regiment* **45** | **43** | *Armoured Divisional Provost Company Corps of Military Police* | **44** | *Royal Corps of Signals* | *Independent Mortar and Machine Gun Company* **64** |
|---|---|---|---|---|---|---|---|---|
| No 268 Forward Delivery Squadron (RAC) | 2nd Household* Cavalry Regiment | 2nd Armoured Recce Battalion Welsh Guards | 77th Field Security Section | Armoured Div. Postal Unit (RE) | Armoured Divisional Signals | 1st Company Royal Northumberland Fusiliers |

| **50** | **60** | **40** | **40** | **80** | **40** | **HQ** | |
|---|---|---|---|---|---|---|---|
| HQ 5th Guards, Armoured Brigade | HQ 32nd Guards Brigade | HQ Divisional Artillery Royal Artillery | HQ Div. Engineers Royal Engineers | HQ Divisional RASC | HQ Divisional RAOC | HQ Divisional REME | Royal Army Medical Corps |
| **51** | **61** | **74** | **42** | **81** | **97** | **99** | |
| 2nd Armoured Battalion Grenadier Guards | 5th Battalion Coldstream Guards | 55th Field Regiment | 148th Field Park Squadron | 310th Armoured Brigade Company | Ordnance Field Park | 5th Armoured Brigade Workshop | 19th Light Field Ambulance **89** |
| **52** | **62** | **76** | **41** | **83** | | **100** | |
| 1st Armoured Battalion Coldstream Guards | 3rd Battalion Irish Guards | 153rd (Leicestershire Yeomanry) Field Regiment | 14th Field Squadron | 224th Infantry Brigade Company | Mobile Laundry and Bath Unit | 32nd Guards Infantry Brigade Workshop | 128th Light Field Ambulance |
| **53** | **63** | **77** | **46** | **82** | | **73** | **93** |
| 2nd Armoured Battalion Irish Guards | 1st Battalion Welsh Guards | 21st Anti-Tank Regiment | 615th Field Squadron | 535th Divisional Transport Company | | Units Light Aid Detachments | 8th Field Dressing Station |
| **54** | | **78** | **52** | | | | **92** |
| 1st Motor Battalion Grenadier Guards | | 94th Light Anti-Aircraft Regiment | 11th Bridging Troop | | | | 60th Field Hygiene Section |

*Above.*
**The Guards Arm.Div. is entering St-Martin-des-Besaces on 31 July: this Sherman Vc Firefly probably belongs to the 2nd Irish Guards, who were leading the division with infantry from the 5th Coldstream Guards. Except for some damaged house roofs, the village seems to have suffered little from the fighting.** *(IWM B8293)*

## Operation *Bluecoat*

For this offensive planned to follow the American progression southwards and cover their west flank, 8th Corps had the leading role with 30th Corps on its left. The objective was a long ridge of hills between St-Martin-des-Besaces and Thury-Harcourt, culminating with Mont Pinçon which offered the enemy an overlooking position. The attack by 11th Arm.Div., 15th Inf.Div. and 6th Guards Tk.Brig. began on 30th July and met first an encouraging success, even though 30th Corps was labouring to follow on the left. Guards Arm.Div. entered the fray on the 31st in the morning, in a new hilly bocage landscape, and the 2nd Irish Guards/5th Coldstream Guards group took the lead towards St-Martin-des-Besaces, heading for St-Charles-de-Percy and the River Souleuvre in the distance. The ridge was reached in the evening, and on 1st August the advance resumed towards Hill 238 and 192, against increasing opposition from 21.Pz-Div. which was finally driven out after violent fighting. The Grenadier Guards group consolidated the position, and 32nd Guards Brig. was brought in as reinforcement to send 1st Welsh Guards towards St-Denis-Maisoncelles in order to maintain

*Below.*
**From St-Martin-des-Besaces, the Guards advanced on 1 August towards the River Souleuvre. The division now entering the bocage country incited the crews to thoroughly camouflage their tanks, a rare practice until then. Foliage and hessian tape are efficiently used to break the angular shape of this Sherman.**
*(Tank Museum 4812/A4)*

contact with 11th Arm.Div. 3rd Irish Guards and a *Coldstreamers'* Squadron had to repel the enemy in Le Tourneur and seize the Souleuvre river bridge there. In spite of heavy defensive fire, the attack succeeded but Le Tourneur was only reached at night. The assault resumed in the night of 2 August against the strongly held village, the attackers managed to get to the river and the Royal Engineers from 615th Field Squadron realised that the bridge was intact; it was under the control of 3rd Irish Guards before

A Sherman named "Black Sod" is climbing up a ditch during Operation Bluecoat, in early August: this nickname, written on the driver and machine-gunner armours, is known to have been given to a Sherman from N°2 Squadron, 2nd Irish Guards, whose tanks had names beginning with the letter B.
*(Tank Museum 4836/B1)*

dawn. After this rather easy success, order was given to seize Vassy, 20 km further south!

5th Arm.Brig. took the lead again, and the Grenadier Guards group headed for Montcharival (probably an English alteration of Montchauvet) and, beyond that, for Mont Pinçon. 2nd Irish Guards/ 5th Coldstream Guards pushed on towards St-Charles-de-Percy then Montchamp and Estry. The Cathéolles bridge was crossed without difficulty, but the defence put up by 21.Pz-Div. was being strongly reinforced with 9.SS-Pz.Div. Hohenstaufen. In the morning, N°1 Squadron of 2nd Welsh Guards were travelling towards Montcharival, climbing up along the bends of the little river running in the valley, when the leading Cromwell was suddenly knocked out just before the village, obstructing the road. The river and the trees on each side precluded any by-passing, and the Welsh Guards had to move back to be relieved by the Grenadier Guards. N°3 Squadron meanwhile moved past St-Charles-de-Percy and found the road to Courteil was blocked by antitank guns. They turned away further east towards Maisoncelle, which was also strongly defended

by the Germans. An exit was found further south, and patrols were sent towards Estry, while N°1 and 2 Squadrons joined up. The Grenadier Guards had mopped up the surroundings of the hamlet of Drouet, but they failed before Arclais, were driven back by a hard counterstroke and had to dig in. Because of this failure, 2nd Irish Guards/5th Coldstream Guards could not advance any more and had to stop in view of the Germans who copiously shelled them. The tanks finally managed to open the road towards St-Charles-de-Percy, but they were stopped in Courteil like the Welsh Guards. They followed the same route as the latter, and arrived in La Marvindière at night.

*Below.* **On 2 August, the Guards Arm.Div. is passing through Cathéolles to cross the Souleuvre river bridge. A Sherman V, well protected with spare track links, is raising a dust cloud while going through the Caen – Vire and Le Bény-Bocage – Montchauvet crossroads. Two days later, Churchills from 6th Guards Tk.Brig. were also photographed on this seemingly busy location.**
*(Tank Museum 4811/C1)*

On 3 August in the morning, all the elements of 5th Guards Arm. Brig. were committed, it was so the turn of 32nd Guards Brig. to break open a passage towards Montchamp and Estry, with the 3rd Irish Guards and a Squadron from the 1st Coldstream Guards in the lead. The infantry without transport means had to walk up to St-Charles-de-Percy. Progressing by fits and starts, the group succeeded in seizing Courteil and stopped before Maisoncelle for the night. The Grenadier Guards in Drouet were meanwhile enduring three violent counterstrokes from the Hohenstaufen. The area around the hamlet remained insecure, and a hill occupied by the Germans was overlooking the very close country, but its slopes were too steep and wooded for the tanks. It fell to the infantry of 44th Brigade (15th Inf.Div.) helped by the 1st Welsh Guards to conquer this position, which they did when the enemy finally withdrew. On its side, the 3rd Irish Guards had seized Maisoncelle and the *Coldstreamers* had destroyed a Panther and a StuG in La Marvindière. But general counterattacks on the whole front meant that the positions had to be consolidated: the infantry then did most of the clearing job,

sometimes supported by a *Coldstreamers'* Squadron when Panzers were met. An attempt to seize Montchamp thus failed despite the destruction of a Panzer IV with a PIAT and the arrival of the Coldstream Guards tanks to drive back the Hohenstaufen's Panthers.

On the same day, the 2nd Welsh Guards, 2nd Irish Guards and 5th Coldstream Guards had made progress towards Estry and Le Busq, but fierce defence put up by 9.SS-PzDiv. forced them to fall back. Even the 153rd (Leicester Yeomanry) Field Regiment from the divisional artillery was threatened near St-Charles-de-Percy and had to be protected against the Panthers by the 21st Anti-Tank Regiment's SPGs: three Panthers were destroyed, and a fourth was claimed by two Troops of 1st Coldstream Guards who came up as reinforcements. If the progression was good, the situation of the leading elements was very difficult, and 29th Arm.Brig. (11th Arm.Div.) even had to bring in part of the supplies they required from its adjacent positions.

## The thrust south-eastwards

From the 4 August onwards, the front was quieter in the Guards Armoured Division's sector, although the unit endured losses to the enemy mortar and gun harassing fire. The wounded had to be evacuated by emergency means, but the Germans abandoning Montchamp on 5 August lifted the pressure on this area. On 6 August, the 5th Coldstream Guards, supported with indirect fire from the Irish Guards Shermans, tried in vain to seize Estry and had to stop in Les Ecublets. The same attempt by 15th Inf.Div. on 7 August also failed. It appeared that the Vire – Estry line was very strongly defended, the Germans protecting their attack westwards (Operation *Lüttich*). Holding the front was the order of the day, thus allowing the units to take a short rest in rotation. In the salient threatened by the 10.SS-PzDiv. Frundsberg, 5th Guards Brig. was given control of half of the front left by 11th Arm.Div. moving eastwards.

On 11 August began Operation *Grouse* with the Vire – Vassy road, and further away Mont Cerisy and Tinchebray, as objectives. The main axis was followed by 32nd Guards Brig. towards Chênedollé and Le Boulay-aux-Chats, with strong artillery support, and back-up from the Churchills of the 3rd Scots Guards (6th Guards Tk.Brig.) The 1st Welsh Guards, 3rd Scots Guards and 2nd Irish Guards captured the hills between Le Bas Perrier and Pierres, to the heavy cost of one hundred casualties. The rest of the division was then to reach the Viessoix – Chênedollé road, but progression was slow because of mines and isolated attacks by Panzerfaust teams. The fate of the 3rd Irish Guards/1st Coldstream Guards group was much worse: it took part in an action considered as secondary south of Sourdevalle, with practically no artillery support (a single Field Bat-

*Top, left.*
**Still at Cathéolles crossroads, a long Guards Arm.Div. column is stopped along the road: it includes Shermans as well as Carriers from 1st Company Royal Northumberland Fusiliers, identified by the tactical sign 64. It was the divisional Mortar and Machine-gun Company. Note the white star painted on the tarpaulin covering a spare wheel on the first Carrier.**
*(Tank Museum 4835/D5)*

*Left.*
**On the Caen – Vire road, near St-Charles-de-Percy, Churchills from 6th Guards Tk.Brig. are passing by Sherman Vs from 1st Coldstream Guards. The writer Robert Boscawen, who was a member of this unit and whose book is in the bibliography, has recognized his tank (N°2, without rear stowage box), preceded by the N°2A of Sergeant Brough, and followed by N°2B of Sergeant Caulfield.**
*(Tank Museum 4799/C4)*

# REGIMENTS ACCORDING TO THE ORDER OF PRECEDENCE

## 2nd Armoured Battalion, Grenadier Guards

**- Origins:** First regiment of "Lifeguards of Foot" raised in 1640 against the Scots. Successor regiment raised in 1642 for the Civil War, then "Royal Regiment of Guards" formed in 1656 in Holland against Cromwell. In 1662, "King's Regiment of Guards" raised in 1660 by Colonel Russell in England was amalgamated with "Royal Regiment of Guards" back from Holland. Given precedence as First Regiment of Guards in 1666, and ranked as senior regiment of Horse. In 1673 and 1677, formed with the Coldstream Guards a composite battalion in Holland and in America. Organized in three battalions, became "1st Regiment of Foot Guards" in 1689. Some battalions fought in Flanders in 1691-92 and 1701. New composite battalion with the Coldstream Guards in 1702, serving at Cadiz, Gibraltar, then back in Flanders in 1708. After return to England in 1713, the battalions served separately in Gibraltar, in Germany, in Britain, until 1768. In North America in 1776 for the War of Independence, with the Coldstream and Scots Guards. Returning in 1782, the battalions were again separated and fought in Holland, at Valenciennes and Ostend, until 1799. 1st and 3rd battalions served in Sicily, Spain and Holland until 1809. Spanish War between 1810 and 1813, fought in Belgium in 1814-15, then became "1st or Grenadier Regiment of Foot Guards" after the victory at Waterloo. The three battalions served separately in all the conflicts in which was committed the United Kingdom: Peninsula (1826), Canada (1837-40 and 1862), Malta and the Crimea (1854), not to mention many appearances in Ireland. The regiment became "The Grenadier Guards" in 1877. Still separated, the battalions fought in Egypt and in Sudan (1882, 1885 and 1898), in Gibraltar (1897), in South Africa (1900). 1st and 2nd battalions were sent to France in 1914, with 7th and 2nd Divisions respectively, and a 4th battalion was raised (disbanded in 1919 with 5th reserve battalion). The four battalions formed the Guards Division in 1915, and took part in the campaigns of the Marne, Aisne, Somme, fighting at Ypres, Loos, Passchendaele, Cambrai, Arras... The three maintained battalions were sent in rotation to Egypt from 1930 to 1937.

**- 1939-44:** 2nd battalion in France in 1939 then evacuated via Dunkirk in 1940. Became armoured regiment in September 1941, within 5th Guards Arm. Brig. (Guards Arm.Div.) Fought from Normandy to Germany with this unit. Sometimes nicknamed *"The Boneshakers"*

## 1st Armoured Battalion, Coldstream Guards

**- Origins:** Regiment raised in 1650 by General Monck, against the Scottish royalist army, thus nicknamed the *Coldstreamers*. Helped restore the Monarchy in London in 1660, reconstituted as "Royal Regiment of Guards" the following year, part of the Royal Bodyguard. Fought with the Navy against the Dutch in 1665, given precedence as Second Regiment of Foot Guards in 1666. "The Coldstream Regiment of Foot Guards" in 1670, sent to America in 1677 then to Flanders. Organized in two battalions, formed a composite regiment with the Grenadier Guards and set sail for Tangiers in 1680. In Flanders in 1689-92, then in Cadiz (1702), in Gibraltar (1704), in Spain (1705). After the combats in Flanders in 1708, both battalions returned to England and were separated in 1713. The one or the other took part in all conflicts: Germany (1742), Flanders (1747), Britain (1758). Composite force with the Grenadier and Scots Guards in 1776 for the War of Independence in America. 1st battalion was chiefly committed during the following years: Holland (1793 and 1799), Spain (1800 and 1809-11), Malta and Egypt (1801), Germany (1802). 2nd battalion took part in expeditions against Ostend (1798), the Scheldt estuary (1809), Tarifa (1811), and valiantly fought at Waterloo in 1815. Both battalions then served in England and Ireland. Became "The Coldstream Fusilier Regiment of Foot Guards" in 1831. 2nd battalion was sent to Canada in 1837, 1st battalion in Malta and the Crimea in 1854. Frequent service of the regiment in Ireland until 1877, then became "The Coldstream Guards". Both battalions served, separately or not, in Egypt (1882-85), in Gibraltar and South Africa (1899), and in Ireland. A 3rd battalion, formed in 1897, was sent to France with 2nd battalion within 2nd Division (1st battalion with 1st Division). 4th pioneer and 5th reserve battalions were raised in 1914-15, then disbanded in 1919. The regiment took part in the battles of the Marne, Somme, Ypres, Langemarck, Saint-Quentin... The three remaining battalions then served in Constantinople (1922), Shanghai (1927), Egypt (1932) and Palestine (1936).

**- 1939-44:** 1st and 2nd battalions were sent to France in 1939 within independent infantry brigades, and were evacuated via Dunkirk in 1940. 1st battalion became armoured battalion in 1941, attached to 5th Guards Arm.Brig. (Guards Arm.Div.), which landed in Normandy in June 1944.

Nicknamed *"The Coldstreamers"* or *"The Coleys"*.

## 2nd Armoured Btn, Irish Guards

**-Origins:** Regiment raised in 1900 by order of Queen Victoria to commemorate the bravery of the Irish regiments in South Africa; detachments served there in 1901. Sent to France in 1914 with 2nd Division. A 2nd reserve battalion, raised in 1914, became 3rd battalion in 1915, a new 2nd battalion joining the Guards Division in France. The regiment took part in the battles of Mons, Marne, Aisne, Ypres, Langemarck, Loos, Poelcappelle, Cambrai, Somme, Hasbrouck, Arras, Sambre... Back in England in 1919, the 2nd and 3rd reserve battalions were disbanded. Action in Constantinople (1922), Gibraltar (1923), Egypt (1936) and Palestine (1938-39).

**- 1939-44:** 2nd battalion was reformed in 1939, and 1st battalion set sail for Norway in 1940. After having served as Bodyguard for Queen Wilhelmina of the Netherlands, 2nd battalion reached Boulogne to be evacuated some days later. Converted to armoured battalion in 1941, within 5th Guards Arm.Brig. (Guards Arm.Div.) Took part in the whole North-West Europe campaign with this unit.

Nicknamed *"The Micks"* or sometimes *"The Bog Rats"*.

## 2nd Armoured Recce Battalion, Welsh Guards

**- Origins:** Three-battalion regiment raised in 1915 by order of King George V, by transfer of personnel from other Guards regiments. 1st battalion joined the Guards Division in France, fought on the Somme, and at Flers, Morval, Ypres, then Passchendaele, Cambrai, Bapaume, Arras... 2nd and 3rd battalions were disbanded in 1919. Served in Egypt (1929) and in Gibraltar (1939).

**- 1939-44:** 2nd battalion was recreated in 1939, and fought in Boulogne in 1940. Converted into armoured battalion in 1941, joined in September of the same year 5th Guards Arm.Brig. (Guards Arm.Div.), and landed in Normandy with this unit.

Nicknamed *"The Taffys"* or sometimes *"The Daffy Taffs"*.

---

tery of eight guns). But this area was notably defended by a great number of antitank guns and several Panzers, which furthermore enjoyed a perfect view on the attackers. During a short but dreadful fight, under constant shelling, the *Coldstreamers* lost three quarters of their tanks (there were only eight left out of the normal 19 in N°2 Squadron), and the two infantry companies suffered 70% losses, a single officer surviving the battle.

8th Corps came into the Army reserve on 12 August, and its role was limited to the holding of the north-eastern side of the pocket taking shape around Falaise. The tanks were not very useful for these missions, some were dug in on the first line and the others were in reserve for possible counterstrokes. For 48 hours, "aggressive" patrols were carried out by day and night, and since infantry was in short supply, 2nd Household Cavalry without their armoured cars were used in this role. The German retreat was obvious on 15 August, and only mines and booby-traps were left. The Guards Arm.Div. was put in Army reserve on the 16th, and the brigades

returned to their original organization. The sappers were in charge of mine-clearing and building of Bailey bridges, and the whole division took part in burying the many dead – both human and animal - which littered the countryside and were infecting it. The losses were gradually made up; personnel were transferred from the Irish to the Welsh Guards since more Irish than Welsh reinforcements were arriving.

Several changes of senior officers were made, for instance Lieutenant Colonel Hobart, second in command, left to join his RTR regiment, and was replaced by Lieutenant Colonel Hornung from 32nd Guards Brig., himself substituted for by Major Fitzalan-Howard. On 23 August the order to move up towards Condé-sur-Noireau for a few days rest arrived. The division came under control of 30th Corps from the 27th onwards, and headed for Laigle, along broken-up roads and over half-destroyed bridges. It was to concentrate before 30 August near the River Seine, and the 2nd Grenadier Guards crossed the river first on the 29th, leading the Guards Arm. Div. in pursuit of the retreating Germans.

# 4th ARMOURED BRIGADE

**F**ROM THE VERY BEGINNING OF SECOND WORLD WAR, the 4th Armoured Brigade was in close association with the Mobile Division of 1938, which became the 7th Armoured Division in January 1940, for they shared common origins.

Initially known as 4th Heavy Brigade, it fought within this division from April 1940 onwards, and became independent in June 1942 for Operation *Crusader*. Billeted in Cairo, 4th Arm. Brig. was originally composed of 7th, 8th and 11th Hussars, and 1st Battalion, Royal Tank Regiment. It was committed as early as January 1940 when Mussolini attacked Libya and Egypt, and then participated in most of the battles of the early North African campaign: Fort Capuzzo, Sidi Barrani, Beda Fomm, Operations *Battleaxe* and *Crusader* (Sidi Rezegh), and Gazala

*Black jerboa in a white circle, on a black square background (inspired from the red jerboa of the 7th Armoured Division). Often simplified in a black jerboa on a white square background.*

in May 1942, including the more famous battles of Tobruk, Alam El Halfa, El Alamein, and Tunis.

Having fought in North Africa from the beginning, 4th Arm. Brig. made use of every existing armoured vehicle, from antiquated Rolls-Royce armoured cars, Vickers tanks, Cruisers A9 and A13, Crusaders, Matildas, to American Honeys (Stuarts), Grants and Shermans. Many armoured regiments served with it: 2nd, 3rd, 4th, 5th, 6th and 7th Battalions RTR, 12th Lancers, 3/4th County of London Yeomanry (*Sharpshooters*), Royal Scots Greys. For the Sicily campaign, the brigade's composition was again modified: 3rd CLY, 44th RTR, then 50th RTR incorporated in August. In September, 46th RTR joined the brigade in Italy, for the Tarento landings and the fighting on the Sangro and Moro rivers. According to Montgomery's will, 4th Arm.Brig. embarked in January 1944 at Naples to return to England, in order to prepare for the assault on North-West Europe. For some members of the brigade, who had not seen their families

*Top.*
**This Sherman ARV I of HQ Squadron, 3rd CLY (diamond and tactical sign 123) is duly "waterproofed", the protection around the hatch of the compartment being particularly interesting. It may have been photographed in England prior to D-Day, or else in Normandy just after the Invasion. The 4th Arm.Brig. insignia is visible on the right of the differential and final drive housing.**
*(Tank Museum 353/C1)*

*Left.*
**It is the turn of 44th RTR or the Royal Scots Greys (is the square on the turret red or yellow?) to pass through Reviers, while an infantry unit (probably belonging to 50th Inf.Div.) tramps along the same road. The square indicates B Squadron, number 4 identifying n°4 Troop: this kind of turret markings was typical of 4th Arm.Brig.** *(Tank Museum 2713/D4)*

*Next page.*
**Shermans II of 3rd CLY (cf. tactical sign 123 on the left tank, and A Squadron triangle on the turrets) are landing from an LCT on Gold Beach, on 7 June. Quite unusually, the turret bin of the Sherman on the right is equipped with two fire extinguishers, which are normally carried on the hull.** *(Tank Museum 353/D1)*

for nearly five years, going back home was more than welcome.
But with this went a difficult return to the life in barracks they had
forgotten while enduring the harsh conditions of the Mediterranean
theatre of operations.

Brigadier John Currie took command of the brigade in England,
and the armoured regiments were given Sherman IIs, and Fireflies
(Sherman Vc) armed with the formidable 17 pounder gun. The men
regretted their diesel-powered Shermans III that they regarded as more
reliable and less prone to caught fire when hit. 4th Arm.Brig. concentrated its efforts on close cooperation tactics between tanks and infantry,
with its Motor Battalion, 2nd Battalion King's Royal Rifle Corps (2nd
KRRC) in M5 and M9 half-tracks. Companies in this battalion and the
three armoured regiments were married up according to a permanent
pre-arranged distribution: A/3rd CLY, B/44th RTR, and C/Scots
Greys. Artillery support was provided by the 4th Royal Horse Artillery.

## Landing and Operation *Epsom*

Under control of 1st Corps, the 4th Arm.Brig. landed between
7 and 10 June in Normandy, in support of 50th Infantry Division,
but was not involved in any noteworthy fighting for two weeks.
The units gathered together between Colomby-sur-Thaon and Bény-
sur-Mer only took part in some long range shooting. For Operation
*Epsom*, the thrust of 8th Corps towards Bretteville-sur-Laize, the brigade came under command of 11th Arm.Div.: the armour had to
push through Saint-Manvieux and Cheux, previously taken by 15th
Inf.Div., then cross the Odon River, and finally capture Hill 112. On
the 26th of June, the first day of *Epsom*, Brigadier Currie was killed
by a shell splinter and replaced by Lieutenant Colonel Carver. The
*Sharpshooters* with 10th Hampshire Light Infantry (HLI) attacked
towards Mouen, through minefields and against dug-in tanks from 21.
Panzer-Division. They lost eight tanks, but claimed to have destroyed

two Tigers, two SPGs and four Panzer IV (as there was no Tiger at that time in this area, they were probably Panthers). In any case, four Panthers were knocked-out by 3rd CLY and 44th RTR on 27 June.

The next day, 44th RTR protected the flanks of 29th Arm.Brig. (11th Arm.Div.) to push on to Hill 112; the force came near Evrecy and Esquay after stiff fighting, but was unable to capture the villages. A Squadron met enemy tanks and antitank guns around Esquay, and C Squadron were heavily shelled when attacking towards Hill 113, losing seven Shermans in the process (three more were knocked-out in the afternoon). The task of dealing with numerous German armoured vehicles in Evrecy was left to the artillery. The advance of 44th RTR was not easier westwards, as they lost 13 tanks in a day, with three more damaged. On 29 June, a German counterattack drove away 11th Arm.Div. and 4th Arm.Brig. from the heights of Hills 112 and 113, so they had to start all over again. Carver questioned the officering of the troops involved, and replaced four officers in command, even Desert war veterans, in a few days. The brigade was next put in reserve, but not far enough from the front to avoid shelling

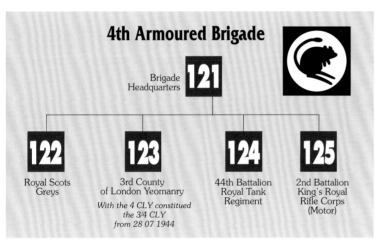

# 4th Armoured Brigade

Brigade Headquarters **121**

**122**
Royal Scots Greys

**123**
3rd County of London Yeomanry
*With the 4 CLY constituted the 3/4 CLY from 28 07 1944*

**124**
44th Battalion Royal Tank Regiment

**125**
2nd Battalion King's Royal Rifle Corps (Motor)

from German mortars and Nebelwerfers; it came afterwards under the command of 53rd Inf.Div.

## The thrust to the River Orne

For Operation *Jupiter*, while the 31st Tank Brigade's Churchills were supporting 129th and 130th Inf.Brig. of 43rd Wessex Inf.Div., 4th Arm.Brig. with 214th Inf.Brig. had to attack beyond Hill 112 to seize Maltot; the Scots Greys and 2nd KRRC were leading behind a powerful artillery barrage. After 9th RTR had nearly all its Churchills destroyed, the men of 43rd Inf.Div., overwhelmed by enemy fire, had begun to fall back when German Panzers, including some Tigers of SS-PzAbt.101 and 102, appeared. The *Scots Greys* held the line on 9 and 10 July, but could not advance. On the 11th, B Squadron attacked with 5th DCLI against troops from 10. and 9. SS Pz-Div., and succeeded in reaching Hill 112 at last. They were nevertheless ordered to withdraw in the evening, because there were only four serviceable Shermans left in the Squadron! But the Germans had suffered too: ambushed lower down, A Squadron had destroyed four SPGs with help from 114th Antitank Battery's M10s. 3rd CLY clashed with Panthers in Eterville while supporting 2nd Seaforth: A Squadron and

their Fireflies succeeded in knocking out or damaging a total of 12 enemy AFVs. However, no advance had been made by 11 July, and during the ten following days, the brigade under control of 12th Corps worked in support of 43rd and 53rd Inf.Div. in the Odon valley. It left the front on 27 July to reach Carpiquet airfield, where 4th CLY of 7th Arm.Div., greatly weakened by the early Normandy campaign, were amalgamated with their parent regiment 3rd CLY to form 3/4th CLY in 4th Arm.Brig. Assimilation was not so easy, as 4th CLY were previously equipped with Cromwell tanks. Furthermore, redundant personnel having to be posted to other units obeyed reluctantly.

## Ending the campaign in Normandy

Kept out from *Goodwood*, 4th Arm.Brig. was in action again on 28 July with 2nd Canadian Corps, the *Scots Greys* losing four tanks while supporting 4th Canadian Inf.Brig. around Ifs and Verrières. Coming under control of 3rd Inf.Div. on the 3rd of August, the brigade skirted round Vire from the east in four days. 44th RTR were in action between 6 and 11 August near Le Pissot and on the Tinchebray road, and they lost several tanks before being relieved by 3/4th CLY. Reflecting the temporary dispersal of the brigade for immediate needs, the *Scot Greys* secured 11th Arm.

(IWM B8785)

45

# REGIMENTS ACCORDING TO THE ORDER OF PRECEDENCE

## The Royal Scots Greys

- **Origins:** Regiment raised in 1681 by General Dalziel under the name of "The Royal Regiment of Dragoons of Scotland", sent to London in 1685 at the time of the Great Revolution. Became "The Royal Regiment of Scots Dragoons" in 1692. In Flanders in 1694-95, and again in 1702. Fought at Ramillies in 1706, became "The Royal Regiment of North British Dragoons" in 1707, with grey horses as mounts, fought at Malplaquet in 1709. Participated in the siege of Lille in 1708, then returned to England and Scotland in 1713. In Flanders in 1742, became "The 2nd (Royal North British) Regiment of Dragoons" in 1751. A Light Troop took part in raids on St Malo and Cherbourg. In England and Scotland from 1763. In Holland and France in 1793-94, then returned to England. Known as "2nd Dragoons" in 1815, fought in Belgium and notably at Waterloo. In United Kingdom until 1854, the regiment fought then in the Crimea (Balaclava et Sebastopol). Became "The 2nd Dragoons (Royal Scots Greys)" in 1877. A detachment in Egypt in 1884, then in Ireland in 1887. In South Africa in 1899, returned to England in 1904, and sailed for France in 1914, then for Belgium (Mons, Ypres, Arras, Bapaume...). Became in 1921 "The Royal Scots Greys (2nd Dragoons)" and was sent to Egypt and Palestine, then to India in 1922.

- **1939-44:** The regiment was motorized in 1941. Under direct control of GHQ, Middle East Forces from January 1940 to January 1941, and also in May and July 1943. Incorporated from March to July 1941 into 6th Cavalry Brigade in North Africa, then from September to November 1942 in 4th Light Arm.Brig. Under control of 15th Army Group for the campaign of Italy in September 1943, the Royal Scots Greys joined 4th Arm.Brig. in February 1944, for the invasion of Normandy. Nicknamed "*The Greys*".

## 3rd County of London Yeomanry

- **Origins:** In common with "4th County of London Yeomanry". Raised in 1900 for the Boer War by the Earl of Dunraven; became "3rd County of London Yeomanry (Sharpshooters)" in 1901. Elements fought in 1915 at Gallipoli and in Egypt. Often amalgamated with other cavalry, machine-gun or even cyclist units, during First World War. Absorbed 4th CLY, and spent the last months of 1918 in France. Reconstituted in 1920, then assigned to Territorial Army in 1922, became armoured car company before being armoured regiment in 1939.

- **1939-44:** Having absorbed the 4th Regiment, 3/4th County of London Yeomanry fought in Egypt and North Africa from 1941 to September 1942 within 22nd Arm.Brig. of 7th Arm.Div. Both regiments' destinies parted again in September 1942, 3rd CLY being then directly under control of GHQ, Middle East Forces. Incorporated into 4th Arm.Brig. in July 1943 for the combats in Sicily and Italy. Landed in Normandy in June 1944 with this brigade, and was amalgamated again in July with their parent regiment, 4th CLY, to form 3/4th County of London Yeomanry.

Nicknamed "*The Sharpshooters*".

## 44th Battalion Royal Tank Rgt

- **Origins:** In common with the whole Royal Tank Regiment, see 1st RTR. Formed in 1939 from 6th Battalion "The Gloucestershire Regiment", Territorial Army.

- **1939-44:** Part of 21st Army Tank Brigade in United Kingdom, from September 1939 to September 1940. Joined in January 1941 1st Army Tank Brigade serving in North Africa and then in Palestine, until May 1943. Incorporated in July 1943 into 4th Arm.Brig. for operations in Sicily and Italy. Landed in Normandy with this brigade in June 1944.

---

Div.'s left flank for the end of operation *Bluecoat*, at Forgues, Sourdeval and Vaudrey. 4th Arm.Brig. were then carried on tank transporters to Evrecy, coming under control of 53rd Inf.Div. within 12th Corps, and struggled on 14 and 15 August to cut the German retreat between Condé-sur-Noireau and Falaise, exerting a strong pressure to tighten the encirclement of the enemy.

Lieutenant Colonel Carver succeeded in convincing the senior command that a swift pursuit was starting up, and that his brigade had to lead the race: instead of the usual cooperation for minor pushes, the tanks dashed by the infantry without waiting for them. 44th RTR thus cut the road to Falaise, followed by the *Scots Greys* and the *Sharpshooters* going by through Bonnoeil and Pierrepont. But the Germans were still dangerous: a counterattack on 16 August near Trepel badly hit the 2nd KRRC, despite help from 3/4th CLY. The situation on the

17th was difficult too for 44th RTR and the *Scots Greys*, who were confronted with very pugnacious remnants of 1., 2. and 9.SS Pz-Div. More and more retreating troops were being captured as the roads they were using to withdraw were cut by surprise by the British.

The crossing of Rouffigny was tricky for the *Sharpshooters*, who lost five tanks but destroyed two German SPGs in the process. The village was cleaned up in two days, as were Pierrefitte and Nécy where the last Tigers were seen. 44th RTR were in Ronai by 18 August, and the following day, the brigade's tanks took position on the heights overlooking the roads, and enjoyed a real shooting party, with the Germans retreating in a hurry. 4th Arm.Brig. also advanced towards Saint-Clair and closed the bottleneck still remaining between American and British troops, capturing 3000 prisoners on the way. 44th RTR occupied Aubry-en-Exmes on 20 August and came in touch with the American in Chambois and the Canadians in Magny: the Falaise pocket was closed. Marching at a rapid pace all the way from Trun, and supporting 53rd and 15th Inf.Div., 4th Arm.Brig. then pushed on to the River Seine which was reached on 28 August

**A Sherman Vc Firefly leading an armoured column: here is another type of travelling lock, which could identify a tank from 4th Arm.Brig., but no insignia can be seen. This identification cannot be ascertained however, for Guards Arm.Div. also seems to have used a similar kind of travelling lock.** *(RR)*

# 6th GUARDS TANK BRIGADE

**IN SEPTEMBER 1941, several Guards infantry regiments were converted into armoured or motor regiments to form the Guards Armoured Division. The 6th Guards (Armoured) Brigade of Brigadier Adair (composed of 4th Armoured Battalion Grenadier Guards, 3rd Armoured Battalion Scots Guards, and 2nd Armoured Battalion Welsh Guards) was part of this large unit.**

By autumn 1941, the structure of the armoured division was changed, and no longer included more than a single armoured brigade. The 6th Guards Arm.Brig. was thus incorporated into 15th (Scottish) Division. Soon after, 2nd Welsh Guards were replaced by 4th (Motor) Battalion Coldstream Guards, the latter becoming a Tank Battalion like the other two regiments. Brigadier Verney of the Irish Guards replaced Brigadier Adair at the same period. Known as Tank Brigade from early 1943, the unit was equipped with Churchills instead of its Covenanters, although early models of this new tank were hardly suitable for warfare.

By the middle of 1943, training was mainly intended for improving cooperation with the infantry, because some Infantry Divisions were to receive an armoured brigade. The idea was given up in September 1943, and 6th Guards Tk.Brig. thus became independent, and was incorporated into the 2nd Army. The heavy losses suffered by the Foot Guards in Italy nearly caused the brigade to be disbanded, first in June 1943 and then again in January 1944, but the matter turned out all right. The unit was equipped with new Churchills Mk VI armed with a 75-mm gun, but there were not enough of them to replace all the old 6 pounder-equipped Mk IV (Mk VIIs arrived later as replacements). The brigade came under

*Top.* **Having been brought late to Normandy, 6th Guards Tk.Brig. was only committed on 30 July: a column of tanks of the 4th Grenadier Guards (cf. tactical insignia 152) is heading towards the gathering line before the attack. The Churchill in the foreground, riding with its turret in rearward position, is a 6 pounder-equipped Mk IV, as shown by the gun counterweight.** *(Tank Museum 4799/B1)*

White shield bared by a blue/white/blue band
(unit colours), with a golden sword.

the control of 21st Army Group for the Normandy invasion. Although it embarked on 19 July only, it actually sustained its first losses on 24 June when a V1 crashed on the workshops' gathering area, causing the death of 51 men.

## The arrival in Normandy and Operation *Bluecoat*

The 6th Guards Tk.Brig. landed on 20 July 1944 on Gold and Juno beaches, to concentrate in the vicinity of Bayeux. One of the first visits made by the officers was to a cemetery gathering the vehicles that had been destroyed during the battle for Caen. At the sight of tank hulls with holes punched by the German 75-mm or 88-mm guns, the officers ordered that the Churchill's armour was to be reinforced with added steel plates or spare track links. The first recces were carried out from 24 July onwards, but the brigade was eventually committed on the 30th only.

For Operation *Bluecoat*, the 15th Inf.Div. (8th corps) was appointed to attack from the ridge of Caumont-l'Eventé, with support from 6th Guards Tk.Brig., to provide cover for the Americans against the German 326.ID: the objective was another ridge located 6 1/4 miles to the south, in a dense bocage country. The left flank was secured by 43rd Inf.Div. and 8th Arm.Brig. Since launching the operation was becoming urgent, no reconnaissance or preparation were carried out: by night and in the middle of confusion, the brigade reached an ill-prepared starting line on 28 July. Moving up with 227th Inf.Brig., the 4th Grenadier Guards had to advance with Crocodiles and Flails to Lutain Wood (this spot no longer exists) and Sept-Vents. In dust and smoke raised by the artillery barrage, the attack began at 8.00 on 30 July, and Sept-Vents was occupied soon after. Five tanks were damaged by mines. The enemy was no longer present in Lutain Wood, and Crocodiles had to intervene to dislodge the Germans from trenches and hedges in the vicinity. In spite of serious losses in infantry and tank commanders through sniping, the objective was captured soon after Sept-Vents, and many prisoners were taken.

The 4th Coldstream Guards continued the offensive from Sept-Vents,

Another 4th Grenadier Guards Churchill moves up with 15th Inf.Div. infantrymen in an oat field. The brigade insignia can be clearly seen on the rear of the tank, as can be the code
on the turret: Troop number (3) in the A Squadron triangle (N°1 Squadron in the Guards). Spare track links
cover the turret sides. *(Tank Museum 4834/D3)*

but the infantry was delayed by mortar fire and snipers. A second artillery barrage was ordered for 9.30, the Coldstream Guards then pushing on to Hervieux, still without infantry. The 3rd Scots Guards met the same difficulties on the left, and the infantry could not advance on difficult terrain and against strong enemy positions. The Coldstreamers made good progress, led by N°3 Squadron on the right and N°1 Squadron on the left. The mopping-up of any place that could be used by Germans to hide or entrench was complete by midday. Meanwhile, the Scots Guards waited in vain for their infantry and launched the attack on their own. The Right Flank was stopped at Les Loges, but the Left Flank reached its objective at 14.30: the breakthrough had been successfully carried out.

Since the infantry was still unable to keep up with the armour, the commanding officers of 6th Guards Tk.Brig. and 15th Inf.Div. decided that the tanks would have to go on alone. The Coldstreamers took the lead, while the Scots Guards were bringing forward 2nd Glasgow Highlanders. Le Bois du Homme was bombed by Lancasters and Halifaxes, and the

Coldstream Guards advance met little opposition along the Caumont – St-Martin-des-Besaces road. N°3 Squadron were held up by the enemy at La Morichèse, lost a tank against a Panther, and turned off eastwards across country to reach Hill 309 at 16 o'clock despite several Churchills getting bogged down.

The Grenadier Guards and the transports of 15th Inf.Div., held up in a traffic jam back at Hervieux, only started at 16.30. A Churchill was

*Bottom, left.*
**On 2 August, Churchills are transporting infantry south of Caumont, for the following stages of Operation Bluecoat. Tactical sign and unit insignia have been obliterated by the brigade itself, and not by the censor on the photograph: before particular offensives, orders were given to take out such distinctive signs from vehicles and uniforms, to keep the operation secret.** *(Tank Museum 1774/D2)*

*Below, right.*
**In early August, a Churchill of C Squadron (or N°3 Squadron), 4th Grenadier Guards, is passing by the dismantled wreck of a Panzer IV Ausf.H in the Estry area. It is once again a 6 pounder-armed Mk IV: from its presence on the wartime photographs, this old variant seems to have equipped 6th Guards Tk.Brig. in greater numbers than other Churchill units.** *(Tank Museum 4834/D4)*

knocked-out by an 88 gun at La Morichèse, and the infantry dismounted from the tanks to catch up with the *Coldstreamers*. As for the Scots Guards, holding on to the hill of Les Loges, they were joined by the Argyll and Sutherland Highlanders, but without any antitank support or transport. Enemy shelling at 18 o'clock was followed by a counterattack from the left rear, although this area was in theory secured by 43rd Inf. Div. Three Guards tanks were destroyed by antitank guns, and suddenly three Jagdpanthers of schwere Panzerjäger-Abteilung 654 charged and knocked-out eight more Churchills in a matter of minutes. The defensive fire of the Guards was in return rather effective, for two Jagdpanthers were damaged and abandoned later by the withdrawing attackers.

The Coldstream Guards had advanced beyond Hill 309, and they received constant infantry reinforcements during the night, with antitank guns having to be pulled by men since the ground was impassable for Carriers. The next day was spent bringing up supplies for the tanks with half-tracks, under intermittent shelling from the German artillery. After a quiet night, 1 August began with two violent counterattacks supported by armour from 21.Pz-Div. Although both were driven back, they revealed the danger of the brigade's advanced position. A final counterattack, disclosed in advance by the questioning of deserters, was repelled by the artillery alone.

During the battle south of Caumont, the Grenadier Guards had taken

**Another view of Churchills, probably belonging to the 3rd Scots Guards, during Bluecoat: this one, of which the front is protected by spare track links, carries at least eight soldiers. In the background can be seen strips of white tissue (indicating that this passage has been cleared of mines and then delimited by the Engineers), and the tower of St-Pierre-Tarentaine's church.**
*(Tank Museum 4799/C1)*

part in the attack against Montcharival (the name of this hamlet cannot be found on present day maps, it was probably a misrepresentation of Montchauvet) and the River Souleuvre, in support of 6th KOSB and 6th Royal Scots Fusiliers. The assault resumed on 3 August towards Le Tourneur, on difficult terrain where tanks got stuck in the mud: in one of these tanks, completely bogged down, the crew spent the whole night struggling hard with feet in the water against the Germans, until they were freed on the following day! On the very same day, N°1 Squadron supported 8th RSF in difficulty against enemy armour, knocked-out a Panzer IV, and helped to capture Montcharival before night. The first commitment of the brigade had been rich in lessons: casualties were limited, but still too high regarding tank commanders, and instructions were given to weld armour plates at the back of the tanks' cupolas. The 6 pounder and 75-mm guns of the Churchills were not powerful enough to defeat the Panther's and Tiger's armour, even with the new discarding sabot ammunition. Moreover, although the Churchill's armour was rather thick, it was vulnerable (except the frontal armour) to the fire of either the 75-long or 88 German guns.

## 6th Guards Tank Brigade

Brigade Headquarters **151**

**152** — 4th Tank Battalion Grenadier Guards

**153** — 4th Tank Battalion Coldstream Guards

**154** — 3rd Tank Battalion Scots Guards

### The battles of August 1944

The end of the offensive phase of Operation *Bluecoat* was marked by the departure of Brigadier Verney to 7th Arm.Div., his place being taken by Lieutenant-Colonel Sir Walter Barttelot from the Coldstream Guards. The 6th Guards Tk.Brig. was scattered in support of various infantry units of 15th Inf.Div., and was tasked with continuing the advance by limited attacks. On 7 August, in the morning mist, the Grenadier Guards with 2nd Gordon Highlanders left Montcharival for Estry: light opposition

# REGIMENTS ACCORDING TO THE ORDER OF PRECEDENCE

## 4th Tank Battalion, Grenadier Guards

- **Origins:** In common with the Grenadier Guards Regiment, see Guards Arm.Div. 4th Battalion raised in 1915, sent to France within Guards Division, and disbanded in 1919.

- **1939-44:** 4th Battalion reformed in 1940. Became armoured battalion in 1941 known as "4th Armoured Battalion, Grenadier Guards", incorporated in 6th Guards Arm.Brig. in September 1941; was designated Tank Battalion when the brigade became Tank Brigade. Landed in Normandy with this unit, which was now independent Tank Brigade.

The Grenadier Guards are sometimes nicknamed *"The Grannies"* or *"The Tow-Rows"*.

## 4th Tank Battalion, Coldstream Guards

- **Origins:** In common with the Coldstream Guards Regiment, see Guards Arm.Div. "4th (Pioneer) Battalion" raised in 1915, and disbanded in 1919.

- **1939-44:** 4th Battalion reformed in 1940, became motorised in 1941. Converted into Tank Battalion in February 1943 when incorporated into 6th Guards Tk.Brig., which was equipped with Churchill tanks. Fought within this same unit during the whole campaign in North West Europe.

Nicknamed *"The Coldstreamers"* or *"The Coleys"*.

## 3rd Tank Battalion, Scots Guards

- **Origins:** Regiment raised in 1639 by the Marquis of Argyll in the Highlands, became Royal Regiment in 1642. Life Guards unit (bodyguard) of King Charles II in 1650, took part in the battle of Worcester, disbanded in Scotland in 1651. Two companies raised in 1660 by the Earl of Linlithgow formed the nucleus of the "Scots Regiment of Foot Guards". Fought against the Covenanters in 1679, and became "Scottish or Third Regiment of Foot Guards" in 1685, composed of two battalions. Sometimes separated, the two battalions were committed in Flanders and Spain in 1689 and in 1705. The unit became "3rd Regiment of Foot Guards" in 1711. Fought in Spain (1719), in Germany (1742), and became "3rd Scotch Foot Guards" in 1751. Took part in the expedition in Britain in 1758, then served in Germany (1760) and in America during the War of Independence (1776), with a composite regiment including the Grenadier and the Coldstream Guards. Fought in Holland in 1793-99. 1st Battalion sent in Spain, and to Gibraltar and Malta (1800), then to Egypt (1801), Germany (1805), and Denmark (1807). Still separated, both battalions served in Spain and in Holland (1809-13). 2nd

Battalion fought at Waterloo (1815) and in the Peninsula (1826). The regiment became "The Scots Fusilier Guards" in 1831. 1st Battalion was in the Crimea in 1854, 2nd Battalion in Canada in 1862. Became "The Scots Guards" in 1877. In Ireland in 1880, 1st Battalion left for Egypt in 1882, joined by 2nd Battalion in 1884 to take part in the Gordon Relief expedition. In 1899-1900, sent to South Africa. A 3rd Battalion formed in 1899 was disbanded in 1906. The two Battalions left were sent to France in 1914, with 1st and Guards Divisions, and a 3rd (Reserve) Battalion was raised. The regiment took part in the battles of the Marne, Aisne, Ypres, Festubert, Somme, Flers, Passchendaele, Cambrai and Bapaume; remained afterwards for occupation duties in Germany until 1919. 3rd Battalion then disbanded. 2nd Battalion in China in 1927 in Palestine in 1936, 1st Battalion in Egypt in 1935.

- **1939-44:** A training battalion was raised in 1939, then a 3rd Battalion in 1940. 1st Battalion was sent to Norway in 1940, and became motorised when returning to England. 2nd Battalion fought in North Africa in 1941; 3rd Battalion was converted into Armoured Battalion. Integrated into 6th Guards Arm.Brig. in September 1941, under the name "3rd Tank Battalion, Scots Guards", when it became Tank Brigade in February 1943. Landed in Normandy with this unit. Sometimes nicknamed *"The Jocks"*.

---

was expected, but it turned out to be tough; a minefield and an antitank gun slowed the Churchills, and Panzers as well as mortar stonks stopped the attack. Scots Guards' Left Flank, which was following with 10th Highland Light Infantry, had to wait until 13.15 to take over. It lost one tank on a mine, another against a Panther. The clearing of machine-guns nests was interrupted by night because of the infantry heavy losses. Right Flank was not luckier, for it was shot at by enemy self-propelled guns as soon as it began to progress in the valley of Montchamp. Two Troops advanced with the Argyll and Sutherland behind a smoke screen, a Panther which destroyed a Churchill was driven back by PIAT fire. On the same day, the Coldstreamers made little progress from St-Pierre-Tarentaine, and an attempt to take Lassy with the Glasgow Highlanders ended up in the loss of five tanks.

The repeated assaults of the Grenadier Guards towards Estry on 8 and 9 August were not successful either, despite the support of six AVREs and six Crocodiles, against a defence reinforced with many antitank guns. The regiment restricted itself to holding its position, and the enemy withdrew on its own on the 12th. The Grenadier Guards were relieved by 11th Arm.Div., whilst the *Coldstreamers* and *Scots Guards* were operating in the Vire area, with 3rd Inf.Div. and Guards Arm.Div. respectively.

## Chênedollé

The *Scots Guards* quickly came back into battle by taking part on 11 August with 1st Welsh Guards infantry (Guards Arm.Div.) in an attack from Presles towards Chênedollé, between Vire and Vassy. The bombardment by heavy bombers was cancelled because of the thick fog, and early in the morning, supported by armoured bulldozers and four AVREs, the Churchills of 3 Squadron advanced down a lane under sporadic fire from the enemy artillery. Whereas the left column made good progress, the right one was held up by four Panthers and a company of infantry. Two of the Panzers were knocked out, and the attack resumed successfully, for Le Bas-Perrier was almost surrounded. Left Flank started at 7.30, lost a tank, while Right Flank and S Squadron was escorting infantrymen from 5th Coldstream Guards.

The attack succeeded when Chênedollé was reached in the evening, the Churchills having progressed in line in front

of the infantry to protect them; several hundred Germans were killed or wounded.

The brigade came next under command of 3rd Inf.Div., but the main part of the fighting took place now in the 30th Corps sector. On 18 August, Brigadier Barttelot left for a conference at 3rd Inf.Div. headquarters, but his Scout-Car blew up on a mine: both he and his driver were killed. The loss of this former 4th Coldstream Guardsman was a severe blow for the brigade. He was replaced two days later by Colonel Greenacre from the Welsh Guards. On 23 August, at the time when the Falaise pocket was tightening, 6th Guards Tk.Brig. was billeted between Flers and Tinchebray, and could at last carry out the essential tasks: maintenance, washing, resting… New tanks were delivered, and crews were trained on rafts for the crossing of a lake. Drivers were sent on battlefields to recover German AFVs for testing and evaluation. They took advantage of this trip to bring back more prestigious vehicles (Mercedes, Volkswagens) that they kept for the following moves. The brigade's campaign ended with inspections and visits of officials, while the faster units were picked out for the pursuit of the Germans beyond the River Seine.

*Next page, from top to bottom.*
**On 4 August, Churchills from 6th Guards Tk.Brig. meet their Sherman "cousins" of 1st Coldstream Guards (Guards Arm.Div.) on the Vassy road, near St-Charles-de-Percy. The fact that both units had to take opposite directions, and yet both were taking part in the same battle at the same period,**
**is not a favourable indication of the way the battle was conducted on the British side…** *(IWM B8600)*

**A 4th Grenadier Guards Churchill is rumbling along the hamlet of Catheolles, on the road to Vire, on 4 August. Regarded as a slow tank, the Churchill had a maximum speed of only 26 km per hour, but probably exceeded that speed on a sloping road like this.** *(Tank Museum 4799/B3)*

**The 3rd Scots Guards operated in support of Guards Arm.Div., and then of 3rd Inf.Div., during the battle for Chênedollé. Although they were mainly formed with men without experience of battle, the crews of 6th Guards Tk.Brig. quickly learned the veterans' tricks, such as fixing crates and boxes on their tanks to carry everything that could not find space inside (not to mention spare track links, here from Shermans, for added protection).** *(RR)*

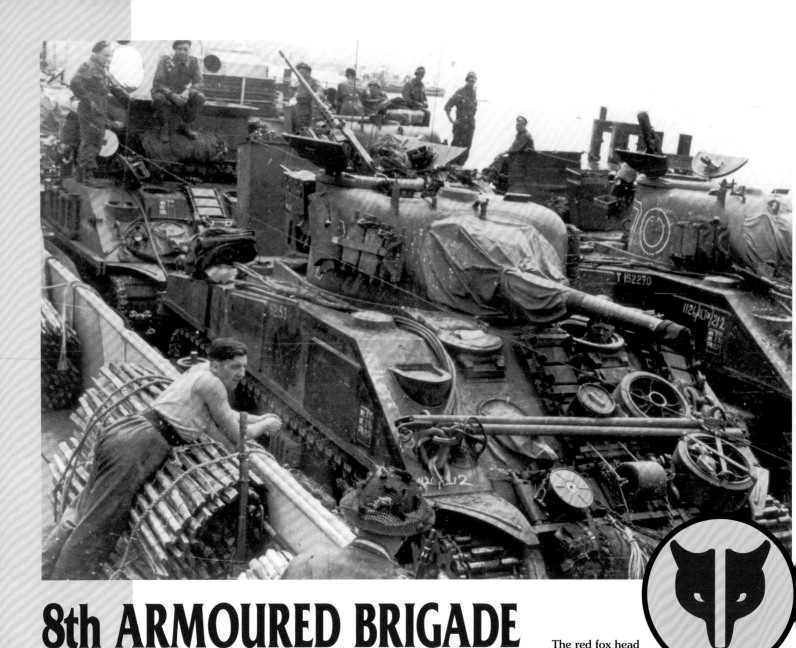

# 8th ARMOURED BRIGADE

The red fox head
on yellow background, derived
from the 10th Armoured Division insignia
(a red fox head on a black background).

THE CAVALRY BRIGADE WAS FORMED IN 1940 in Palestine within 1st Cavalry Division and was denominated 8th Armoured Brigade in July 1941. Already attached to 30th Corps, it left for North Africa in early 1942 and won fame at Alam El Halfa and El Alamein.

Independent in November, it took part in numerous battles until the end of the campaign in May 1943: El Agheila, Medenine, Tripoli, the Mareth line, Tunis. The Household Cavalry Regiment, Royal Scot Greys, Nottinghamshire Yeomanry, Staffordshire Yeomanry, 3rd RTR and 1st Regiment, The Buffs all served within its ranks. The 8th Arm.Brig. was one of the experienced units chosen by Montgomery to be brought to England at the prospect of the landings in Normandy. Back home in England, the regiments were taken in hand by their colonel so that the men lost their bad Desert habits, regarding uniform and hierarchy, for instance…

For Operation *Overlord*, 8th Arm.Brig. was composed of three armoured regiments (4/7th Royal Dragoon Guards, 24th Lancers, Nottinghamshire Yeomanry) and a motorized infantry battalion (12th Battalion King's Royal Rifle Corps). 4th and 8th Arm.Brig.

*Title.* **Some hours before the Invasion, tanks probably belonging to 8th Arm.Brig. are waiting for the order to set sail in their LCT. The Shermans are overloaded with equipment, and the crews seem to be ready to go. A Sherman ARV Mk I with its full Deep Wading Equipment is following the tank in the foreground.**
*(Tank Museum 5636/E3)*

were actually the only ones to be given an infantry unit. The 147th Field Rgt Royal Artillery (Essex Yeomanry), equipped with 105-mm Priest self-propelled guns, was also incorporated into the brigade. 8th Arm.Brig., commanded by Brigadier Bernard Cracroft, was mainly equipped with Sherman IIIs together with Sherman Vc Fireflies to strengthen its antitank capacity, but two Squadrons in two regiments (4/7th RDG et Sherwood Rangers) were converted to Sherman IIs and IIIs Duplex Drive, to take part in the initial assault.

## 6 June at dawn

In support of 50th Infantry Division, the 8th Arm.Brig. landed in the Gold sector: 4/7th Royal Dragoon Guards with 69th Inf.Brig. on King Red beach, in front of La Rivière and Saint Léger, the Sherwood Rangers on the left with 231st Inf.Brig. on Jig Green and Red beaches, in front of Port-en-Bessin and Le Hamel. Flails from the Westminster Dragoons and Churchill AVREs from 81st and 82nd Assault Squadrons of Royal Engineers were there to open the road. 24th Lancers in reserve was to go ashore in the evening. Because they had to land in the first hours of the assault, some Squadrons were at sea as early as on 2 June, thus spending more than four days in bad weather.

4/7th RDG's Sherman DDs were intended to be launched 3 km from the beach to reach the shore at H - 5 min (7.20), but the bad sea conditions forced the Navy to bring them in to a distance of 200 m only, and even so seven tanks were drowned or disappeared in water-filled bomb craters. On the beach crowded with troops, vehicles and debris, the two leading Squadrons quite easily found an exit however, for the mined obstacles had been thoroughly cleared by frogmen and Royal Engineers. Against the German 716.ID which was still resisting, the tanks' work mainly consisted of shooting at the bunkers' embrasures until the troops inside surrendered. Two tank commanders of A Squadron were killed by snipers; B Squadron advanced more easily up to the River Seulles, but lost four Shermans which were destroyed by antitank SPGs whilst going on towards Brécy. In the Sherwood Rangers' sector, eight Sherman DDs launched about 500 m from the shore (instead of 4 miles) rapidly sank. Enemy 75 and 88-mm guns immediately knocked out four tanks on the beach, two others blew up on mines. The dune line was however crossed rather quickly, and the regiment advanced towards Le Hamel. The village was seized with help from 1st Battalion Hampshire Regiment, after having held out during the whole afternoon. The 24th Lancers' tanks began to land in the evening, but the regiment was only at full strength on the next day.

## Early days in the bocage

After having eliminated some resistance nests, the Sherwood Rangers were the first to enter Bayeux on 7 June: the welcoming population was enthusiastic, for the city was fortunately captured without damage, a rare achievement during the Normandy campaign. C Squadron, 4/7th RDG, which were advancing on the Bayeux – Caen road, lost two Shermans brewed up by antitank guns. The just-landed 24th Lancers met one of the worst threats of the bocage: a tank was destroyed at point blank range by a Panzerschreck. The regiment cleared the area around Bazenville, where the brigade HQ was to set up. On 8 June, it tried to break through east of Villers-Bocage via Putot-en-Bessin, Cristot and Fontenay-Le-Pesnel, but ran into two adversaries that were to become too familiar: the 12.SS and 21.PzDiv. After tough brushes and the loss of a Sherman, the regiment moved back towards Martragny to re-supply the tanks in fuel and ammunition during the night.

The Sherwood Rangers were tasked on 9 June with the taking of Hill 103, which was well defended by Panzers and SPGs. Several patrols towards this position failed, and tanks were lost, including the first Fireflies. On the same day, 4/7th RDG captured Audrieu and also pushed on towards Hill 103 to occupy it at last. The tank crews discovered on the way a dozen Panthers advancing 4500 yards away: despite the distance, the Shermans shot explosive shells at the enemy tanks, and, scoring a lucky hit on the engine deck of one of them, were the first in the brigade to set a Panther on

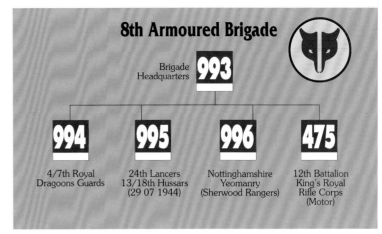

**8th Armoured Brigade**

Brigade Headquarters **993**

| **994** | **995** | **996** | **475** |
|---------|---------|---------|---------|
| 4/7th Royal Dragoons Guards | 24th Lancers 13/18th Hussars (29 07 1944) | Nottinghamshire Yeomanry (Sherwood Rangers) | 12th Battalion King's Royal Rifle Corps (Motor) |

fire. 24th Lancers moving up with 8th Durham Light Infantry (DLI) meanwhile took St-Pierre, near Tilly-sur-Seulles. On the 10th in the morning however, a counterattack by the Panzer-Lehr drove off the British who lost 12 tanks from St-Pierre. The village was recaptured in the afternoon by B Squadron, 24th Lancers, who destroyed two Tigers from Panzerkompanie (Fkl) 316, and four Panthers. On the 10th too, A Squadron, 24th Lancers and two 4/7th RDG Squadrons supported 6th Green Howards in their failed attack on Cristot. Out of the tanks leading the assault, seven were knocked out, the others being repelled towards Hill 103. The Germans supported by four Tigers counterattacked the position, which was held by the infantry with help from Fireflies.

The 12th of June was a bad day for 24th Lancers: while they were spread in front of Hill 103, an attack by Pz-Gr. Regiment 901 (Panzer-Lehr) cost them 10 killed and 15 wounded. HQ were moreover hit by bombardments. On the same day, 4/7th RDG attacked the village of Marcel together with 6th and 9th DLI. The same group pushed on towards Verrières and Lingèvres on the 14th; three Shermans were lost but Verrières was taken and three German AFVs were destroyed by A Squadron 4/7th RDG, whilst five Panthers threatening the infantry were disabled by B Squadron. 8th Arm.Brig. then came under control of 49th Inf.Div. on 14 June, and rested for two days.

On 16 and 17 June, 24th Lancers supported 146th and 147th Inf. Brig. in the vicinity of Cristot and Boislande park, and claimed to ha-

**Some days after D-Day, a Sherman named Virgin is getting ashore, coming out of a Landing Ship Tank (LST) on the Mulberry harbour of Arromanches. It belongs to a Squadron of 8th Arm.Brig. HQ, as indicated by the tactical sign 993 coupled with the unit insignia, a red fox head on yellow background.** *(RR)*

A Sherman Vc from 8th Arm.Brig. is heading for St-Léger on 11 June. It bears the triangle of an A Squadron on the turret side. The marks of the brackets for the Houseboat device are still visible on the hull side, as on many early production Fireflies. *(IWM B5416)*

*Right.* On 13 June, a Sherman II Duplex Drive probably belonging to 8th Arm.Brig. is passing the wreck of a Panzer IV, destroyed by a PIAT according to the wartime caption. The photograph was certainly taken in the sector of Tilly-sur-Seulles, where the brigade was fighting at that time. The DD propellers have been simply taken off, and not swung upward, to avoid any damage. *(IWM B5446)*

*Bottom.* The following photograph in the same report shows another Sherman clearly belonging to the 24th Lancers, as witnessed by the tactical sign 995 below the brigade insignia. It is a Firefly once again, as shown by the second hatch on the turret top, and it has lost its rear stowage box (unless it has been moved to the front). *(IWM B5417)*

ving destroyed or damaged four Tigers there: actually, a single Tiger was lost this day by sSS-PzAbt.101; the other tanks were probably Panzer IVs. On 18 June, the Sherwood Rangers moved up with 6th and 7th Duke of Wellington north of Fontenay-Le-Pesnel. Infantry was driven back from the recently captured position in Boislande park, but the tanks soon after regained it in spite of a stonk… from British artillery! 4/7th RDG fought alongside Durham Light Infantry towards Tilly-sur-Seulles, and then the brigade was pulled out for a five days' rest in Folliot, in order to take on reinforcements. The 12th KRRC only joined up with the brigade at that moment.

## Operation *Epsom*

The storm striking the Normandy coast on 19 June destroyed the American Mulberry artificial harbour, and delayed Operation *Epsom*, which started on the 25th only, for several days. Four infantry and one armoured divisions, as well as four Tank or Armoured brigades were committed. On the right flank, 8th Arm.Brig. had to help 49th Inf.

Div. (Sherwood Rangers with 147th Inf.Brig., 4/7th RDG and 24th Lancers with 146th Inf.Brig.) for the advance towards Fontenay-Le-Pesnel, Tessel, Brettevillette and Rauray. C Squadron, Sherwood Rangers attacked at 11.00, losing five tanks hit by antitank fire coming from the woods, and in the thick fog, they lost contact with their infantry. They went on progressing towards Fontenay, and also supported an AVRE Petard in razing the German HQ that was set up in a castle to the ground. On 26 June, 4/7th RDG and 24th Lancers attacked from the west and completed the mopping-up of Fontenay, with support from 12th KRRC. The *Sherwood Rangers* soon after drove through Fontenay which was said to be cleared: an A Squadron Sherman came face to face with a Tiger at less than 50 m, and managed to shoot five shells one after the other, only one of them hitting the Panzer's turret ring. The turret stopped, the crew baled out and the Tiger was captured almost intact! A photograph of this tank exists, however sSS-PzAbt.101, the only unit of that type in this area, did not register any tank loss on that particular day… Altogether, 14 enemy tanks were destroyed or captured, for four Shermans lost.

On 27 June, B Squadron lost another three tanks in Rauray; only seven were left available instead of the normal complement of 19. But they captured nine German AFVs, including an abandoned Tiger on the 24th.

For their part, 24th Lancers had a bad time in Tessel wood, and then took defensive positions in Boislande park on 28 June. The regiment made up for it on 1 July while actively supporting Tyneside Scottish in Rauray: 31 German tanks were destroyed or disabled in the neighbourhood, and even if some dated back to previous combats, it was a splendid testimony of the stubborn defence put up by 24th Lancers against the counterstrokes mainly launched by 2. SS-Pz-Div. "*Das Reich*". So Operation *Epsom* came to an end: the British armoured unit had lost 124 tanks against 86 Panzers destroyed, but they kept control of the battlefield.

## Combats in July

In early July, most of 8th Arm.Brig. was at rest after having endured grievous casualties in a month's fighting: 432 killed or wounded,

including 73 officers. It was nevertheless back in action from 8 July, first supporting 50th Inf.Div. in Hottot. 4/7th RDG was with 231st Inf.Brig. on the Caen – Caumont road, supported by 141st RAC's Crocodiles. Then they were attacked by Typhoons on the 12th, while fighting alongside 2nd Devonshire! In the meantime, C Squadron, 24th Lancers were operating with 11th DLI from 49th Inf.Div. The *Sherwood Rangers* had been pulled out from the front on the 4th only, so they stayed longer at rest. Still very weak, the brigade was pulled back for two weeks to the north-east of Caumont: the frontline was held by infantry, so that armour at the rear could regain strength while maintaining a close watch. On 23 July came terrible news: 24th Lancers were to be disbanded at the end of the month. The whole bri-

**On 30 June, in an orchard near Rauray, Sherman IIIs and a Humber Scout Car from 8th Arm.Brig. have been photographed beside the grave of a German Waffen-SS soldier in the foreground. The light colour diamond stands for an HQ Squadron, probably 24th Lancers (Second Regiment).**
*(IWM B6218)*

gade felt concerned, and in spite of senior officers intervening to the highest levels of command, the disbanding was confirmed. This brave regiment, with an excellent record, had to give over on 29 July to 13th/18th Hussars, the latter also coming from the disbanded 27th Arm.Brig. Out of 600 24th Lancers members, some were distributed between the brigade's two other regiments, others were posted to 11th and 7th Arm.Div., or in 4th Arm.Brig., the rest of them joining replacement units.

## Operation *Bluecoat*

The 13/18th Hussars, which had so gallantly fought in June, joined up with 8th Arm.Brig. for the launch of Operation *Bluecoat*, scheduled for 30 July. They provided support to 50th Inf.Div. advancing towards Saint-Germain-d'Ectot, whilst the *Sherwood Rangers* and 4/7th RDG moved up with 43rd Inf.Div. towards Briquessard, supported by Flails and Crocodiles from 79th Arm.Div. Opposition consisted of only infantry, and on the following day, B Squadron of the *Sherwood Rangers* seized Cahagnes. 12th KRRC occupied two important crossroads near Robin, with 4/7th RDG: the latter, during a fight on 1 August near Bois du Homme, destroyed two Jagdpanthers from schwere Panzerjäger-Abteilung 654, and captured two others that had been left bogged down. In Jurques, the village ruined after RAF bombardments had to be by-passed by the Sherwood Rangers and 7th Hampshire, who took La Bigne in the evening.

On 2 August, the *Sherwood Rangers* made difficult progress with 43rd Inf.Div. towards Ondefontaine against 10.SS-PzDiv., and lost two tanks and several killed and wounded, mainly NCOs and officers. The village was reached on the following day, at the bottom of strongly-defended Mont Pinçon. The British units were under constant fire, night and day, from mortars and artillery set up on

*Left to right.* **On 1 or 2 August, a Sherman is going through Cahagnes without disturbing an abandoned horse, which had probably seen much worse over the few days! The tank almost certainly belongs to the Sherwood Rangers who seized the village on 31 July. The same photograph preserved in the Imperial War Museum is larger, and shows that the road sign on the left bears the 7th Arm.Div. insignia, but this unit was almost exclusively Cromwell-equipped.** (*Tank Museum 2707/B5*)

**In mid-August, mechanics are working on the engine of a Sherman from 8th Arm.Brig. (see formation insignia). The tactical sign cannot be seen. The tank is a Firefly Vc, as indicated by the rear travelling gun lock and the spaced bogies.** (*RR*)

**A Sherman III from 24th Lancers is passing in front of an abandoned Panther Ausf.A between Caen and Tilly-sur-Seulles, on 30 June. The wartime caption mentions erroneously that it is a Tiger, and said that the regiment was attached to 49th Inf.Div., the unit with which the regiment operated at that time.** (*IWM B6226*)

these heights. An attack by the whole brigade was scheduled on 6 August, to take Condé-sur-Noireau: 4/7th RDG and the *Sherwood Rangers* were once again in support of the 43rd Inf.Div.; two days of continuous fighting were necessary to capture the village of La Varinière only. However, A Squadron, 13/18th Hussars discovered a crossing site over the antitank ditch at the bottom of Mont Pinçon, and rushed from the west on to the slopes, ignoring the enemy fire, to reach the summit in the evening with only six Shermans, three having been lost during the attack. The position was cleared with the back-up of B Squadron and 4th Somerset Light Infantry.

# REGIMENTS ACCORDING TO THE ORDER OF PRECEDENCE

## 4th/7th Royal Dragoon Guards

**Origins:** Regiment formed in 1685 as "Arran's Regiment of Cuirassiers", in northern England, fought in Flanders and at Namur in 1691 and 1695. Became "The Prince of Wales's Own Regiment of Horses" in 1715, then "The 4th (Royal Irish) Dragoon Guards" in 1788. Often committed against Irish rebels between 1795 and 1806, fought in the Peninsula War in 1812-13. Alternately in England and in Ireland between 1814 and 1882, served in the Crimea (Balaclava) in 1854. Sent to Egypt in 1882, then to South Africa in 1906. Fought in France from 1914 onwards (Marne, Ypres, Somme), and became "The 4th Royal Irish Dragoon Guards" in 1921, then was amalgamated with "The 7th Dragoon Guards (The Princess Royal's)" to take the name of "The 4th/7th Royal Dragoon Guards" in 1936 and so become a light tank regiment in 1937.

**- 1939-44:** In England within 2nd Inf.Div., with a Squadron in Palestine in 1939; the regiment was with 27th Arm.Brig. (9th Arm.Div.) in France and Belgium in 1940, then was evacuated via Dunkirk. Remained in England until 1944, before joining 8th Arm.Brig. in March for the campaign in North-West Europe.

Sometimes nicknamed *"The Fire Brigade"*.

## 24th Lancers

**- Origins:** Unit initially raised as "Regiment of Dragoons" by Colonel Morris in 1716, disbanded in 1718. Reformed as "24th Light Dragoons" in 1794, to be disbanded again in 1802.

In 1794, a regiment named "27th Light Dragoons" was formed; it served in India (Hindustan) and was given the name "24th Light Dragoons" in 1803, prior to being disbanded in 1819.

**- 1939-44:** The "24th Lancers" were reformed in 1940 with cadres from "9th Queen's Royal Lancers" and from "17th/21st Lancers". In England with 29th Arm.Brig. (11th Arm.Div.) from 1941, incorporated into 8th Arm.Brig. in February 1944, and took part in the landing and early fights in Normandy before being disbanded on 29 July 1944.

## Nottinghamshire Yeomanry

**- Origins:** A first troop of cavalry volunteers was raised in 1794, which took the name of "The Nottinghamshire Yeomanry Cavalry (Sherwood Rangers)" in 1828 then "The Nottinghamshire Imperial Yeomanry (Sherwood Rangers)" in 1900, in South Africa. Known as "The Nottinghamshire Yeomanry (Sherwood Rangers) TF", two regiments were formed and served at Gallipoli in 1915 (with 1st Mounted Division), then in Macedonia (1916), in Palestine (1917) before disbanding in 1918. A regiment was reconstituted in 1920 and joined the Territorial Army in 1922. **- 1939-44:** Within 5th Cavalry Brigade in Palestine in 1940, then incorporated into 8th Arm.Brig. in August 1941, and fought in North Africa until 1943 (Alam El Halfa, El Alamein, Tripoli, Enfidaville). Repatriated to England with this brigade for the campaign in North-West Europe.

## Operation *Blackwater* and the pursuit to the Seine

A limited-range operation was arranged on the following days to capture Le Plessis Grimoult and Danjou. 4/7th RDG with Duke of Cornwall's Light Infantry rushed from the top of Mont Pinçon, took Le Plessis Grimoult, and were the first in the campaign to capture a Tiger II, from sPzAbt.503. Then their B Squadron, 12th KRRC and 43rd Reconnaissance Regiment cleared around Danjou. The brigade was directed towards Condé three days later, in support of 50th Inf.Div.

On 11 August, the advance was difficult for 13/18th Hussars who lost seven tanks, and for 4/7th RDG. To make up the tank crew losses, the Squadron HQ antiaircraft section was disbanded on 14 August. Proussy was captured on the same day, and the *Sherwood Rangers* with 43rd Inf.Div. crossed the River Noireau, losing seven Shermans in the process, but were unable to take the Condé bridge intact.

Operation *Blackwater* ended on the following day, with the occupation of Berjou, while the *Sherwood Rangers* were dashing towards Sainte-Honorine-La-Chardonne.

The brigade rested for a few days, mainly for its many damaged AFVs to undergo repairs: for example, there were only 25 tanks left in 4/7th RDG instead of the usual 61. Only 13/18th Hussars went on progressing rapidly behind the Germans who were retreating to escape from the Falaise pocket: Putanges and the forest of Gouffern were passed through in order to reach Breteuil. At top speed, the other regiments followed a short while later, and the material losses were now caused by track, bogie or engine problems. On 23 August, most of 8th Arm.Brig. was reunited for a new advance via Courcelles, Cagnes, Bailleux, and finally Laigle. The forest of Laigle was cleared by 4/7th RDG with help from the FFIs, then the brigade waited three days so that 43rd Inf.Div. could set up a bridge to cross the River Seine at Vernon, which they did on the 27th.

# 27th ARMOURED BRIGADE

**F**ORMED IN APRIL 1940 from divisional Cavalry regiments (1st Fife and Forfarshire Yeomanry and East Riding Yeomanry), the 1st Armoured Recce Brigade was renamed 27th Armoured Brigade in November of the same year.

It then consisted of the following regiments: 4th/7th Royal Dragoon Guards, 13th/18th Royal Hussars and East Riding Yeomanry. Assigned to 9th Arm.Div. until June 1942, the Brigade commanded by Brigadier Prior-Palmer was next incorporated into 79th Arm.Div. in October. It was chosen in April 1943 by the divisional commander, Major General Percy Hobart, to be equipped with amphibious Duplex Drive tanks (Sherman II, III and Vs). The development and testing of these AFVs, first designed on Valentine then Sherman chassis, were carried out in great secret in Scotland, in south Wales and on the isle of Wight, with help from the Navy. The crews progressively learnt to master the difficult water-launching and tricky handling of their "boats".

Montgomery decided in October 1943 that the DD tanks would

A white and yellow sea horse on a blue shield, colloquially nicknamed "*the pregnant pilchard*".

lead the forces landing in Normandy, and on the 15th, 27th Arm.Brig. came under direct control of 1st Corps, which was to seize the landing beaches, reach the River Orne and capture Caen. However, liaisons with 79th Arm.Div. were still close and regular. At that time, East Riding Yeomanry was substituted for 148th Battalion, Royal Armoured Corps. The brigade was appointed with the support of 3rd Inf.Div., with which it trained for a few months. In February 1944, Staffordshire Yeomanry was substituted for 4th/7th Dragoon Guards, and East Riding Yeomanry came back to fill the place of 148th RAC: the two regiments leaving with their DDs were to join 8th Arm.Brig., which was part of the first assault force. With D-Day approaching, the first parties of the brigade embarked on 2 June at Southampton, but they only left harbour on the 5th, because of the delay caused by weather conditions.

## On D-Day

The 27th Arm.Brig., with 190 Shermans and 33 Stuarts, was under command of 3rd Inf.Div., and was to get ashore on Sword Beach, on the left of the Invasion forces. 13/18th Hussars was the spearhead with 8th Inf.Brig., followed by Staffordshire Yeomanry

*Title.* **Sherman DD n°48 from 13/18th Hussars is supporting 8th Inf.Brig. on 6 June. Just landed, it still has its full floating skirt and has folded-up propellers. Photographs taken in this area on D-Day are often of low quality, since fighting was then raging and reporters had not much time to bother with exposure or pose...**
*(Tank Museum 5646/F3)*

### 27th Armoured Brigade

| Brigade Headquarters | **50** | |
|---|---|---|
| **51** | **52** | **53** |
| 13/18th Hussars | Staffordshire Yeomanry | East Riding Yeomanry |

and 185th Inf.Brig. Facing defences manned by 716.ID and two regiments of 352.ID, a first group of four LCTs each bringing four Sherman DDs from 13/18th Hussars' A and B Squadrons headed for the beach in front of La Brèche d'Hermanville, to support 2nd East Yorkshire and 1st South Lancashire, while C Squadron was fighting with 1st Suffolk before Périers and Colleville. The DD tanks were to be launched 6,300m from the shore, but the sea was too rough, and they left the LCTs only 4,500m from the beach: 34 of the 40 transported tanks were launched, but two collided with other landing crafts and drowned, five were overwhelmed by waves, and four were rapidly knocked out by enemy fire upon arrival on the shore. Only 23 tanks were thus left which, once their floating skirt was lowered, began to shoot at the German defences with their 75-mm gun and machine-guns. The slowly rising tide drowned the engine in some tanks, but they went on firing until their ammunition was exhausted. Not a single one of the Flails which had landed before the DDs was still operational, and the tank commanders were hesitating about advancing on mined ground.

A defensive position nicknamed Strongpoint Cod was particularly troublesome with its three 7.5 and 5cm guns, three mortars and several machine-guns. 13/18th Hussars however dealt with it, and the beach being almost cleared at 8.30, they were able to start progressing towards Hermanville, Lion-sur-Mer and Colleville.

*Above.* **The 27th Arm.Brig. went on progressing towards Hermanville in the morning of 6 June. Although the wartime caption says these tanks belong to 13/18th Hussars, close examination of the first Sherman reveals the tactical sign 52 of Staffordshire Yeomanry. It is a Sherman III, as indicated by the large rear armour plate and closely spaced bogies.** *(IWM B5021)*

*Below.* **Shermans of 27th Arm.Brig. are moving through Douvres-la-Délivrande on 8 June, before the eyes of the town's children. No insignia can be seen, except maybe the circle of a C Squadron on the transmission housing. Remnants of Bostik waterproofing can be made out around the gun mantlet and hull machine-gun.** *(IWM B5267)*

The Colleville battery was attacked at 13.00 with 1st Suffolk and Crabs from 22nd Dragoons, but it was only taken on the following day. Staffordshire Yeomanry soon after completed their landing and moved up with King's Shropshire Light Infantry: C Squadron towards Beuville, B Squadron towards Périers, and A Squadron in reserve. The Périers ridge was captured at 15.00, but Beuville resisted. A counterstroke from 21.PzDiv. was stemmed by Staffordshire Yeomanry, it turned away and finally reached Lion-sur-Mer, but the Panzers were threatened with encirclement so they pulled away. The 21.PzDiv. lost nearly 70 tanks on 6 June, and 27th Arm.Brig. accounted for a fair number of these, although Caen was still out of reach.

## Holding the beachhead

The German counterattack that was expected on 7 June did not materialize, so the advance towards Caen resumed at 10.00: Staffordshire Yeomanry supporting 185th Inf.Brig. reached Hérouville, then met an antitank ditch and strong opposition from 21.PzDiv.: after the loss of three tanks, the progression stopped. Tigers were reported at Ranville at 16.00, and two 13/18th Hussars Squadrons were sent there to protect the Orne river bridge. The recently landed East Riding Yeomanry came to cover the brigade's right flank in contact with the Canadians. 8 June was quiet, except four attacks from German fighter-bombers, and consolidation of the beachhead continued. A confused battle took place in Cambes on 9 June, during which East Riding Yeomanry lost their first three tanks whilst supporting Royal Ulster Rifles. On the next day, paratroopers from the 6th Airborne were again attacked at Ranville, and B Squadron, 13/18th Hussars restored the situation: 200 prisoners were captured, and a hundred dead enemy were counted on the battleground. Activity on 11 June was limited to infantry patrolling, and 13/18th Hussars' A Squadron were committed on the 12th at the paratroopers' side for the successful attack on Biéville. B Squadron, moving

up with the Black Watch to assault a castle south of Biéville, lost three tanks.

The three regiments remained in their positions from 13 to 22 June, although enduring frequent artillery shelling on day and Luftwaffe bombing at night, causing worrying casualties, mainly officers. Lieutenant Colonel Harrap, commanding 13/18th Hussars, was killed on 16 June when his Jeep ran into a Panzer IV on a lane corner. The complement of various units was delayed because of the storm raging on 19 June on the Mulberry harbours. Skirmishes happened during reconnaissance patrols carried out to prepare Operation *Perth* against Ste-Honorine-la-Chardonnette, for which the brigade came under control of 51st Inf.Div. On 23 June, A Squadron, 13/18th Hussars, supported 5th Cameron Highlanders for the attack: entering the village, the crews spotted the presence of 35 enemy AFVs on the right, and shot at them from a distance. Several German assaults were repelled during the day, with help from the Navy and Typhoons, and the regiment claimed in the evening to have knocked out 13 Panzers (including 10 for A Squadron) and two half-tracks, without a single loss! From 24 to 26 June, the brigade got ready to take part in

operations *Mitten* and *Aberlour*, for which Staffordshire Yeomanry and East Riding Yeomanry were to support 8th and 9th Inf.Brig. (3rd Inf.Div.) against Le Landel, chateau de La Londe, and La Bijude.

Operation *Mitten* began at 15.30 on 27 June, and Staffordshire Yeomanry and 8th Inf.Brig. soon realised that about 30 enemy AFVs were present around the chateau de La Londe. C Squadron attacked mortar positions west of Lebisey, while A Squadron was running into dug-in tanks: three or four of them were destroyed, but

*Above.* **On 13 June, a Firefly (probably Sherman Vc) from 27th Arm.Brig. by-passing the village of Bréville. Even if the tactical sign 51 is barely visible on the transmission housing, the shoulder flash of the two crew members confirms that the tank belongs to 13/18th Hussars. Very early in the campaign, spare track links were carried on the glacis plate to improve its protection.**
*(IWM B5470)*

*Below.* **Near Saint-Contest, Shermans (probably M4A2) from 27th Arm.Brig. prepare to support 59th Inf.Div. infantrymen during Operation Charnwood. Bombardments have heavily damaged the town church on the right, as well as the trees in the background.** *(IWM B6758)*

antitank SPGs were holding up the Staffordshire Yeomanry, damaging two of their Shermans. During the assault which resumed on the following day, the regiment knocked-out two enemy tanks, and watched other AFVs manoeuvring without shooting. East Riding Yeomanry in support of 9th Inf.Brig. lost six tanks in the afternoon, mainly to antitank guns.

On their side, Staffordshire Yeomanry registered the loss of three other Shermans at the end of the day. But infantry bore the brunt of the losses, although destroying at least three Panzers: consequently, Operation *Aberlour* was cancelled.

The brigade was sent back from 29 June to 7 July in order to prepare for Operation *Charnwood*, and 13/18th Hussars which had been the most often committed regiment since D-Day were at rest in Luc-sur-Mer to reorganize, and were temporarily replaced by 148th RAC from 33rd Arm.Brig.

## Operation *Charnwood*

After a preliminary bombardment in the evening of 7 July by Lancasters, Operation *Charnwood* was launched on the 8th at

4.20, with 27th Arm.Brig.'s armoured regiments supporting the following units: 13/18th Hussars with 176th Inf.Brig., Staffordshire Yeomanry with 185th Inf.Brig., East Riding Yeomanry with 197th Inf.Brig., and elements of 22nd Dragoons (Crabs), 141st RAC (Crocodiles) and 5th Assault Rgt (AVRE) under command. The attack of 3rd Canadian, 59th and 3rd Inf.Div. north of Caen made rapid progress against the defences of 12.SS-PzDiv., 21.PzDiv. and 16. Luftwaffe Feld-Division. Galmanche, La Bijude and Lebisey were seized by 10.00, but the advance slowed down afterwards as the resistance stiffened, with notably many snipers: East Riding Yeomanry lost six killed or wounded tank commanders in Galmanche. 3rd Inf.Div. finally succeeded in entering Caen, and the Canadians made good progress on their side. The attack resumed on 9 July against resolute opposition. St-Contest was taken by the 197th Inf.Brig./East Riding Yeomanry group, then a convergent assault from 33rd Arm.Brig. and 3rd Canadian Inf. Div. enabled them to conquer half of Caen. In spite of coordination problems between 27th Arm.Brig. and 59th Inf. Div., who did not know each other very well, most parts of the city were occupied by the evening. In comparison with the infantry's heavy losses (more than 1300 men), the armour had suffered rather little: 13/18th Hussars for instance had lost six tanks but destroyed as many Panzers. The brigade withdrew until 15 July for a relative rest, and prepared afterwards for the next great offensive.

## Operation *Goodwood*

The role of 27th Arm.Brig. for *Goodwood* was to hold the left flank of 8th Corps, which was undertaking the main offensive, with 3rd Inf.Div., 13/18th Hussars with 8th Inf.Brig., Staffordshire Yeomanry with 185th Inf.Brig., East Riding Yeomanry with 9th Inf.Brig. were also escorted by Flails from the Lothian & Border Horse Yeomanry. Under the harassing shelling from the German artillery and Nebelwerfers, 13/18th Hussars opened the attack at 7.45 towards Touffréville and Sannerville, which was under control at 11.00; Staffordshire Yeomanry and 185th Inf.Brig. then headed

# REGIMENTS ACCORDING TO THE ORDER OF PRECEDENCE

## 13th/18th Royal Hussars (Queen Mary's Own)

- **Origins:** Resulting from the amalgamation in 1922 between "13th Hussars" (deriving from "13th Regiment of Dragoons" created in 1697, known as "13th Regiment of (Light) Dragoons" from 1795), and "18th Royal Hussars (Queen Mary's Own)" (deriving from "18th Light Dragoons" formed in 1715). The 13th/18th Hussars were in Scotland and in England in 1925-27, then in Egypt in 1929, and in India in 1931. Became "13th/18th Royal Hussars (Queen Mary's Own)" in 1935, converted into light tank regiment in 1938.

- **1939-44:** With 1st Inf.Div. from September 1939 to March 1940, evacuated via Dunkirk. Joined 27th Arm.Brig. in July 1940, remained in England until D-Day. After the brigade disbandment, joined 8th Arm. Brig. in August 1944.

## Staffordshire Yeomanry

- **Origins:** Troops from "Staffordshire Volunteer Cavalry" raised in 1794, forming a regiment in 1798, "The Staffordshire Regiment of Gentlemen and Yeomanry". Sub-titled "The Queen's Own Royal Regiment" in 1838, became "The Staffordshire Imperial Yeomanry" in 1900 and sailed for South Africa. Became "The Staffordshire Yeomanry (The Queen's Own Royal Regiment) TF Hussars" in 1908. Three battalions (including one bicycle battalion) formed in 1914-15, in Egypt, then in Palestine and in Damascus (1917). Two battalions disbanded in 1918; the cavalry regiment was reconstituted in 1920 as "The Staffordshire Yeomanry (The Queen's Own Royal Regiment) TF". Territorial Army in 1922.

- **1939-44:** In Palestine and in Syria in 1940-41, with 6th Cavalry Brigade, became armoured regiment in August 1941 within 8th Arm.Brig. Back in England, transferred to 27th Arm.Brig. in February 1944, landed in Normandy with this unit, and when the latter was disbanded, became independent regiment in August 1944 and was then incorporated into 79th Arm.Div.

## East Riding Yeomanry

- **Origins:** Regiment raised in 1794, "The East Riding of Yorkshire Yeomanry Cavalry", disbanded in 1801. Reformed in 1803, disbanded again in 1814. Recreated in 1902 as "Wenlock's Horse", became "The East Riding of Yorkshire Imperial Yeomanry" in 1903, then "The East Riding of Yorkshire Yeomanry TF (Lancers)" in 1908. Three battalions (including one bicycle battalion) formed in 1914-15, the 1st in Egypt then in the Sinai Desert (1916), in Palestine (1917) with Yeomanry Mounted Division. Became "102nd Light Machine Gun Battalion" and fought in France in 1918. After disbandment or amalgamation of 2nd and 3rd battalions, reconstituted in 1920: "The East Riding of Yorkshire Yeomanry TF", Territorial Army in 1922 and became armoured car regiment, RAC. Renamed "The East Riding Yeomanry RAC TA" in 1935.

- **1939-44:** Two Cavalry regiments in 1939, the 1st fought in France in 1940, was evacuated via Dunkirk then amalgamated with 2nd regiment because of losses. Integrated into 27th Arm.Brig. in April 1940. Meanwhile, part of "East Riding Yeomanry" was converted to infantry battalion in 1940, then to parachute battalion (10th Battalion, The Green Howards) in 1943. The armoured regiment landed in Normandy with 27th Arm.Brig., and after the latter's disbandment in August 44, joined 33rd Arm. Brig.

---

for the railway line Caen – Lisieux. Crabs proved to be very useful when anti-personnel minefields were met north of Touffréville. At 16.00, C Squadron, 13/18th Hussars were in Banneville-la-Campagne, but they had lost four tanks to dug-in Panzers, although managing to knock-out or capture three antitank guns, four mortars and a Panzerjäger with 8th Inf.Brig. In the evening, East Riding Yeomanry supported 9th Inf.Brig. towards Troarn, but the advance became very difficult: the armour lost contact with King's Own Scottish Borderers about 19.00, and the infantry had to dug-in.

On 19 June at midday, Staffordshire Yeomanry and 185th Inf. Brig. advanced towards Le Prieuré, which was soon taken, then to Le Quai. While 13/18th Hussars was in reserve, East Riding Yeomanry continued to support 9th Inf.Brig. towards Troarn without much success, for they met a long antitank ditch and a strong defence line reinforced with Panzers and SPGs, between Hubert-Folie, Frénouville and Troarn. Tigers were even reported but made no intervention

in the sector. Tank and infantry losses made the assault stop, and two small enemy counterstrokes launched in the evening against Le Quai were repelled. East Riding Yeomanry was still blocked before Troarn on 20 July, and torrential rains in the afternoon interrupted the fighting: they were to last for 36 hours, and thus put an end to Operation *Goodwood*.

## The end of the road

Thunder struck on 22 July: because of the important losses endured by the British armoured units since D-Day, the 27th Arm.Brig. was to be disbanded. It seems that from the beginning, the high command had not hoped that this unit would be kept since it had expected the brigade to suffer much heavier losses during the landing. The regiments were pulled out of the frontline, and it was known as early as 23 July that the 13/18th Hussars was to be incorporated into 8th Arm.Brig., and that the Staffordshire Yeomanry would be repatriated to England and come under control of 79th Arm. Div. The fate of East Riding Yeomanry was not sealed yet, but in the meantime, they were ordered for 25 July, together with 13/18th Hussars, to help 148th RAC to secure the left flank of the 2nd Canadian Corps' attack on Tilly-la-Campagne.

The regiments were left out of battle on the 25th, but they nonetheless suffered losses (including a damaged Sherman and Stuart) caused by enemy artillery shelling. Relieved by 33rd Arm.Brig., the two regiments withdrew west of the River Orne while Staffordshire Yeomanry were preparing to set sail to England on 27 July, after having handed over their tanks to 13/18th Hussars. The brigade disbandment was effective on 30 July, 13/18th Hussars being substituted for 24th Lancers within 8th Arm.Brig., while East Riding Yeomanry simply rested and trained for a few days, prior to joining 33rd Arm.Brig. on 16 August in replacement of 148th RAC.

The brigade headquarters personnel was mainly dispatched between these two regiments staying in Normandy, or else joined 8th Arm.Brig. HQ.

# 31st TANK BRIGADE

**T**HE 31ST ARMY TANK BRIGADE was created on 15 January 1941 in England, under the command of Brigadier G.S. Knight. It initially included 9th and 10th RTR only, which were joined by 141st RAC in November 1941.

Intended to be equipped with infantry tanks, the brigade was one of the first units to be issued with the new Churchill in mid-1942, some 9th RTR members having even taken part in the final development at the side of Vauxhall workers. Known as Tank Brigade in May 1942, it lost again 141st RAC from July 1942 to February 1943. The ultimate formation from March 1943 onwards was: 7th RTR, 9th RTR, and 141st RAC, but the latter were equipped with Churchill Crocodile flame-throwers, and were most of the time under control of 79th Arm.Div. (it was the case in Normandy). Attached

between June 1942 and September 1943 to 53rd Inf. Div., with which it trained intensively, the brigade became independent afterwards.

### Arrival in Normandy and Operation *Epsom*

Forward parties from 31st Tk.Brig. were shipp on 16 June 1944, but most of the unit set sail on the 18th from Gosport, and landed on the following day on Juno Beach, in the middle of the storm. The landing was completed on the 22nd only, and the brigade lost its first tanks when six 7th RTR Churchills were drowned with their LCT after it hit a mine. Gathering together around St-Gabriel, east of Bayeux, 31st Tk.Brig. came under control of 15th Inf.Div. (8th Corps). For Operation *Epsom*, the brigade was reduced to two regiments (7th and 9th RTR) but reinforced with elements from 79th Arm. Div. (Flails, AVREs, Crocodiles). 7th RTR were to support 46th Inf. Brig. on the right; 9th RTR's A and B Squadrons moved up with 44th Inf.Brig. on the left, while C Squadron were behind with 227th Inf. Brig. The objective was the Caen – Fontenay-le-Pesnel road level with St-Manvieu and Cheux.

After reconnaissance on the start line near Bretteville-l'Orgueilleuse, on 26 June the attackers rushed at 7.30 behind a heavy artillery barrage, making good progress against the Hitlerjugend of which only snipers remained. 7th RTR was however delayed by minefields south of Mesnil-Patry, losing nine tanks. Cheux was seized at 10.00, but Haut-du Bosq resisted, defended by Panthers from 2 Pz-Div. 44th Inf Brig took St-Manvieu after hard street fighting against the I Hitlerjugend,

Verticaldiaboloformed with two green isosceles triangles.

## 31st Army Tank Brigade

Brigade Headquarters **990**

**991** — 7th Battalion Royal Tank Regiment

**992** — 9th Battalion Royal Tank Regiment

**993** — 141st RAC

*Title.* **It is a pity that the exact location of this photograph in Normandy is uncertain, for it shows a rare Churchill Mk III armed with a 75-mm gun (sometimes referenced to as Mk III\*), with old-pattern tracks moreover. That this tank belonged to 31st Tk.Brig. is however certain, from the tactical sign beginning with 99 (probably 991 for 7th RTR).**
*(Tank Museum 1780/E2)*

with support from 9th RTR's A and B Squadrons and 141st RAC's Crocodiles. The brigade lost its first man killed and three Churchills. 11th Arm.Div. then got through the captured positions to continue the assault. C Squadron from 9th RTR attacked with 227th Inf.Brig. at 19.15 only, in the rain, towards the Caen – Tilly road. Despite the lack of the expected air support, and the presence of many enemy antitank guns, the assaulting force moved beyond Cheux but the tank losses mounted: there were only six operational Churchills by nightfall.

Orders were issued on 27 June to seize crossing sites on the River Orne, but bad weather precluded any air support. Artillery contribution from 3rd Canadian Inf.Div. allowed C Squadron, 7th RTR to support 10th Highland Light Inf. towards Gavrus. They were harassed from the start line by Panzer IVs and Panthers, but destroyed three of these. The rest of 7th RTR concentrated to support 43rd Inf.Div. which was fiercely counterattacked. C Squadron, 9th RTR were fighting with 2nd Argyll and Sutherland Highlanders, while A and B Squadrons were helping 46th Inf.Brig. in the attack towards Grainville-sur-Odon and Mouen, losing two tanks to Panthers. 11th Arm.Div. did the bulk of the job on 28 June, but 31st Tk.Brig. was still supporting the infantry: B Squadron, 9th RTR knocked-out three Panthers whilst defending 9th Cameronians; A and B Squadrons, 7th RTR took part in tough fighting with 44th Inf.Brig.

On the following day, they faced the 1.SS-Pz-Div. at the Grainville – Mondrainville crossroads. By 18.00, the enemy had gained ground and 12 Churchills had been lost, so C Squadron came up to form a defensive position. On their side, C Squadron, 9th RTR reinforced A and B Squadrons in Colleville at dawn, and the crews had to be on the alert all day long under a hail of artillery shells and mortar bombs. A big counterstroke was repelled at 18.00, two Panthers that infiltrated into

*Above.* **The 7th RTR's tactical sign 991 can be clearly seen besides the bridge classification disc (40 tons) on the original photograph taken on 26 June, in the early morning mist, when operation Epsom started. It is a command tank as indicated by the three antennas instead of the usual two. Here again, note the old-pattern tracks.** *(IWM B5993)*

*Below.* **On 26 June, the plain south-west of Caen was not too attractive in the fog: a Troop of three Churchills is advancing, turret in the three o'clock position. They have not yet got in touch with 15th Inf.Div. that they are to support during the offensive.** *(RR)*

Grainville damaged two Churchills, but the position was held despite another attack on Haut-du-Bosq.

30 June was spent in consolidating the positions, and C Squadron, 9th RTR in support of 130th Inf.Brig. at Haut-du-Bosq, repelled soon after midday an attack from 9.SS-Pz-Div. and 60 AFVs. *Epsom* came to an end: it only succeeded in a slight 5 miles advance west of Caen, but above all it enabled three more German armoured divisions to be tied up in the British sector.

## Operation *Jupiter*

In early July, 31st Tk.Brig. was still providing support and protection to infantry units: 43rd Inf.Div. with 9th RTR, and 15th Inf.Div. then 53rd Inf.Div. with 7th RTR. From the 5th onwards, it enjoyed a brief rest period, although undertaking recces to prepare Operation *Jupiter*. For this offensive aimed at the famous Hill 112, 31st Tk.Brig. was in support of 43rd Inf.Div., 7th RTR with 129th Inf.Brig. towards the hill itself, and 9th RTR with 130th Inf.Brig. towards Eterville and Maltot.

*Left.* **A Churchill Mk IV or VI, armed with a 75-mm gun, is providing protection for a column of 15th Inf.Div., the insignia of which can be seen on the Jeep, together with the tactical sign 62 identifying 7th Seaforth Highlanders. The tank front is adorned with a "busty bust" which seems to represent a Queen of England!**
*(IWM B6002)*

The attack opened at 2.30 on 10 July, with 7th RTR and 129th Inf. Brig. progressing towards Le Bon Repos: the objective was reached at 12.30, but C Squadron were stopped by four dug-in Tigers supported with Panthers. After violent clashes, eight Churchills were left on the battlefield by the evening, but 7th RTR claimed to have knocked out nine Panzers (an optimistic tally, even if SS-sPzAbt. 102 eventually lost three Tigers on Hill 112). B Squadron, 9th RTR were meanwhile leading 5th Dorsetshire towards the chateau de Fontaine, with Achilles TDs in cover against a dozen Panthers from 10.SS-Pz-Div. Opposition only consisted of machine-guns and snipers, and the objective was reached at 6.14 for the loss of a single tank. C Squadron immediately advanced towards Eterville with 4th Dorsetshire, and the village was seized at about 7.35. A Squadron and 7th Hampshire then got through the gained positions, heading for Maltot, but four Jagdpanthers destroyed two Churchills, and Tigers in ambush put harassing fire on

**Two Churchills (Mk IV or VI) from 31st Tk.Brig. are moving up along a Norman road on 27 June: the ruins of Bretteville-l'Orgueilleuse or Norrey-en-Bessin can be seen in the background. The look of the sky and the soil shows how bad the weather really was for Operation Epsom. The unit with the tactical sign 124 on two-colour background, painted on the board lying on the ground, is unknown.** *(IWM B6054)*

the assailants. A Squadron could just field nine tanks at about noon against the German counterattacks, and only four Churchills were still able to fire a bit later: the position held, however. The attack resumed at 16.40 towards Hill 112 (with A Squadron, 7th RTR) and towards Maltot (with C Squadron, 9th RTR); the latter village was reached by 4th Dorsetshire, but Panzers infiltrated to the rear and forced the infantry to withdraw. The day had been very tough for 9th RTR, who had suffered 65 casualties, i.e. more than the quarter of their total losses during the whole North-West Europe campaign.

While 9th RTR remained on the ridge on 11 July, 7th RTR's B Squadron successfully supported 15th Inf.Div. on the Caen – Eterville road. The brigade was in action until the 25th, mostly in a defensive role, but 7th RTR attacked with 129th Inf.Brig. on the morning of 22 July, up to Maltot which was reached at 22.00. C Squadron made slight progress on next day against the 272. and Frundsberg divisions, but could not get beyond Maltot: they lost eight Churchills for a single destroyed Tiger. 7th RTR were relieved by 153rd RAC on 25 July to reorganize, and the brigade came under command of 59th Inf.Div. on the morrow. 9th RTR operated with 176th Inf.Brig. against possible counterstrokes around Fontenay-Le-Pesnel, and 7th RTR came back on 29 July to support the failed assault of 197th Inf.Brig. on Le Coisel. The attack resumed on the following day and failed again, B Squadron losing two

*Above.* **On 28 June, a 31st Tk.Brig. Churchill, maybe from 7th RTR, is preceding infantrymen before passing through a hedgerow. Fighting is probably very close, men seem tense. Once again, the crew has festooned the tank turret with various boxes; artillery aiming posts can even be seen on the rear turret bin, unless these are parts of the ramrod.** *(Tank Museum 4835/A2)*

*Below.* **Heading to Eterville, Stuart IIIs (M3A1) from 31st Tk.Brig. are passing through a Norman village on 10 July at dawn. On these vehicles in good condition, the antenna is particularly tall: after the fighting, it was not rare to see only a short stump of antenna remaining.**
*(IWM B6815)*

# REGIMENTS ACCORDING TO THE ORDER OF PRECEDENCE

## 7th Battalion, Royal Tank Regiment

- **Origins:** In common with the whole Royal Tank Regiment, see 1st RTR (7th Arm. Div.). The 7th Battalion derived in 1918 from G Battalion, Tank Corps, formed in 1916 as a company in the Machine Gun Corps, and which fought at Cambrai in 1917. In support of 3rd French Inf.Div. at Morcuil in 1918, disbanded in 1919. Recreated as "7th Battalion, Royal Tank Corps" in 1937, then "7th Battalion, Royal Tank Regiment" in 1939.

- **1939-44:** In France in 1940 with 1st Army Tank Brigade, temporarily amalgamated with 4th RTR, then evacuated via Dunkirk. Dispatched to Egypt in January 1941 under control of GHQ, Middle East Forces, then attached to 4th Arm.Brig. in May and June. Fought with 32nd Army Tk.Brig. at Tobruk from September 1941 onwards. After capture and destruction in July 1942, reformed in early 1943 from 10th RTR, within 31st Army Tk.Brig. from March 1943 onwards. Fought with this unit during the

whole Normandy campaign.

## 9th Battalion, Royal Tank Regiment

- **Origins:** In common with the whole Royal Tank Regiment, see 1st RTR. I Battalion, 3rd Brigade, Machine Gun Corps formed in 1916 became 9th battalion in 1918. Disbanded in 1920, recreated as "9th Battalion, Royal Tank Regiment" in 1940.

- **1939-44:** In England in January 1941 with 31st Army Tk.Brig., landed with this unit in Normandy.

## 141st Regiment, Royal Armoured Corps

- **Origins:** In common with the whole Royal Armoured Corps. The RAC was formed in 1939, by integration of all RTR regiments and almost all those of the armoured cavalry. It was authorized in early 1941 to raise its own regiments, by conversion of infantry units, numbered 107 to 163. After a maximum of 33 regi-

ments in 1942, the RAC only fielded 20 in 1943, and 13 were present for the Normandy campaign. 141st RAC was formed in 1941 by conversion of "7th Battalion, The Buffs (Royal East Kent) Regiment", raised itself in 1940 and deriving from "3rd Regiment of Foot", created in 1572 in London.

- **1939-44:** Incorporated into 31st Army Tk.Brig. in November 1941, converted into flame-thrower Crocodile-equipped regiment in early 1944. More or less independent, either directly attached to 79th Arm.Div. or to its 30th Arm.Brig., either to 31st Tk.Brig. Because it was the only regiment with flame-throwing tanks in Normandy, it was used in many different operations, scattered all over the area, depending on demand. Nicknamed "*The Buffs*".

Churchills in the process.

## Operation *Totalize* and the thrust towards the Seine

In early August, 31st Tk.Brig. and 59th Inf.Div. were still holding their positions, even managing to gain ground as the Germans withdrew; the losses were now mainly caused by mines. The brigade was attached to 49th Inf.Div. (1st Corps) on 4 August, and had to move up eastwards of the beachhead on the 6th, to join 1st Canadian Army: it was given the task of securing the left flank of the Canadian breakout towards Falaise. 9th RTR alone were committed with 146th Inf.Brig. on 8 August, when Operation *Totalize* started, to protect the 51st Inf.Div.'s attack on Secqueville. On the 9th, 7th RTR moved up with 70th and 147th Inf.Brig., and 9th RTR with 146th Inf.Brig. to converge on Vimont, and the Squadrons supported the slow infantry progression in rotation on the following days, in spite of machine-guns, mines and mortars. 31st Tk.Brig. came under control of 2nd Canadian Corps from 13 August onwards and provided cover for Operation *Tractable*, 7th RTR losing two Churchills in Urville. With the spreading German withdrawal, 9th RTR was used on 15 August to support 2nd Canadian Inf.Div. towards Falaise, and Villers-Canivet was reached in the evening: by the 16th, the British forces had made a 40 miles advance in 30 hours! Meanwhile, 7th RTR were in support of 146th Inf.Brig. (49th Inf.Div.), and half-a-Squadron helped in seizing the Dives river bridge in Mézidon.

The 31st Tk.Brig. was informed that it was soon to join 79th Arm. Div. and be equipped with Crocodiles; 7th RTR was attached to 34th

Tk.Brig. (12th Corps) from 17 August on: they were to stay in the Montigny area near Falaise until 31 August, to reorganize and carry out essential maintenance. 9th RTR replaced them at the side of 49th Inf.Div. for the defence of the Mézidon bridgehead on the River Dives. Whilst waiting to cross the river, the regiment looked for crossing sites on the River Vie, often in vain. C Squadron succeeded on the 20th through the use of the bridge set up by 51st Inf.Div., and then managed to catch up with the Hallamshire Battalion in spite of mines and antitank guns: two of the latter were destroyed for the loss of one tank, and three Churchills bogged down. From 21 August onwards, 9th RTR, (now the single regiment in the brigade) were constantly in action, supporting King's Own Yorkshire Light Inf. and Duke of Wellington Rgt at Crèvecœur and Cambremer against the weakening resistance of machine-guns, mortars and antitank guns (but no Panzers). 144th RAC came under temporary control of 31st Tk.Brig. until 31 August, and supported 49th Inf.Div. as soon as a class 40 bridge was built on the River Touques on the 24th. The advance towards Pont-Audemer on the next day was stopped since no bridge was available in Cormeilles; a tank of C Squadron, 9th RTR was destroyed by a Panzerfaust in Epaignes, and two enemy antitank guns were disabled. The rejoicing liberated villages were slowing down the progression as much as mines and blown bridges, and the operations were stopped on 26 August for the brigade to reequip and train. 9th RTR eventually left to join 34th Tk.Brig. for the attack against Le Havre, and 31st Tk.Brig. had to reorganize with new regiments.

Operation Jupiter against Hill 112 was the second major offensive involving 31st Tk.Brig.: on 16 July, a column of Churchills is moving up to attack Evrecy. The first tank, with a C Squadron circle on the turret, is a Mark V equipped with a 95-mm howitzer, and is also a command vehicle (see the three antennas). *(IWM B7584)*

# 33rd ARMOURED DIVISION

A vertical diabolo formed with two isosceles triangles, black below and green above.

**3RD ARMY TANK BRIGADE was created on 30 August 1941. At that time it comprised a single regiment, 43rd RTR, to be joined in October by 144th and 148th RAC.**

The first Valentines reached the units for training, since the brigade was to be equipped with infantry tanks. Becoming Tank Brigade in June 1942, it was issued with Churchills in the meantime. It was assigned to 3rd Inf.Div. from June 1942 to April 1943, then became independent again. 43rd RTR left for 79th Arm.Div. in August 1943, then it was the turn of 148th RAC in October, these regiments being replaced by 1st Northamptonshire Yeomanry and East Riding Yeomanry. Eventually, the brigade was reequipped with Sherman Is and IIs: the Churchill was the fruit of an ancient concept, and its construction was a heavy strain on production capacities in Great Britain, who preferred to focus on more recent machines such as the Cromwell. On the other hand, the Sherman mass-produced in the USA was available in great numbers. The experience with these two different tank types, and with the tactics involved, was to be very useful for the brigade during the fighting in Normandy. In March 1944, the returning 148th RAC was substituted for the East Riding Yeomanry who joined 27th Arm.Brig. Re-denominated 33rd Armoured Brigade on the very same month, the raw and untried unit embarked in Portsmouth from 11 June 1944 onwards, in order to go and fight in Normandy under the command of Brigadier H.B. Scott.

## Three week's wait

1st Northamptonshire Yeomanry began to land on 13 June in front of Asnelles-sur-Mer and Le Hamel (Gold Beach), and was soon followed by the other units. 33rd Arm.Brig. assembled south of Bayeux and came under command of 7th Arm.Div. Concentration was almost complete on 16 June, and the brigade moved up towards Baugy woods on the 19th, to prepare for the battle for Caen. Its taking part was however cancelled, and the units remained in reserve, mostly unscathed from the mortar and artillery shelling, but enduring Luftwaffe night attacks which caused the first 1st Northamptonshire Yeomanry casualty on the 21st. Crews grew more and more

### 33rd Armoured Brigade

**From 13 June to 15 August 1944**

| | Brigade Headquarters **172** | |
|---|---|---|
| **173** | **174** | **175** |
| 1st Northamptonshire Yeomanry | 144th RAC | 148th RAC |

**Fom 15 August 1944 to 18 January 1945**

| | Brigade Headquarters **151** | |
|---|---|---|
| **152** | **153** | **154** |
| 1st Northamptonshire Yeomanry | East Riding Yeomanry | 144th RAC |

*Title.* **Although a bit fuzzy, this shot of 144th RAC tanks taken on 8 July, at the start of Operation Charnwood, is interesting in showing three different Shermans: in the foreground, a middle-production Sherman I already fitted with the late cast transmission housing; in the middle an older Sherman I with the bolted transmission; and in the background a Sherman I Hybrid.** *(IWM B6633)*

impatient, barely calmed down by the disappointing fire tests with 75-mm guns on captured Panthers. The brigade joined 30th Corps on 26 June, and was informed that it was to operate regiment by regiment in support of various infantry divisions. The first commitment happened when C Squadron, 1st Northamptonshire Yeomanry supported 6th Green Howards (50th Inf.Div.) during a local attack and knocked out their first Panther.

The regiment then came under control of 49th Inf.Div., whilst 144th and 148th RAC were in counteroffensive defence on the 29th. The brigade was set on defensive positions in St-Léger in early July, on the Caen – Bayeux road. From 3 July onwards, 148th RAC crossed the

*Above.*
**On 8 July, a Sherman from 33rd Arm.Brig., the insignia of which can be seen on the left rear, is passing by a column of infantry from 185th Inf.Brig. (3rd Inf.Div.) It is a Firefly as indicated by the large stowage box on the hull rear, and the second hatch on the turret roof.** *(IWM B6639)*

River Orne and relieved 13th/18th Hussars at the side of 51st Inf.Div., north-east of Caen.

## The battle for Caen

Operation *Charnwood* to take Caen was launched on 7 July, and on the left flank, 33rd Arm.Brig. worked in support of 9th Inf.Brig. (3rd Inf.Div.) from the 8th onwards: 1st Northamptonshire Yeomanry with 2nd Royal Ulster Rifles, and 144th RAC with King's Own Scottish Borderers attacked in succession towards Lebisey wood, after a pounding by 460 RAF heavy bombers. The assault began at 8.00, Lebisey was cleared, and the tanks advanced towards Hill 64 despite bomb craters. Two 1st Northamptonshire Yeomanry Stuarts were destroyed by antitank guns while reconnoitering, whilst A and B Squadrons claimed one Panzer IV each. A Sherman and a Firefly were again lost before the resistance of 16. Luftwaffe Feld-Division was overcome. In the rear, 144th RAC met little opposition. On 9 July, patrols in the same area began at 5.30, 144th RAC seized the enemy-free village of Couvre-Chef. 1st Northamptonshire Yeomanry destroyed a Panzer IV, and in the evening, their B Squadron preceded by a bulldozer tried in vain to enter Caen, but ruins and craters were everywhere.

148th RAC took part on 10 July to Operation *Stack* with 51st Inf. Div. (B Squadron and 153rd Inf.Brig. on the right, A Squadron and 152nd Inf.Brig. in the middle, C Squadron and 154th Inf Brig. on the left): the objective was to seize and clear the Colombelles works, where the Germans had dug in the mine galleries and were using the chimneys as observation post. The defence supported by Tigers proved to be too

**Still on 8 July, near Lebisey, a Sherman belonging to 33rd Arm.Brig. according to the wartime caption is speeding past another stopped Sherman. The three antennas and the man wearing an infantry helmet behind the tank commander's head, suggest that it may be a tank used as an artillery observation post.** *(IWM B6642)*

strong. In a single day, ten Shermans were knocked out and infantry casualties were very heavy for mediocre results: only part of the objective had been reached. The regiment was then put in defence up to 16 July, in the Ranville and Ste-Honorine-la-Chardonnette area. It was then withdrawn towards Colleville and left at rest until 21 July, by which time it came under control of 32nd Guards Brig., waiting for the latter to be relieved by 154th Inf.Brig. in Cagny.

The 33rd Arm.Brig. joined 1st Corps on 13 July and prepared for a 59th Inf.Div. attack from Audrieu and Loucelles towards Noyers. The operation was launched on the 16th: on the right, 1st Northamptonshire Yeomanry moved up with 176th Inf.Brig., their A Squadron and 7th South Lancashire attacked Hauts des Forges that they captured together with 310 prisoners. Two Tigers and six other Panzers appeared, and a Panther was destroyed. 144th RAC was progressing on the left with 177th Inf.Brig. and met minefields: seven tanks were rapidly disabled. Flails from the Westminster Dragoons came up to clear the ground at 13.00, and the attack then resumed towards Noyers: an antitank gun and two Panzerschrecks were knocked-out, and a Panther was captured by the evening. A hail of mortar shells forced tanks and infantry to withdraw slightly. The battle continued on the next day, 1st Northamptonshire Yeomanry destroyed two antitank guns and a Panzer IV and captured 100 prisoners while helping the infantry. A few tanks lost their tracks on mines north-west of Noyers, and a Sherman totally burned up with its whole crew, unfortunately. For their part, 144th RAC destroyed a Panther and an antitank gun, and inflicted heavy losses on the German infantry.

Fighting lost intensity on 18 July, but A and C Squadrons, 1st Northamptonshire Yeomanry made more progress with 1/7th Warwickshire Rgt towards Brettevillette, whilst 144th RAC lost a tank in Noyers and seized the village thanks to selective support from artillery and from AVREs and Crocodiles. The infantry was nevertheless stopped about 16.00, the fighting going on around the railway station. 33rd Arm.Brig. was in reserve from 19 to 21 July, and then moved up westwards of Cristot on the 22nd. It came back under 1st Corps control on the morrow, and rested in Langrune-sur-Mer then Démouville (although 1st Northamptonshire Yeomanry took part in a short-range attack on 20 July towards Landelle with 59th Inf.Div.) 148th RAC were again assigned to the brigade on 26 July, but they remained with 49th Inf.Div. near Hérouvillette.

## Totalize, the breakout to Falaise

33rd Arm.Brig. moved up on 3 August towards Cormelles and joined 51st Inf.Div. under control of 2nd Canadian Corps in order to secure the left flank of Operation *Totalize*. The offensive was to go off by night, so the leading tanks were fitted with compasses and luminous directional devices. The brigade was to lead the attack with 154th Inf.Brig. (1st Northamptonshire Yeomanry and 1st Black Watch on the left, 148th RAC and 7th Black Watch in the rear, 144th RAC and 5th Argyll and Sutherland on the right). The idea was to move on Cramesnil, St-Aignan-du-Cramesnil and Garcelles-Secqueville. In the night of 7 to 8 August, wide columns alternating tanks, armoured troop transports (including the famous Canadian Kangaroo on

*Above.* **A column of Sherman Is from 144th RAC (see tactical sign 174 and 33rd Arm.Brig. insignia on the last tank's rear) is preparing to attack towards Caen. Note that the big red numbers outlined in white were not typical of 27th Arm.Brig., as many authors seem to believe, although they are also reproduced here in white or yellow on the turret bin.** *(IWM B6658)*

*Above.* **33rd Arm.Brig. was also in Saint-Contest on 9 July: the Shermans here belong to 144th RAC, as indicated by the tactical sign 174 barely visible on the left front of the leading tank. Oddly enough, this Sherman carries a spare wheel on the turret side. The village has already considerably suffered from shelling and fighting** *(RR)*

*Below.*

**An old Stuart III from 144th RAC (see tactical sign 174 barely visible on the left front) is heading towards Caen on 9 July, and is passing by a Jeep and an upturned German cart. Note on the left of the superstructure a white letter T, already visible on the Sherman of the preceding photograph: was it a particular identification?** *(IWM 6748)*

*Above.* **The report about 144th RAC continues: followed by a Humber Scout Car the rear load of which is covered with a tarpaulin displaying a large white star, Sherman Is bearing numbers 20 and 23 take a dirt track in the Norman countryside. On the right can be seen the gun barrel of a Panzer IV, and the village burning in the distance is Epron.** *(IWM 6750)*

Priest chassis) and special 79th Arm.Div. AFVs rushed forward behind a huge ground and air bombardment, through darkness, smoke and dust. A Squadron, 1st Northamptonshire Yeomanry in the spearhead ran into SPGs, destroyed three, but lost two Shermans and three Kangaroos prior to their reaching St-Aignan. 144th RAC quickly came to a standstill, having three leading tanks knocked-out by Panzerfausts, but the infantry seized Cramesnil about 7.00. 148th RAC's group headed towards Tilly-la-Campagne, later followed by 7th Argyll and Sutherland. A destroyed Sherman temporarily blocked the Garcelles road: the village was captured about 5.00, but fierce resistance from 89.ID prevented the infantry from seizing Tilly. Reinforcement from a 148th RAC Squadron, which got rid of a Panzer, was indispensable to occupy the village.

The late morning on 8 August was quiet: the objectives had been reached, but a violent German counterstroke was launched in the afternoon against the Canadians. 1st Northamptonshire Yeomanry quickly reacted: a single gunner, Trooper Ekins, in an A Squadron Firefly, succeeded in destroying three Tigers in 12 minutes! The regiment claimed five Tigers, four Panthers, six Panzer IVs and five SPGs for the loss of 20 tanks. 144th RAC claimed to have knocked-out two Tigers or Panthers. These tallies do not seem to be exaggerated, for the sSS-PzAbt.101 reported to have lost seven Tigers on the same day. At 18.00, 148th RAC and 153rd Inf.Brig. seized Secqueville with support from Crocodiles. The first stage of Totalize ended on 9 August with good results, even if the continuation was less successful. The brigade remained on its positions to support the infantry while Poles and Canadians continued the offensive, then it withdrew towards Bras (although 148th RAC helped 152nd Inf.Brig. to clear Poussy). 144th RAC alone were in action on 10 August, to mop up the woods south-east of St-Sylvain with 154th Inf.Brig. A Tiger and an antitank gun were destroyed during a counterattack in the afternoon.

Enemy mortars and artillery brought about casualties on the following day; 144th RAC were relieved by 148th RAC on 13 August, and sell led in Cramesnil to reorganize, while 1st Northamptonshire Yeomanry and 152nd Inf.Brig. were securing 2nd Canadian Corps flank. 144th RAC were called back on 14 August to set up a bridgehead on the River Dives with 2nd Derbyshire Yeomanry (51st Inf.Div.) A Squadron led the advance towards Le Hamel on the 5th, opposition petered out and the progression was swift. 148th RAC, the commander of which, Lieutenant Colonel Cracroft, had been killed by the enemy artillery on the day before, took part on 14 August in a successful attack of 154th Inf. Brig. towards Le Bû-sur-Rouvres. The regiment learnt on the 15 Au-

gust that it was to be disbanded, and soon began to hand over its tanks to East Riding Yeomanry which were replacing it. Part of the personnel joined one of the 33rd Arm.Brig.'s regiments, others were assigned to replacement units. The disbandment was definitive on 27 August.

## The long road to the Seine

East Riding Yeomanry were located near St-Pierre-sur-Dives, on 16 August, while C and HQ Squadron, 144th RAC were fording the River Dives despite a bogged-down Sherman. 1st Northamptonshire Yeomanry moved up with 154th Inf.Brig. towards Lisieux, A Squadron and 7th Black Watch leading. Antitank guns, snipers and four ambushed Tigers stopped their advance by the evening, but they resumed on the morrow, knocking out an antitank gun and an SPG, although they just progressed $7^{1/2}$ mile for the loss of 10 damaged or destroyed tanks. At 13.30 on 18 August with 2nd Seaforth Highlanders, B Squadron, East Riding Yeomanry started the attack to seize the Oudon river bridge, but the latter blew up upon their arrival. A Scissors bridge could not be deployed; the infantry however managed to ford the river and enabled a Bailey bridge to be erected, allowing some tanks to cross

72

# REGIMENTS ACCORDING TO THE ORDER OF PRECEDENCE

## 1st Battalion, Northamptonshire Yeomanry

- **Origins:** Regiment raised by the Earl Spencer in 1794 as "The Northamptonshire Yeomanry Cavalry", disbanded in 1828. "The Northamptonshire Imperial Yeomanry" was re-created in 1902, and became "The Northamptonshire Yeomanry TF (Dragoons)" in 1908. Two regiments formed in 1914 were distributed in Squadrons with 4th, 8th and 61st Inf.Div. in France. 1st regiment was in Italy in 1917, 2nd regiment was disbanded in 1918. Reconstituted in 1920, became "25th (Northamptonshire Yeomanry) Armoured Car Company, Royal Tank Corps TA" in 1922.

- **1939-44:** Converted into Armoured Regiment in 1939, under the name "1st Northamptonshire Yeomanry" (2nd Northamptonshire Yeomanry was formed as duplicate). In England with 20th Arm.Brig. from September 1939, then assigned to 42nd Arm.Div. from April to October 1943. Incorporated then into 33rd Arm.Brig., with which it took part in the whole North-West Europe campaign.

## 144th Regiment, RAC

- **Origins:** In common with the whole Royal Armoured Corps, see 31st Tk.Brig. Armoured regiment formed in 1941 by conversion of "8th TA Battalion, The East Lancashire Regiment".

- **1939-44:** Joined 33rd Arm.Brig. in England in November 1941, and took part in the Normandy campaign with this unit.

## 148th Regiment, RAC

- **Origins:** In common with the whole Royal Armoured Corps, see 31st Tk.Brig. Regiment formed in 1941 by converting infantry regiment "9th TA Battalion, The Loyal Regiment".

- **1939-44:** Incorporated into 33rd Arm.Brig. in November 1941, but joined 27th Arm.Brig. from October 1943 to January 1944. Returned in March 1944 to 33rd Arm.Brig. for the Normandy landings.

---

and set up a small bridgehead. For several days, friendly fire from the Allied aircraft increased because of the fast advance: Mustangs, Spitfires and Lightnings were harassing spearhead units, in spite of identification signals and smoke, and were causing absurd human losses.

Advance resumed on 19 August to reach Lisieux: against irregular defence, 144th RAC and East Riding Yeomanry crossed the River Vie. The latter's A Squadron started to attack with 5th Seaforth Highlanders at 6.15 on the 20th, and one Sherman was destroyed by a Panzerschreck. C Squadron took over at 9.00 with 5th Queen's Own Cameron, lost a Firefly but suppressed any opposition with help from the artillery. The village of La Corne was taken in the evening by 5th Seaforth Highlanders, A Squadron losing a tank. A counterstroke was driven off on the next day, and St-Pierre-des-Ifs was seized. For two days, 144th RAC supported 153rd Inf.Brig. towards La Bosquetterie, and 1st Northamptonshire Yeomanry did the same with 154th Inf. Brig. towards Lisieux, which was reached by the evening of the 22nd, enemy resistance having almost vanished. But the Germans came back on the following day, and C Squadron, 144th RAC lost two tanks while supporting 5/7th Gordon Highlanders in the town. The regiment was relieved at 13.00 to be lent to 31st Tk.Brig. in support of 49th Inf.Div.

1st Northamptonshire Yeomanry went on clearing Lisieux with 154th Inf.Brig., and East Riding Yeomanry rested until 27 August.

On 24 August, 1st Northamptonshire Yeomanry were holding the flank of the Falaise pocket while 144th RAC were helping 147th Inf. Brig. in crossing the River Touques south of Cormeilles. A B Squadron tank blew up on a mine, two others forded at La Valette. A bridge was built during the night of the 25th, allowing A Squadron, 144th RAC and 11th Royal Scots Fusiliers to cross over. The River Risle was in sight on the next day, west of Ruelles, and the regiment crossed it at Appeville on the 27th. On the same day, C Squadron, 144th RAC reached Quillebœuf on the Seine, among debris and wreckages left by the fleeing enemy. The regiment remained in the Bourneville area, while East Riding Yeomanry and 1st Northamptonshire Yeomanry concentrated in St-Georges-du-Vièvre, crossed the River Risle and reached Flancourt and Appetot. Up to 31 August, they helped to mop up the river outskirts in Yville-sur-Seine, Ambourville and Bourg-Achard, while 144th RAC gave chase to German stragglers in the forest of Brotonne, moving back under brigade control on 30 August. Waiting to cross the River Seine, the members of 33rd Arm.Brig. could enjoy a warm welcome from the Norman civilians, free at last.

*Left.* **In the vicinity of Lebisey on 9 July, a Sherman Firefly from 33rd Arm.Brig., whose diabolo can be clearly seen on the transmission housing (one can make out the 144th RAC tactical sign 174 on the left), is raising a dust cloud while rushing towards Caen.** *(IWM 6751)*

**Operation *Totalize* was, after *Charnwood*, the other important commitment of 33rd Arm.Brig.: on 7 August, the eve of the attack, an officer is distributing rations. The turret of the Sherman I is camouflaged with hessian tape. Two tank crew helmets are hanging from the commander's hatch: in this brigade, crews seem to have widely used this kind of protection (see the previous photograph).** *(IWM B8796)*

# 34th TANK BRIGADE

**H**EADQUARTERS OF 34TH ARMY TANK BRIGADE were constituted on 1 December 1941, by converting those of 226th Inf.Brig. They were rapidly joined by three armoured regiments: North Irish Horse, 147th RAC, and 153rd RAC.
The unit became 34th Tank Brigade in June 1942, under the command of Brigadier W.S. Clarke, and was composed of 147th, 151st and 153rd RAC from August onwards; its definitive structure was established in January 1944: 107th, 147th and 153rd RAC (actually, 151st RAC was absorbed by 107th RAC).

As Tank Brigade, it was intended for infantry support and was quickly issued with Churchill tanks instead of the Valentines with which it had started to train. According to the organization charts of an infantry division at that time, which included an armoured brigade, the unit was assigned to 1st Inf.Div. from June to August 1942, then to 43rd Inf.Div. from October 1942 to September 1943, and finally became independent afterwards. The 34th Tk.Brig. was not intended for taking part in the first assault wave for the invasion of France, but for holding the beachhead: accordingly, it focused its training on cooperation with infantry, maybe more in defence than in attack. It was one of the first units to be equipped with the new and better armoured Churchill Mk VIIs and VIIIs, armed with a 75-mm gun or a 95-mm howitzer, although it retained older Mk IIIs. Waterproofing the tanks and vehicles began as early as the end of May 1944; however the brigade remained a full month on its assembling area, for the units only started to embark on 2 July.

## First combats in Normandy

After landing before Bernières-sur-Mer, in Juno beach sector, the regiments gathered together around Lantheuil, between Bayeux and Caen. The officers visited neighbouring units which had been fighting in Normandy for a month, in order to glean information and advice, then the brigade was put on the alert on 7 July under the command of 1st Corps, but it was not committed in the battle for Caen. Back in Lantheuil, it prepared for Operation *Greenline* scheduled for 15 July: as indicated precisely in the war diary, it was an attack to draw the enemy's attention in order to ease the breakout east of Caen (Operation *Goodwood*). The brigade was operating in support of 15th Inf.Div. in its progression towards Esquay and Evrecy, with help from Crocodiles and AVREs from 79th Arm.Div.

H Hour was at 21.45 on 15 July: 107th RAC and 2nd Glasgow Highlanders advanced from the east of Baron under an artillery barrage,

*Title.* **For its first battle in Normandy, 34th Tk.Brig. assembled from 17 July onwards for Operation Greenline, acting as a cover for Goodwood. A 147th RAC column of Churchills (see tactical sign 157) is travelling towards the start line. The first tank is a Mark VII as confirmed by the rounded driver hatch and the strengthened turret. Note the number 7 in a square (B Squadron) on the muzzle cover, and the white star painted on top of the mudguard.** *(IWM B7636)*

towards Le Bon Repos and Esquay. Even before the assault began, German mortars pounded the attackers and the brigade sustained its first losses in men and equipment (four tanks). The objective was seized at 22.30, but dust and nightfall precluded the tanks from shooting at clearly identified targets, so the infantry were forced to dig in in Esquay. 147th RAC were expected to be committed during the night, but the minefields had not been cleared, the first tank blew up, and the infantry had to continue the attack on their own.

On 16 July, 153rd RAC moved up at 5.30 with 8th Royal Scots and both advanced towards Gavrus and Bougy against German infantry armed with machine-guns and two antitank guns. Bougy was captured at 12.30, and then a dozen Focke-Wulf 190s raided the attackers and were followed by an armour-supported counterstroke by infantry. Two Tigers and three Panthers were knocked out, but 153rd RAC lost ten Churchills and many others damaged, mainly within A Squadron, and also sustained heavy casualties: 86 killed or wounded!

147th RAC had to move up with 158th Inf.Brig. (53rd Inf.Div.), which was under control of 15th Inf.Div., to resume the attack on Evrecy on 17 July. 153rd RAC were in support with only two composite Squadrons considering their heavy losses.

Although the operation only opened at 21.00, the units were barely ready to go, the tanks did not succeed in finding their associated infantry, and the advance was carried on in disorder. In a matter of hours, A Squadron, 147th RAC lost eight tanks to Panthers in ambush on Hill 112 and managed to reach Evrecy, but the infantry found it

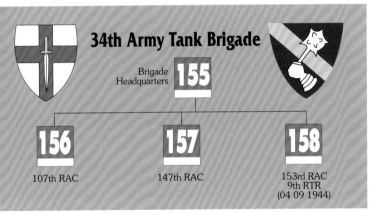

difficult to progress as they were slowed down by machine-guns and explosive shelling. Artillery support was insufficient to enable the now-weakened infantry to follow the armour, and the latter had to fall back at night, having lost a total of 11 tanks.

The only success of the attack was the capture of a lot of prisoners. On the following day, A Squadron 107th RAC were manoeuvring north of Hill 112 when they were shot at by a Tiger: three Churchills were destroyed before the Tiger was silenced. Nevertheless, the latter does not seem to have been destroyed, for SS-sPzAbt.102 did no register any loss on 18 July.

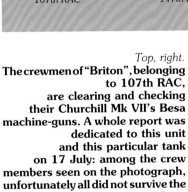

*Top, right.*
**The crewmen of "Briton", belonging to 107th RAC, are clearing and checking their Churchill Mk VII's Besa machine-guns. A whole report was dedicated to this unit and this particular tank on 17 July: among the crew members seen on the photograph, unfortunately all did not survive the Normandy campaign, for "Briton" was brewed-up on 14 August by an 88, but was nevertheless repaired.**
(IWM B7625)

*Right.*
**34th brigade's Churchills, bearing the 2nd Army insignia on the front, are raising dust clouds as they rush to the frontline on 17 July. These crews seem to be more seasoned: they do not wear helmets anymore as those seen on the first photograph, and they have fastened spare track links to the front of their tanks.**
(IWM B7641)

## In defence north-west of Caen

From 19 July onwards, 107th and 147th RAC occupied defensive positions against possible counterstrokes (such as the one that happened on 21 July, during which 147th RAC lost a tank while supporting 5th Welch Rgt). 153rd RAC were withdrawn from the frontline on the 20th in order to receive the necessary reinforcements to compensate for their heavy losses (14 tanks since 15 July); they were followed by 147th RAC on 22 July. Meanwhile, 107th RAC were supporting 160th Inf.Brig. of 53rd Inf.Div. during raids on the German positions at Le Bon Repos and Esquay. The regiment came under control of 59th Inf.Div. on 24 July, and 147th RAC came back on their defensive position. The brigade spent the end of July on a static front, sometimes supporting infantry with direct or indirect fire. The Squadrons were alternately sent to the rear to rest and reorganize. More raids were undertaken in August: on the 2nd, B and C Squadron, 107th RAC moved up with 4th Welch Fusiliers and 2nd Mon-mouthshire towards Esquay and Le Bon Repos, and 153rd RAC operated with 158th Inf.Brig. 107th RAC were then attached to 31st Tk.Brig. on the 4th, under control of 59th Inf.Div.; their B and C Squadrons supported 176th Inf.Brig. for the advance to the River Orne which was reached without major difficulty. The remnants of the brigade were to join up later, for the progression towards Thury-Harcourt. The enemy was progressively withdrawing, and 153rd RAC were set back south of Verson, while C Squadron, 147th RAC lost a Churchill in helping 1st Oxfordshire and Buckinghamshire Rgt (Ox and Bucks) to clear the woods east of Gavrus.

**A lovely but probably posed photograph: the helmeted tank commander is conspicuously watching the sky, searching for hypothetical Luftwaffe aircraft, which were very scarce in daytime. The Churchill has probably blown up on a mine, half-a-wheel can be seen besides the track hanging from the sprocket wheel. It is equipped with an odd additional armour plate around the gun and Besa. A Churchill ARV Mk I is visible in the background.** *(DR)*

## Towards the Orne with 59th Inf.Div.

On 5 August began the movement westwards of the River Orne to reach the positions of 59th Inf.Div. (12th Corps), 107th RAC coming back under brigade command. Their A and C Squadrons prepared to cross the River Orne on 6 August, while 147th RAC were in reserve and 153rd RAC were supporting 177th Inf.Brig. towards Maizet. This attack was continued on the next day towards La Roque which was quickly seized. At 9.10, 107th RAC crossed the River Orne by

**On 14 August, the fighting to cross the River Orne was over, but the tanks needed repairs: a Churchill crew is busy working on its tank tracks, with help from REME members whose Churchill ARV Mk I is visible in the background.
One can see the huge spanners used to adjust the track tension by turning nuts located on each side of the sprocket wheel.**
*(IWM B9162)*

sheer force whilst supporting 176th Inf.Brig. (A Squadron followed by C Squadron with 6th North Staffordshire and 7th Royal Norfolk respectively). A fierce German counterstroke at 19.00 was supported with Tigers and Panthers, and the regiment lost four tanks at least but without moving back. 147th RAC had replaced 107th RAC in defence pending the building of another bridge to cross the River Orne, and they also helped to drive back this counterattack but were not left unscathed: the brigade lost 28 damaged or destroyed tanks on that very day. B Squadron, 107th RAC attempted to resume the advance on 8 August, but they were stopped by mines, and the regiment was relieved by 147th RAC and then put in reserve. 153rd RAC found a new crossing site on the River Orne on the following day, their B and C Squadrons crossed at noon with 197th Inf.Brig. to set up a bridgehead. By the evening, two Troops remained isolated in the van, but the position held. 147th RAC took part in clearing the surrounding woods with 1/7th Royal Warwickshire, then to the seizing of Grimbosq.

# REGIMENTS ACCORDING TO THE ORDER OF PRECEDENCE

### 107th Regiment Royal Armoured Corps

- **Origins:** In common with the whole Royal Armoured Corps, see 31st Tk.Brig. Formed in 1941 through conversion of the infantry regiment "5th TA Battalion, The King's Own Royal Regiment (Lancaster)", deriving itself from "4th Regiment of Foot" raised in 1680 by the Earl of Plymouth.

- **1939-44:** Incorporated into 11th Arm.Brig. from its formation in November 1941 onwards. Absorbed 151st RAC in 1943, then joined 34th

Tk.Brig. in January 1944. Took part with this unit in the whole North-West Europe campaign.

### 147th Regiment Royal Armoured Corps

- **Origins:** In common with the whole Royal Armoured Corps, see 31st Tk.Brig. Formed in 1941 by converting the infantry regiment "10th TA Battalion The Hampshire Regiment", deriving itself from "Meredith's Regiment" raised in 1702, which had become "37th Regiment of Foot".

- **1939-44:** Incorporated into 34th Tk.Brig. in England from its formation in December 1941 onwards, landed with this unit in

Normandy.

### 153rd Regiment Royal Armoured Corps

- In common with the whole Royal Armoured Corps, see 31st Tk.Brig. Armoured regiment formed in 1941 by converting "8th TA Battalion The Essex Regiment", deriving itself from "44th Regiment of Foot" raised in 1740.

- **1939-44:** Incorporated into 34th Tk.Brig. from its formation in December 1941 onwards, took part with this unit in the Normandy campaign until disbandment.

---

On 10 August, 147th RAC completed their crossing of the River Orne with 56th (independent) Inf.Brig. and attacked towards the village of La Forge à Cambo, which was taken at 10.40: 140 prisoners were captured, and German-free Croisilles was reached at 17.15. On the following day, the regiment tried to cross several brooks, including one in Le Moncel: a Churchill was lost but the stream was forded downstream by B Squadron followed by C Squadron, despite a few bogged-down tanks. But Le Moncel was heavily defended, and an attack scheduled for the evening with 2nd Essex was cancelled because of the German artillery pounding. In the meantime, 153rd RAC and 158th Inf.Brig. had reached Fresney-Le-Vieux, but since the infantry could not advance farther, the tanks had to withdraw. The village was seized on 12 August only, the advance then resumed towards Bois-Halbout which was captured about 18.15: a Tiger was knocked-out against a single Churchill lost. The day ended with the seizing of Thury-Harcourt by 56th Inf.Brig. supported by 147th RAC, the latter being relieved by 107th RAC on the morrow to help 1st East Lancashire (53rd Inf.Div.) in La Moissonière. On this 13 August, while 147th RAC were at rest, 153rd RAC were supporting 158th and 71st Inf.Brig.: enemy counterstrokes were routed by the intervention of the artillery alone.

## The end of the fighting in Normandy

During the following days, the three regiments continued to support the progression of infantry eastwards via Donnay, Bonnoeil, Martainville, Treprel, Leffard. The advance became more fluid and German action was often limited to rearguard fighting. The St-Marc-d'Ouilly – Falaise line was reached on 16 August, and 147th RAC were joined by 3/4th CLY (4th Arm.Brig.), but tanks were stopped by 88s before St-Martin-de-Mieux. On the next day, B Squadron, 147th RAC and 1st Ox and Bucks started at 7.30 to cut the Argentan – Falaise road: two SPGs

were destroyed, and the Squadron discovered enemy columns flowing back, but order was given not to shoot. Alerted by suspect movements the artillery pounded St-André wood from which emerged other Panzers including a Tiger and five Panthers: the Churchills enjoyed a successful shooting party, disabling two SPGs and three Panthers without any loss for themselves. A and C Squadrons had remained in the rear, but the former managed to reach a hilltop and to destroy several vehicles among the long enemy columns crawling eastwards. On that very same 17 August, the news arrived that 153rd RAC were to be disbanded: the losses suffered since 6 June had the same consequences in several armoured brigades and it proved impossible to make Montgomery change his mind.

7th RTR came under brigade command on 18 August, whilst 107th RAC were supporting 5th South Staffordshire towards Le Mesnil-Hermel. The Troops operated individually and the losses were limited to some tanks losing their tracks on mines. 147th RAC took part in the successful attacks against Nécy and Pierrefitte. On 19 August, C Squadron, 153rd RAC joined 107th RAC (which had been reduced to two composite Squadrons since the 13th), and on the following days the regiment went on handing over tanks and vehicles to 147th RAC and 9th RTR. There was no tank left on the 21st, and remaining personnel were dispatched between 141st RAC and reinforcement units. The 153rd RAC was officially disbanded on 28 August. 107th RAC came back under command of 34th Tk.Brig. on 20 August, they were put at rest to reorganize until the end of the month. After a few days of respite during which the Falaise pocket was closed, 147th RAC, the only regiment in action within the brigade, had to move up towards Trun on 24 August, but they were stopped by traffic jams. In support of 15th Inf.Div., the regiment reached the River Seine without having to fight. It then had to set up a bridgehead in Les Andelys on 29 August, to allow the crossing of 53rd Inf.Div., but the enemy had withdrawn: the operation was cancelled and 147th RAC themselves crossed the river at 7.45, putting an end to the Normandy campaign of 34th Tk.Brig.

Since the Germans quickly retreated in spite of brutal interruptions, armoured forces progressed more easily to the River Seine from 20 August onwards. Churchills Mk VIIs of 34th Tk.Brig. are speeding as fast as they can on a little Norman road. The first tank is a Mark VII, as indicated by its turret and rounded lateral hatches. Even so late into the campaign, crews of the brigade were still wearing helmets although they were impractical in a tank. *(Tank Museum 4885/B6)*

Cromwell Mk IV. « C » Squadron,
2nd Welsh Guards,
Guards Armoured Division.

**Cromwell Mk IV**

Cromwell Mk IV. Headquarters,
11th Armoured Division.

Cromwell Mk IV. Regimental HQ Squadron, 1st
RTR, 7th Armoured Division

© Nicolas Gohin, 2005

A 2nd Welsh Guards Cromwell Mk IV training in England in May 1944. The clearly visible markings include: the tactical insignia 45 on green and blue background of an Armoured Recce Rgt, the bridge classification disc, the white square of the B (or N°2) Squadron with the letter A of the 1st Troop, and the Guards Arm. Div. insignia.
*(Tank Museum 1800/E1)*

# CROMWELL, CENTAUR & CHALLENGER

**I**N NOVEMBER 1940, the Department of Tank Design issued the specifications for a new Cruiser tank. Two firms submitted a project in January 1941: Nuffield proposed a renewed version of the Crusader, Vauxhall suggesting a light Churchill.

The latter was soon abandoned in favour of the Nuffield A24 tank, six prototypes of which were ordered. The armament was to be the new 6 pounder gun with a coaxial Besa, and an odd triple mounting including a 2 pounder gun, a 3 inch howitzer and a Besa was even considered. A Bren or a Besa were planned for antiaircraft defence. The maximum front armour was estimated to be 65mm for the hull and 75mm for the turret, for an expected weight of 24 tons (5 more than the Crusader, but with an armour increase of 14 to 24mm). Unfortunately, the new tank retained the power drive and Liberty engine of the Crusader, prone to numerous breakdowns.

At that time, Rolls Royce and Leyland were working on a V12 tank engine derived from the Spitfire's and Hurricane's Rolls Royce Merlin, and named Meteor. This engine, 30% more powerful than the Liberty, was chosen for the new Cruiser in April 1941. The A24 Cruiser Mk VII project was given priority in the 1942 program, but the Meteor was likely not to be ready in time, so the Liberty equipped the first models. Another firm, the Birmingham Carriage and Wagon Co. (BCW), was associated with the project since it was designing a heavy Cruiser. The first tests with the Meteor on a Crusader chassis revealed the engine's potential, as the vehicle reached a speed of 47 miles per hour, but the choice of the transmission was difficult between the old epicyclical Wilson, the Churchill's Merrit-Brown, and the new five-speed drive designed by Rolls Royce and Leyland.

The working methods of BCW and Nuffield proving to be incompatible, two distinct projects existed in September 1941, the Nuffield A24, 500 examples already ordered, and the BCW A27

Cruiser Mk VIII, which was developed in parallel with the Meteor engine and the Merrit-Brown drive. The A24 was very close to the Crusader, using the same engine, transmission and running gear. In return, the A27 benefited from a strengthened suspension, even though both tank hulls were similar, and Rolls Royce also improved the cooling, air filter and fuel tanks. Both projects were baptized Cromwell in January 1942, and then the A27 was ready and successfully tested, travelling through 2,100 miles without major breakdown. The A24 was ready in March only, and the tests revealed many faults: ball bearings, cooling, ventilation, etc. Leyland had abandoned Rolls Royce in the Meteor development, which was consequently also delayed because of the strong demand for aircraft engines: Meadows and Rover joined Rolls Royce, but the first A27s had to be equipped with Liberty engines. The denominations were then revised: the A24 became the Cavalier, only intended for training; the A27L was a Liberty-equipped Centaur; the A27M was the future Meteor-equipped Cromwell.

The 6 pounder gun, which was to be the main armament, was already obsolete in early 1943. The 17 pounder gun was almost ready, and would have been the ideal choice, but it was too big to fit in the A27 turret ring. In December 1942, the choice turned to a multipurpose 75-mm gun inspired from the American model and using the same ammunition. Derived from the 6 pounder gun, it retained some elements such as the mounting, and could take the latter's place in any tank, with no other modification than the change of ammo stowage. As often, production was not rapid enough and the first tanks were fitted out with a 6 pounder gun. A close support weapon was always required, and a 95-mm howitzer was chosen in February 1943 to equip 12% of the Centaurs and 10% of the Cromwells. Designed in 1942 for the Mk V version of the Churchill, the weapon was composed of a shortened 3.7 inch tube and the breech of a 25 pounder gun: it could use the very efficient ammunition of the latter, but with a lighter charge in a smaller case, easier to handle in a tank turret. The auxiliary armament remained unchanged (two Besas, hull and coaxial) and the tank carried 51 95-mm rounds.

*Above.* **This wartime photo-mounting shows an early production 6 pounder Cromwell with his ancestor, a Crusader Mk III. Although as compact, the Cromwell had better performances: it was faster, better armoured, soon better armed with a 75-mm gun, and above all mechanically more reliable. On the other hand, its silhouette was even less modern...** *(Tank Museum 1800/B3)*

*Right.* **No, the Cromwell was not a flying tank! Photographed during a demonstration, this late production Mk IV (note the side hatch for the driver and the turret bin) proved the Cromwell automotive capacities... as well as its sturdiness, for the landing was certainly rough for the driver!** *(Tank Museum 1800/E4)*

*(Tank Museum 1800/E4)*

*Left.* **The Cromwell's look was resolutely out-of-date, with the big bolts on its angular turret and the almost total lack of sloped armour. But its main advantage was hidden: its Meteor engine conferred it handling ability, speed and reliability.**
*(Tank Museum 1800/A3)*

*Below.* **The 95-mm howitzer was the only difference between the Close Support version and the Cromwell armed with the 6 pounder or the 75-mm gun, even the coaxial Besa was retained. The censor has erased the unit insignia, only the white square of a B Squadron in an Armoured Recce Rgt remains.**
*(Tank Museum 1802/A3)*

*Right.* **This CS Cromwell is already fitted with the Normandy Cowl, a deflector located on top of the exhaust on the engine deck rear: experience of the first combats showed that without this device, the exhaust gas were sucked up in the ventilation and penetrated into the turret.**
*(Tank Museum 1800/C6)*

*Below.* « Hunter » is a Centaur Mk IV from 2nd Independent Battery, 1st Royal Marines Support Rgt, as indicated by the tactical sign 2 on multicoloured background. The white graduated markings for fire control are evident, as are the lack of hull machine-gun and the special sight on the turret.
*(Tank Museum 1802/B6)*

Priority was given in January 1943 to the Cromwell, more promising than the Centaur. Actually, production included eight Marks and four hull types, and some Cromwells were re-motorized Centaurs. It is hard to tell one Cromwell model from another since some are externally identical. The Mk I was the initial model armed with a 6 pounder gun, and the Mk II was a Mk I without machine-gun and with wider tracks. The Mk III was a 6 pounder Centaur with a Meteor engine, while the Mk IV was either a new Cromwell, or a re-motorized Centaur, armed with a 75-mm gun. The Mk V was a Cromwell Mk I brought up to the Mk IV standard and 75-mm-equipped, the Mk VI being either a re-motorized Centaur or a new Cromwell, armed with the 95-mm howitzer. Other models were introduced during or after the Normandy campaign: the hull types A to F differed in the machine-gunner's hatch, armour thickness, modified air intakes, and so on. The most

frequent models in Normandy were the type B (one- or two-door machine-gunner hatch), type C (thinner armour on the engine deck, modified air intakes) and type D (alteration of the engine deck armour plates).

The Cromwell Mk IV, which was built in greater numbers, weighed 28 tons and was equipped with a 600hp Meteor engine allowing for a maximum speed of 40 miles per hour on road, for a 175 miles average range. The tank carried 64 75-mm rounds (23 in the turret, 41 in the hull) and 4950 Besa rounds. The 76 mm-thick armour was just about acceptable for this period of the war. Its speed and manoeuvrability were the real advantages, allowing a Cromwell crew to escape from the Panzers. The tank was very reliable, but required more maintenance than the Sherman. Baling-out was difficult for the machine-gunner and above all for the driver, and this fault was only partly solved by fitting a two-door- then sliding-hatch for the latter. The recessed gun mounting in the turret, already criticized in the Churchill Mk IV, V and VI, was never modified during production: it cast a shadow indicating the gun's location to the enemy, and was furthermore a shot trap.

Considering the high availability in Shermans, the Cromwell was chosen only to equip the reconnaissance regiments of the three "standard" armoured divisions committed in Normandy, at the rate of 40 gun tanks (75-mm) and 6 Close-Support (95-mm) Cromwells per unit. Moreover, the whole armoured brigade of 7th Arm.Div. was issued with Cromwells, at the rate of 55 tanks (75-mm) and 6 CS (95-mm) in each of the three regiments, and 7 Cromwells in the brigade HQ. In addition, some Cromwells were converted to Artillery Observation Posts or command tanks.

## Centaur Mk IV

The only Centaur version to see combat was issued to a Royal Marines special unit: the RM Armoured Support Group was formed in early 1944 for Commando support on D-Day. It was composed of 1st and 2nd RM Support Rgt each including two four-Troop batteries. A Troop was equipped with a Sherman V and four Centaur Mk IVs armed with a 95-mm howitzer: 80 such tanks had been converted, and were devoid of engine and driver to carry more ammunition, for they were to be put into LCTs in order to shoot from the sea. This strange arrangement was modified by Montgomery following a successful training he attended: thinking it was a pity to bring tanks which were unable to move so close to the beach, he obtained that the Centaurs be reequipped with engines, and the Royal Marines quickly trained the drivers requi-

*Above.*
**This early production Challenger (note the lack of turret ring armour) looks poor and puny besides a Tiger I captured by the 8th Army in Tunisia. Neither the silhouette nor the turret is impressive, and the sensation is even worse if you consider the armour thicknesses painted on both tanks...** *(Tank Museum 1794/C4)*

*Below.*
**The added wheel on the lengthened Cromwell chassis did not succeed in compensating for the incongruous aspect of the Challenger's box-like turret. The latter however housed the excellent 17 pounder gun, which outdid the best German weapons.** *(Tank Museum 3581/D6)*

red. The tank turrets were adorned with white graduated markings which allowed an artillery observer to aim their fire from a distance by radio. A periscope and a special sight were also added for the gunner.

Only 48 Centaurs landed on 6 June 1944, often late compared with the timetable, and they saw little use since the Crabs and AVREs had already provided their support to the infantry. They tackled with an antitank wall in Langrune-sur-Mer unsuccessfully, since their 95-mm firepower was not sufficient. They were more useful to the French Commandos when supporting the assault on the Ouistreham Riva-Bella casino. The orders were to make no use of the Centaurs farther than one mile inland... Nevertheless, they exceeded this limited action range by supporting the Commandos until 24 June, when the RM Armoured Support Group was withdrawn from the front. The Centaurs seem then to have been handed over to the French Army (thus explaining why one of these vehicles is preserved in the Saumur Armour Museum).

## Challenger

A tank armed with the new 17 pounder gun was logically asked for from BCW in 1942, since this firm was already involved in the development of the basic Cruiser, the Cromwell. The mounting and turret were designed by Stothert & Pitt, and BCW modified a Cromwell to be fitted out with a larger turret ring (178cm). The hull was widened, and the chassis lengthened to accommodate a sixth wheel and better distribute the added weight. A certain W.A. Robotham from Rolls Royce probably took part in the project, since he asserted that he did in his memories by relentlessly defending the A30 Challenger, without any good reason to do so... Actually, although the Challenger was designed in order to use as many Cromwell components as possible and ease production, its development was long (more than two years, a rarity in wartime) for disappointing results compared with the modern German tanks.

At the time the Challenger project was initiated, the Tiger was almost unknown to the Anglo-Americans, and it is obvious that this dreadful opponent was not taken into consideration then. The A30 armour was to be the same as on the Cromwell, but the suspension was not strengthened, and the suspension or the engine could not take the added weight. The armour had consequently to be cut down, and mainly on the turret since the chassis could not

be altered: the front was then 63 mm thick instead of 75, and the sides 40 mm instead of 65, even though the turret represented a target twice the size of the Cromwell's. In fact, without experience in the use of the 17 pounder gun in a turret, it was deemed that two loaders were necessary to handle the heavy shells. The turret (also accommodating the tank commander and the gunner) was therefore voluminous although badly arranged. The driver was alone at the front, the machine-gunner's seat being replaced by an armoured ammo stowage box.

Three A30 prototypes were ready in August 1942 for slow and difficult tests. The project was even put into question in January 1943: it was both insufficiently armoured for a tank, and ill-designed for a Tank Destroyer. The controversy delayed the testing, and an order for 200 examples was issued in November 1943 only. The turret ring was unprotected, and a special device enabled for the turret to be lifted up a few millimetres in order to clear it in case of jamming. But the trials showed that this area was really too vulnerable, and 25 mm-thick semi-circular armour was added on the front. Other armour plating with the same thickness was added on the turret sides and on the front vertical surfaces, to match the progress of the enemy's armament. This modification only entered production in early 1944, and the fact that no Deep Wading Equipment had been made for this tank explains why the Challenger only appeared on the Normandy front in August. With 172 examples produced from March 1943 to February 1944, the Challenger equipped the armoured reconnaissance regiments in the Armoured Divisions, but at in unknown numbers: depending on the units, it was counted with the 75-mm Cromwells or the 95 mm CS tanks. Few reports mention its use, but it is known that it was too long (8,14m, nearly as long as a Tiger) for its width, involving track and steering problems. With a weight of 33 tons despite over-thin armour, the A30 running gear (drive sprockets and tracks) was also a weak point. Still, it was fast (30 miles per hour at best) and armed with the formidable 17 pounder, but the Sherman Firefly with the same gun was much more effective.

# SHERMAN MEDIUM TANK

**T**HE WHOLE SHERMAN HISTORY would far exceed the scope of this book, but it is useful to remember that studies to find a successor to the M3 Medium Tank started as early as February 1941, and that is was planned to use as many elements of the latter as possible to speed up production.

The configuration was however altered, by deleting the 37-mm gun and mounting the 75-mm gun with a coaxial .30 machine-gun in a large turret. The M3 running gear, chassis and Wright Continental R975 EC2 engine were retained. The cast-hull T6, the armour thickness of which did not exceeded 76,2mm, was designed for a five-man crew.

The prototype was ready in September 1941 while a welded-hull model was under development, and it still included side doors and the M3's .30 cupola mount, which were abandoned when the tank was standardized as M4 (welded hull) and M4A1 (cast hull). Although the machine-gun cupola was deleted, the Sherman, as it was nicknamed by the British, was still very tall at 2,74m. A ball-mounted .30 hull machine-gun was soon substituted for the two original fixed machine-guns.

The first model to enter production at Locomotive Works in February 1942 was the M4A1. The prototype was quickly modified by strengthening the air filters and exhaust rear protection, by adding a hatch and rotating periscope for the machine-gunner (only the driver was equipped so before), and by fitting three hull and turret ventilation fans to extract powder fumes. Two other rotating periscopes were available for the tank commander and loader. The turret pistol ports were soon deleted, except the little left hatch which was also used to get rid of the spent cases. The M34 combination gun mount, protecting the 75-mm gun base with a narrow mantlet, was also adopted. An M4 periscope improved the gun sighting, and a summary external vane sight was fitted in front of the commander's cupola. In this form armed with a 75-mm gun, the M4A1 production (Sherman II for the British) went on up to December 1943, for a total of 6281 examples, and gradually introduced the other variants improvements.

The M4 (Sherman I) production was initiated in July 1942 by Pressed Steel Car Company. The main differences with the M4A1 concerned the cast hull: for instance, the M4 carried ninety-seven 75-mm rounds instead of 90, but still 4750 machine-gun rounds. Performances were identical: the Continental R975 C1 engine was more powerful and less fuel-consuming than the EC2 and afforded the 33.4-ton Sherman a speed of 24 miles per hour, but the range was limited to 100 miles. A new heavy duty bogie with larger volute springs was introduced in the summer of 1942: the return roller was now shifted backwards and a metal skid supported the track.

The bogie type was to evolve on all other Sherman tanks with vertical volute spring suspension, its shape becoming more and more complicated. As on the M4A1, the first tanks were equipped with direct vision slots at the front, which weakened the glacis already made up of several welded armour plates. They were later replaced with two fixed episcopes for the driver and machine-gunner. Several hydraulic or electrical rotation systems were fitted to the M4 turret, since the most efficient one (Oilgear) was not available in sufficient number to replace the other types (Westinghouse, Logansport). To solve the problem of alignment on the M4 sighting periscope, a more precise direct-vision M55 then M70F telescope was adopted.

*Right.* **The rear of the same tank reveals the additional antenna socket on the right of the turret bustle, and the full mudguard set so often discarded in action. Additional side armour plates were arranged to protect the inner ammunition racks, but their usefulness has always been questioned for the Germans were said to use them as targets!**
(Tank Museum 2711/E5)

*Bottom.* **A Sherman II with Deep Wading Equipment takes part in trials before D-Day: the white Roman numerals indicate the various water depths to be reached so that the waterproofing was validated. On the Sherman II, a single wading trunk was enough for the exhaust and air ducting, but two were required on the Sherman III, for instance.**
(Tank Museum 3008/C4)

The M34 combination mount was extended to protect it, and it soon included the coaxial machine-gun on the M34A1 model in October 1942. A grand total of 6748 M4s was built up to January 1944, and the last ones including a cast front were known as Sherman I Hybrid.

The British were the first to use the Sherman in combat and brought several improvements that were often introduced during production: for instance, a 2-inch smoke mortar in the turret roof became obligatory in June 1943. They discarded the .50 antiaircraft machine-gun and deleted its mount on the turret, since their usual practice was to let specially designed vehicles deal with air-attacks. Many modifications appeared during the M4 and M4A1 production, such as light protective guards, siren, gun crutch, added 2,5mm armour plates on the sides, the turret and in front of the driver and machine-gunner positions. The most obvious improvement was the replacement of the three-piece bolted transmission armour with a one-piece cast housing in mid-43. Its much rounded shape in the beginning became more and more pointed to improve its ballistic qualities.

The development of a welded-hull version of the M4 using the General Motors 6046 diesel double engine of the M3A3 was launched in late 1941. The M4A2 pilot tank (Sherman III) was ready in February 1942 and was soon accepted for immediate production. It proved more powerful than its predecessors with a motorization at least as reliable. It reached a top speed of 30 mph, although consuming less fuel (the range was 150 miles). In return, the air filters and the cooling system were more fragile, but were later improved, after the first trials. The seven welded armoured plates composing the front glacis weakened this part of the tank, but the solution was only found in 1944, by introducing a 63.5 mm single-piece armour plate, at a 47° instead of 56° angle. Because the cast parts were missing, the armour of the driver and machine-gunner positions were often welded on the M4A2. It was on this tank version that was first introduced in December 1943 an oval loader hatch on the turret roof. The USA preferred petrol to diesel engines, and kept the diesel tanks for training or Lend-Lease: the M4A2 was thus mainly delivered to the Russian, British and French armies, even if the US-Marines also used

*Right, center.* **The Sherman I Hybrid is sometimes mistaken for an M4A1 because of the cast front armour, which used the new 47° glacis plate and slanting hatches. This tank was delivered to the British Army, as shown by the serial number T233007, and has already been fitted with a turret stowage box of a type often seen in North Africa or Italy.**
(Tank Museum 20/G6)

*Right.* **Part of the Sherman III production was equipped with welded instead of cast armoured driver and machine-gunner's positions, a good identification method. Seen from the front, the M4A2 was otherwise very similar to the M4, as it had the same number of front armour plates. The first one-piece transmission housing retained the shape of the bolted one.**
(Tank Museum 2875/A3)

The Sherman I was the basic M4 version, but few were delivered to the British for it was one the main models chosen by the US Army. This middle production tank is fitted with two small armour plates in front of the driver and machine-gunner's positions, which protected the welding seam with the glacis plate. *(Tank Museum 2706/B4)*

*(Tank Museum 2875/A3)*

of it since diesel oil was easily available on warships. Five firms completed the production of 8053 M4A2s in May 1944.

The M4A3 was never delivered to the British despite satisfactory testing since the USA saved the production for themselves. But the M4A4 (Sherman V) designed form February 1942 onwards to meet increasing requirements for Sherman tanks formed the largest allotment of American tanks delivered to the Commonwealth. Produced from July 1942 to September 1943 in 7599 examples, by Chrysler in Detroit, the M4A4 used the Chrysler A57 Multibank, a very complicated engine composed of a five-car-engine assembly and totalling 30 cylinders. The M3A4 already using this engine was

chosen as test-bed for the M4A4. This Sherman was heavier (at 39.8 tons) and longer (165mm) than its cousins, but retained the same ground pressure thanks to longer tracks (83 links instead of 79). It was also less powerful with a speed of 25 mph; engine maintenance was trickier in spite of continuous improvements tending to decrease the number of water pumps (one instead of five) and to facilitate access to the pistons and valves. It was thus reserved for Lend-Lease deliveries to the Allies...

The hull was lengthened by 28cm, the bogies being more spaced for a better weight distribution. The front armour only included five welded plates now, but the one-piece cast transmission housing and the 47° glacis plate were never factory-fitted to the M4A4. It was nevertheless equipped with the changes introduced on other versions: added armour, periscopes replacing the driver and machine-gunner's direct vision slots, M34A1 combination gun mount, and so on.

**The M4A4 was the most widespread Sherman version in the British arsenal. Even from this angle the greater interval between the bogies typical of the Sherman V can be seen. This model was never fitted with the one-piece transmission housing, even if replacement in unit workshops was possible since the cast and bolted parts were interchangeable.** *(Tank Museum 2725/B4)*

When they were issued with the various Sherman Marks, the British gave them their own registration codes: Sherman I to V for the M4 to M4A4, the other armament than the 75-mm gun being identified by letters A (76-mm), B (105-mm) and C (17 pounder). Thus, a Firefly on M4A4 chassis was a Sherman Vc. The British also made the Shermans suit their needs, by mounting a rear turret stowage box for example (three types at least existed, the most commonly seen in Normandy being rectangular with a metal hooping round the middle). Another stowage box was also added to the Firefly Vcs rear, but was sometimes shifted to the front, on Firefly Ics and Ic Hybrids notably. The N°19 radio set was substituted for the SRC 508 in the turret bustle, and one of the antennas was located in the original left rear socket, while the other one was fixed on an additional base on the right. Six spare track links were usually carried in two racks on the glacis plate.

Early production tanks that were not equipped with smoke dischargers were fitted out with two 4-inch smoke mortars on the turret's right side. A first aid box was fastened on the right of the rear hull, and on command or Squadron-leaders tanks, a telephone was fitted to the left rear in the summer of 1944 in order to ease the communications between the crew and

the infantry. The command tank version could be recognized by an additional N°19 radio set with its antenna fitted on the glacis right, the main armament being often retained but with fewer rounds. The 75-mm gun was however a dummy on the Artillery Observation Post, the breech and the ammo racks being respectively replaced with map supports, and a N°18 (Artillery) and two portable N°38 (infantry) radio sets.

Despite the national Cromwell and Churchill production, the Sherman was the warhorse in British armoured units, first in Italy, then in Normandy. It was issued as the main tank in two "standard" armoured divisions out of three, and four brigades out of seven, representing 18 regiments, for only eight Churchill- and six Cromwell- equipped regiments. It was moreover used for many conversions, in particular by 79th Arm.Div.: Flail and DD, but also ARV or Firefly. It must be said that Great-Britain received 2096 M4s, 942 M4A1s, 5041 M4A2s and 7167 M4A4s during the war, even if some of these tanks were handed over to French, Canadian or Polish units. The M4A4 was the most widespread type in Normandy, with a strong presence of M4A1s and later M4 Hybrids (especially the Firefly version), but the M4A2 tended to be rarer. No 76-mm armed Sherman was used in Normandy: few were delivered to the British, and they were more often sent to Italy.

It is surprising to notice that in spite of obvious efforts to standardize tanks within a unit, at least when it left England, various Sherman variants were issued together in Normandy, not only at the brigade level, but also in a regiment, or even in a Squadron. This was mainly the consequence of the M4A4 being used as the main conversion basis for the Firefly, but also because of the difficulty in finding available tanks of the right model to make up the losses. Depending on American deliveries, the British did not choose the quantity, the delivery date and the model of the tanks they were issued with: the US Army first fulfilled its own needs for the M4, M4A1 and M4A3 versions.

The Sherman had been a good, modern, reliable and well-armed combat tank when it had first appeared in 1942, but almost no evolution had been introduced for two years, and it had become obsolete compared with the latest German tanks, armour as well as armament speaking. Its reliability and availability in sufficient number compensated for these drawbacks, but it never inspired the British crews with total confidence, above all because it was so prone to catch fire as soon as it was hit.

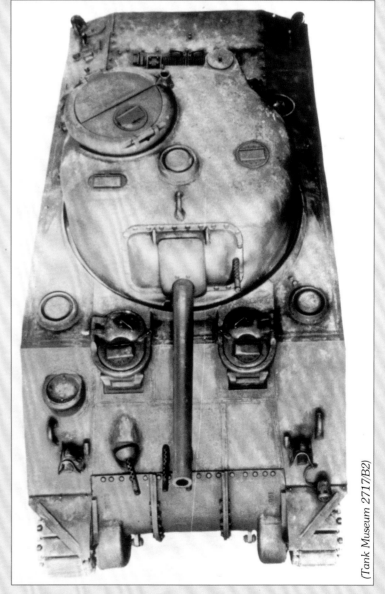

*(Tank Museum 2717/B2)*

**The upper view of an early production Sherman (here an M4A2) shows the front direct vision slots, which could still be seen on some tanks in Normandy. It was not before December 1943 that the additional hatch on the turret roof appeared: so far, the loader had to bale out after the tank commander and the gunner through the main circular hatch.** *(Tank Museum 2717/B2)*

# SHERMAN FIREFLY

**A**LTHOUGH THE **C**HALLENGER was already under development in late 1943, it became urgent for the Royal Armoured Corps to quickly have at its disposal a tank armed with the 17 pounder gun, since the Tiger and last Panzer IV versions had been met in Tunisia and Sicily, and were a sign of the difficult fighting ahead in France.

Even a temporary solution would have been welcome, and that was what was proposed by Major Witheridge: after a year at Fort Knox in the USA, this officer who had gained combat experience in the desert joined the Gunnery School at Lulworth in June 1943 and met Major Brighty there. Both were convinced that mounting the 17 pounder gun in the Sherman turret was possible. Brighty

The second rounded-edge hatch that was added on the turret for the loader can be seen on this photograph, as well as the rear armoured box housing the radio. It included three small rectangular plates on the top, but a model with three round plates also existed.
*(Tank Museum 2995/B1)*

tested this assembly indeed, but the 17 pounder was installed in a fixed mount! Shooting trials showed that the Sherman chassis could withstand the recoil, but a more practical solution had to be found so as not to damage the turret ring.

The biggest problem was recoil, actually: the 17 pounder gun in its towed version was equipped with large and cumbersome cylinders above and under the barrel, and that was the reason why the Challenger turret was so tall. To solve this difficulty, both officers called on WGK Kilbourn, a Vickers engineer attached to the Department of Tank Design. The managers of this organization wanted to cancel the project in favour of the Challenger, but Kilbourn managed to convince them not to do so, arguing that the design was viable and could quickly succeed.

The engineer modified the barrel base in front of the breech to shorten the weapon stroke in the cradle during recoil, and he designed a new mount including two recoil cylinders. The 17 pounder Mk IV was successfully tested on 26 December 1943, and the fact the prototype was ready as soon as 6 January 1944 reveals the urgency dictating the Firefly development. Actually, this name did not appear immediately, and its exact origin is unknown: the Firefly was first known as Sherman 17 pounder, or Sherman C. After approval of the new tank, the War Office put in an order for 2100 examples.

Of course, the Sherman had to be modified to take the 17 pounder

*In title.* **One of the first Fireflies, converted on a Sherman V chassis: the M34A1 mantlet was barely modified by adding six big fastening screws (including four around the barrel), and deleting the small armoured cheeks around the gun base. The long 17-pounder barrel rather improved the Sherman silhouette, which thus became more balanced.** *(Tank Museum 2995/B4)*

*Right.* **This Firefly is fitted, on the mudguards and sides, with attachments for the Houseboat system, designed to receive painted canvas to make the tank seem like a truck. A similar trick had already been used in the desert to conceal the real troop movements from the Germans, but it does not seem to have been necessary in Normandy.** *(Tank Museum 2995/C1)*

*Bottom.* **The rear view of another Sherman Vc reveals the large hull stowage box, used to carry the 17-pounder gun cleaning kit (including cleaning rods). On early Fireflies, the gun crutch was centred on the rear engine deck, and it was later shifted to the left.** *(Tank Museum 2995/A1)*

gun, but not so radically that the conversion could not be undertaken rapidly. The mantlet was similar to the standard M34A1, with a coaxial .30 machine-gun and the telescopic sight N°43.3, but was differing by its fixing through six visible big screws. The 17 pounder breech took a lot of space in the turret: a second hatch for the loader was fitted on the roof, besides the tank commander's cupola. The very long ammunition shells (83cm) were difficult to handle in the turret, and Kilbourn decided to turn the breech through 90° (it thus became horizontal instead of vertical) to ease the loader's task. The N°19 radio set ran the risk of being damaged by the breech recoil if it was mounted to the rear of the turret as on other British tanks. The rear wall was thus cut out and an armoured box housing the radio was fitted on the turret bustle, the device moreover acting as counterweight for the long 17 pounder barrel.

The chassis was modified by deleting the hull machine-gun and plugging its aperture with an armour plate, and substituting ammo stowage racks for the machine-gunner's seat (the crew was now only four). A gun crutch was added on the rear engine deck, first in the centre then on the left. Larger gun travelling locks were also produced in unit workshops (notably 4th Arm.Brig. and Guards Arm.Div.) and installed on the front glacis plate, and those planned for the 75-mm gun on later Sherman Ic Hybrid models were also used. The Sherman Vc officially carried 77 rounds distributed in several racks under the turret ring and on the floor. When fully laden, the 14 or 15-round rack replacing the machine-gun seat could only be reached from outside, through the right hatch. The gun elevated between -5° and +20°, no gyro-stabilizer was provided. The Sherman protection remained the same, added armour plates, although unnecessary since the ammunition were not stowed in the same positions, were still fitted on some Vcs and all Ic Hybrids.

The 17-pounder ammunition was very powerful: the APC (Armour Piercing Capped) and APCBC (APC, Ballistic Capped) could perforate the Tiger I front armour at 1,100m and 1,800m respectively. The discarding sabot APC was even more efficient but less precise, and was only available late and in small numbers. The high-explosive shell was in return often criticized and

justified the 75-mm Sherman being retained. One particular problem was never solved: when shooting, a violent flash at the muzzle brake raised a cloud of dust, blinding the crew and revealing the tank's position. The dangerous flashback at the breech, on the first models, was cured by slightly delaying its opening. The long 17-pounder barrel made the Firefly conspicuous, and the Germans soon learned to knock-out the menacing tank before the other 75-mm Shermans: the parade was to camouflage the gun with hessian tape, to paint part of it in a lighter colour to break its shape, or even to fit a dummy muzzle brake in the middle of the barrel.

A Sherman Vc prototype was ready on 6 January 1944, and after approval, the War Office ordered 2100 examples (the final order stood at 3414 tanks, for an actual production exceeding 2000), which were converted by the Royal Ordnance works in Cardiff, Leeds, Woolwich, Hayes, etc. The production became more and more urgent when it was known that the Challenger had been delayed, and that it was furthermore ill-adapted to the combat tank role. In late May, 342 Fireflies had been completed, and 288 were available in units on the 24 June, against only 120 on 5 May and about 200 on D-Day. Priority was given to the North-West Europe front in order to issue

(Tank Museum 2874/A1)

each four-tank Troop with one and later two 17-pounder Shermans. Each armoured brigade (except Tank Brigades) was generally equipped with 36 Fireflies at the end of June, but some were still missing: 8th Arm.Brig. (which was partially equipped with DD Shermans) only received 22. This relative rarity explains why some gunners had the opportunity to fire the 17-pounder gun only once or twice in training.

The conversion was mainly undertaken on Sherman Vs (M4A4) but also on some Mk Is and later on many Mk I Hybrids. Manufacture was totally dependant on available Shermans, and was thus slowed down when the battle of Normandy took a heavy toll on the reserves. In fact, it is often ignored that there was a shortage of Shermans during the summer of 1944, particularly on the American side, because of the heavy losses. Only the 75-mm Sherman could be used for

**Three Sherman Ic Hybrids are being prepared in Chilwell, a depot in Nottinghamshire. The cast and rounded hull front can be seen on the middle tank. The rear M4 chassis is closed with a sheet metal plate, with Bostik joints, as part of the waterproofing. For several weeks after D-Day, the vehicles were so prepared although they were not to get ashore on the beaches.** (Tank Museum 2994/D5)

**The Sherman Ic (here from 1st Northamptonshire Yeomanry) on M4 chassis was more present in Normandy that one usually thinks: only the spaced bogies and one-piece transmission housing can differentiate it at first glance from a Sherman Vc. It also seems that the added armour in front of the driver's and machine-gunner's positions was seldom fitted to Sherman Vcs.**

the Firefly conversion: the 76-mm tank was ruled out for its different mantlet, and the 105-mm tank because it only had manually operated turret rotation. The Sherman II (M4A1) seems to have been put aside because of its cast armour, which would have not been suited to accommodate the ammo stowage racks, and the M4A2 had become too scarce (it was also planned to use only petrol engine versions, but nobody knows why). All Sherman-equipped units, as well as the 7th Arm.Div.'s armoured brigade, were issued with Fireflies. On the other hand, recce regiments do not seem to have received any, they were to wait until the Challenger was available. The Firefly was a very successful improvised weapon and was the only British effective answer to the Tiger and Panther, but it was always tricky to use because of its weak armour, the conspicuous silhouette of the long barrel and the firing flash.

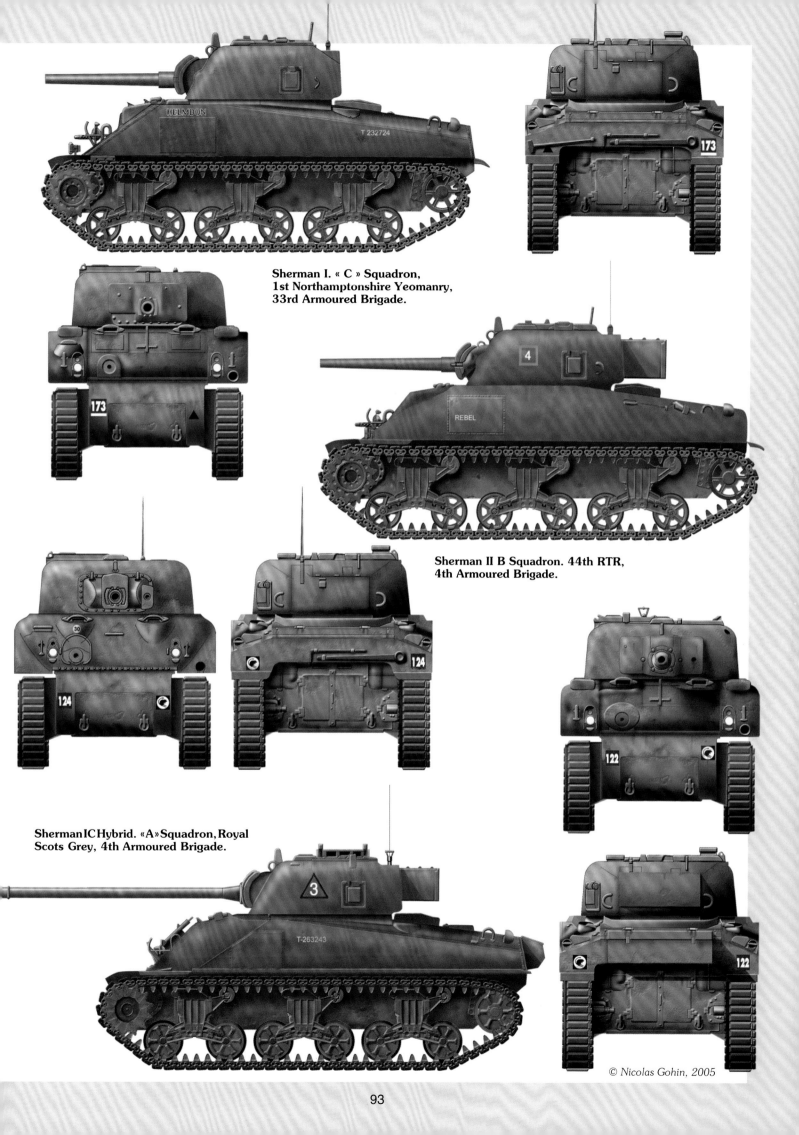

Sherman I. « C » Squadron,
1st Northamptonshire Yeomanry,
33rd Armoured Brigade.

Sherman II B Squadron. 44th RTR,
4th Armoured Brigade.

Sherman I C Hybrid. «A» Squadron, Royal
Scots Grey, 4th Armoured Brigade.

© Nicolas Gohin, 2005

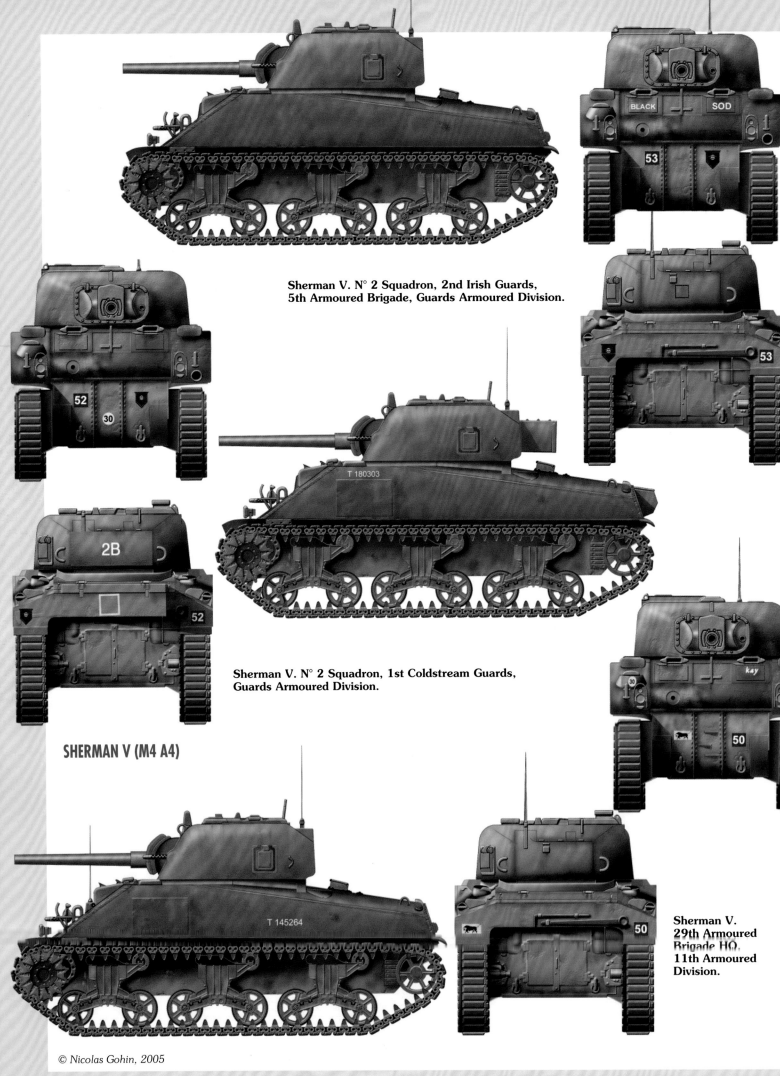

Sherman V. N° 2 Squadron, 2nd Irish Guards,
5th Armoured Brigade, Guards Armoured Division.

Sherman V. N° 2 Squadron, 1st Coldstream Guards,
Guards Armoured Division.

**SHERMAN V (M4 A4)**

Sherman V.
29th Armoured
Brigade HQ,
11th Armoured
Division.

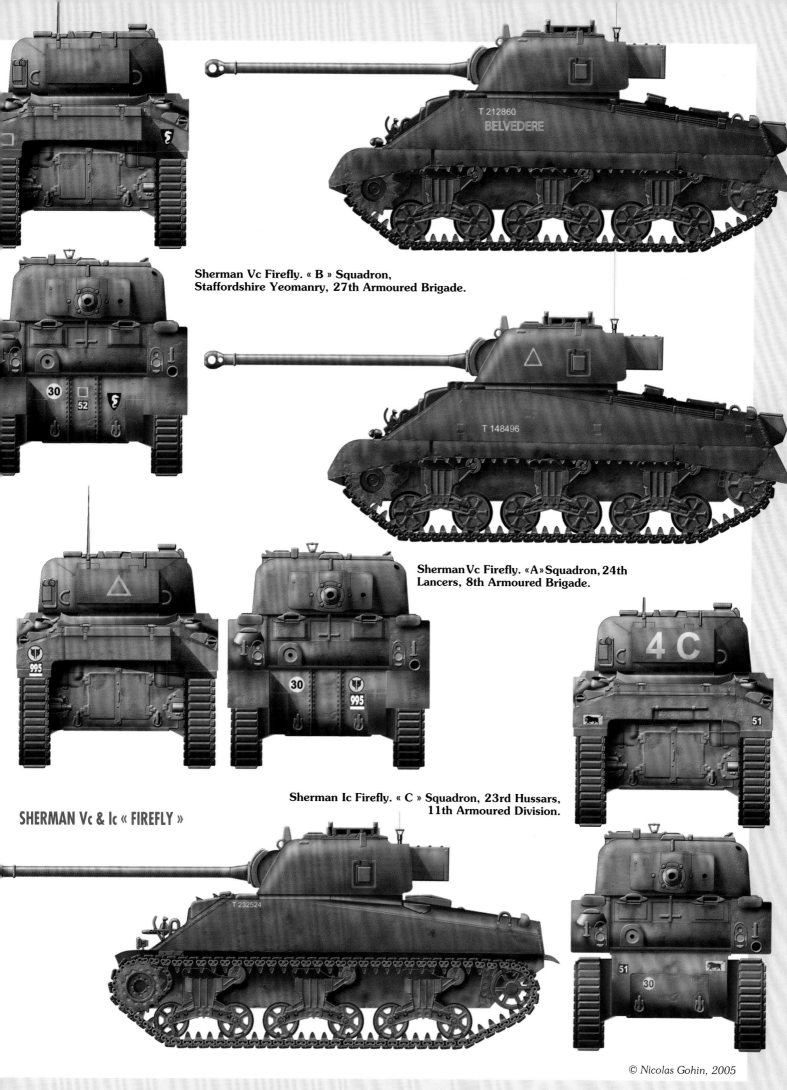

T 212860
BELVEDERE

Sherman Vc Firefly. « B » Squadron,
Staffordshire Yeomanry, 27th Armoured Brigade.

T 148496

Sherman Vc Firefly. « A » Squadron, 24th
Lancers, 8th Armoured Brigade.

Sherman Ic Firefly. « C » Squadron, 23rd Hussars,
11th Armoured Division.

**SHERMAN Vc & Ic « FIREFLY »**

T 232524

© Nicolas Gohin, 2005

# CHURCHILL TANK

**S**EVERAL INFANTRY TANKS were already under development in 1939 (Matilda, Valentine), and a new project was however initialized in September for the A20 heavy tank.

Senior officers of the British Army, most of them having served during World War I, predicted that the campaign in the West would be identical, with trench fighting, fortified positions, and barbed wire entanglements. Logically, the new heavy infantry tank bore a great resemblance to its ancestors of 1916, with its high tracks enveloping the whole hull, and its pair of 2 pounder guns in lateral barbettes. The latter arrangement was given up in June 1940, on behalf of a turret housing one of the guns, the other one being mounted besides the driver. Developed by the Department of Tank Design in association with Vauxhall, who supplied the 12-cylinder engine (actually two coupled Bedford 6 cylinders engines), the project was renamed A22, and the order came that it was to be put into production one year later! This very short time limit was unusual, but wartime necessities required speed in the designing of high-performance armoured vehicles, to the prejudice of adjustment.

The A22 prototype was ready by October 1940, and a first batch of 200 tanks was required for March 1941, out of a total order of 500. In spite of other firms joining in the production (Leyland, BRC&W, Babcock & Wilcox...), these delivery schedules could not be met. Moreover, the first A22, as noted in the technical manual, was hampered by teething troubles that

would have to be progressively corrected, the task of disclosing them being incumbent upon the units. Problems affected the bogies, ball bearings, joints, tracks, drive gear... Divisional workshops frequently had to rely upon makeshift solutions to cure these failings, before they were corrected on later models: for instance, the air louvers, that were positioned downwards and were sucking in dust and leaves, were quickly redesigned facing upwards.

The Churchill (so baptised in September 1941) was a roomy tank, with an individual hatch at least for every one of the five crew members (including lateral doors); it was heavily armoured at that time with a maximum thickness of 102mm at the front, and equipped with 22 bogies for a soft-riding suspension. Speed was not its main quality (16 miles per hour at best since it had to move with the infantry, and its Merrit-Brown 301c gearbox was always fragile. The driver had not the usual levers to steer the tank, but a horizontal bar with two vertical handles instead. The electrically powered turret rotated fast enough, executing a full turn in 15 seconds. Secondary armament included a coaxial Besa machine-gun, and a 2 inch smoke discharger in the roof. The commander's hatch could rotate but was not fitted in a real cupola, and was only equipped with one rear and one front periscope.

The first model to be produced in June 1941 was the Mark I armed with a 2 pounder gun in a cast turret, and with a 3 inch

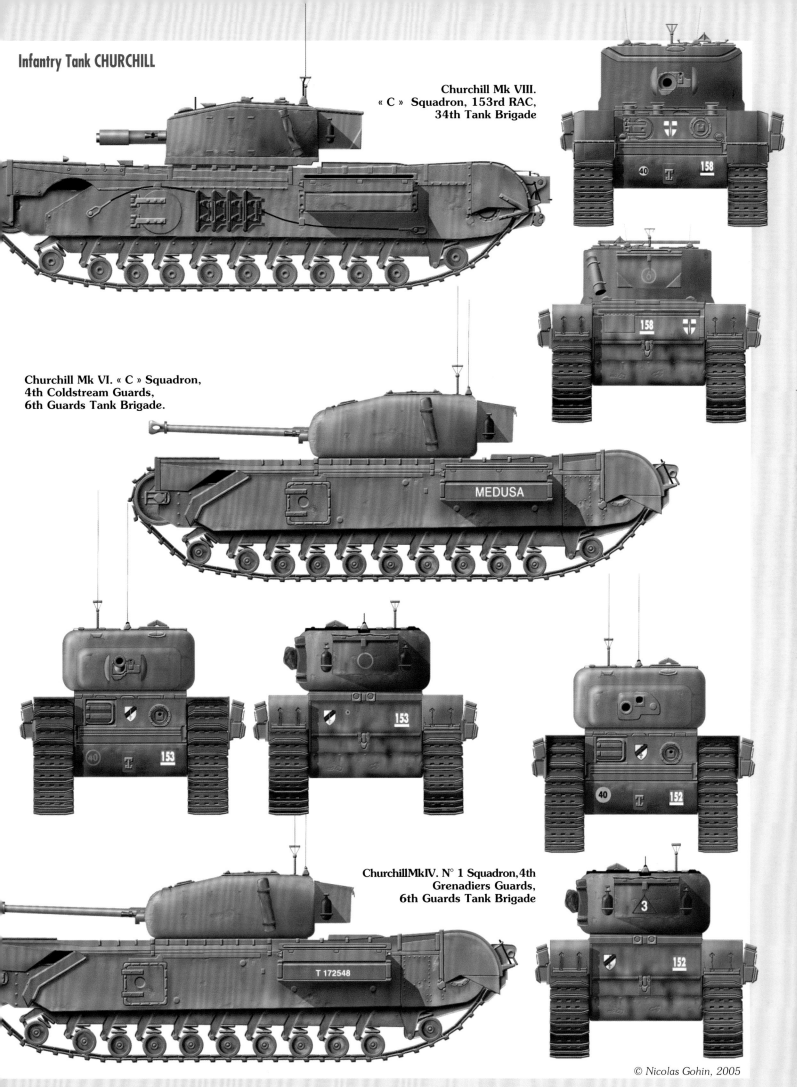

# Infantry Tank CHURCHILL

Churchill Mk VIII.
« C » Squadron, 153rd RAC,
34th Tank Brigade

Churchill Mk VI. « C » Squadron,
4th Coldstream Guards,
6th Guards Tank Brigade.

MEDUSA

Churchill Mk IV. N° 1 Squadron, 4th
Grenadiers Guards,
6th Guards Tank Brigade

T 172548

© Nicolas Gohin, 2005

howitzer in the hull; the use of the latter was very limited for it was given little room, both inside and outside. After about 300 tanks were produced, the howitzer was eventually replaced by a second Besa on the Mark II that was built from the summer of 1941. Except for this change, the Mk II, of which 1100 were produced, was identical to its predecessor. Nevertheless, a small batch of a Close Support version was made, featuring a 3 inch howitzer in the turret and a 2 pounder in the hull. The Mark III introduced two major changes: a more powerful 6 pounder gun was substituted for the 2 pounder, and a welded turret was specially designed for this weapon. The gun was fitted on a recessed mount, which was used on the following models despite being a real shot trap. Although the mock-up was ready by April 1941, this welded turret aroused suspicion: some experts thought that the welding seams would be too vulnerable to enemy fire, and that it would be impossible to guarantee the quantity and quality of the armour plates required. In spite of strengthened and levelled welding seams, these doubts were confirmed during trials, and the production did not exceed 700 Mark IIIs. Another visible change from the Mark III onward was the stowage box being moved from the side of the turret to the rear of it.

Produced from October 1942, the Churchill Mark IV thus reverted to a cast turret that had to be 500kg heavier to match the armour thickness of its welded counterpart. The top of the

tracks was now entirely covered with mudguards, also used as tread ways by the crew or the infantry on board. Although it was considered as obsolete by the Tank Board, there was still an order put for 3500 Churchills. It seems that there was at that time, on some Mark IVs as well as on earlier models, a variant of the 6 pounder using a free elevation mounting, i.e. the gunner put his shoulder in a horseshoe cushioned part fixed to the gun, and aimed the latter in this way, operating the trigger through a simple pistol grip. This archaism that would only disappear with the 75-mm gun was retained to correspond to the fire-while-moving theory, which was no longer in use for many months. Aiming was greatly improved on most Mk IVs through a standard geared, manually operated elevation, and a foot trigger. The Mark V entering production in December 1942 was actually a Mark IV armed with a 95-mm howitzer, this weapon having been developed from a shortened 3.7 inch barrel fitted with a 25 pounder breech, to obtain a Close Support version.

The Churchill chassis had remained unchanged on the three primary models, but was improved through an important Rework Scheme starting with the Mk IV. Actually, bringing the older productions to the standards of the new ones would go on during the whole career of the Churchill. The main modifications introduced by late 1942 were the fitting of mudguards above the tracks, and the alteration of air admissions and exits. But other details were progressively improved, such as the bogies, the brakes and some engine parts, to reach a grand total of 71 changes. In September 1943, a new step was passed in the Churchill's history with the Mark VI, very similar to the Mk IV on the surface, but which was armed, at last, with a 75-mm gun developed from the 6 pounder, giving it the same firepower as a Sherman, with an excellent high-explosive shell in particular. This gun became standard on the Churchill, and in the wake of the rework scheme, it was retrofitted on 242 Mk IIIs and 820 Mk IVs (the 75-mm Mk IV thus became almost impossible to distinguish from the Mk VI).

The following version was developed from May 1943 onwards, and was so radically modified that it was given the denomination A22F. The chassis was larger now, and front armour thickness was increased to 152mm, more than on a Tiger I, and, above all, more than on any Allied tank. The floor was reinforced against mines, the hatch armour was increased, and the lateral and driver's hatches took a circular shape to resist antitank guns better. In particular, a new composite turret was designed (it is not known if it was by the Tank Board or Babcock & Wilson): the roof was welded on the cast turret with strengthened lower sides. Turret pistol ports were deleted, new tracks were fitted, and the gear-

*Left.*
**A new cast turret was adopted on the Mark IV, with a 6 pounder gun Mk 5, thinner and longer than the previous Mk 3.**
**The fully covering mudguards were the main alteration to the tank silhouette; they were also used as tread ways by the crew and accompanying infantry.**
*(Tank Museum 1780/A4)*

*Right*
**Once again, this Churchill Mk VI can only be identified by its serial number T31464. The mudguards and the big cast turret gave a modern touch to the Churchill, its early models being otherwise similar to World War I tanks. What seem like rods on the turret sides are just lashes fixed to the fastening rings for covers and bedrolls.**

*Previous page, left.*
**The Churchill Mk III could be easily recognized by its roomier welded turret housing a 6 pounder gun. Although the turret seemed stronger, the welding seams turned out to be weak. The coaxial machine-gun was now moved to the left of the gun, and would remain so on later models.**
*(Tank Museum 1781/C3)*

*Above, right.*
**When the Mk IV was retrofitted with a 75-mm gun from late 1943 onwards, it became almost impossible to distinguish it from the new Mk VI. Here, only the serial number T173028 can be used to allot this particular vehicle to an Mk IV series. The turret insignia identifies the training camp of Lulworth, in charge of testing the new armoured vehicles.**
*(Tank Museum1774/C6)*

*Above.*
**The Churchills Mk IV to Mk VI had the same cast turret, and the same arrangement of the engine deck. On the other hand, the circular auxiliary fuel tank was characteristic of the Mk IV. The turret stowage box with asymmetrical bevelled indentations was typical of early - and middle- production Churchills, it cleared the access to the driver and radio operator hatches even when the turret was in the 6 o'clock position.**
*(Tank Museum 1780/A2)*

*(Tank Museum 1774/C3)*

The cast turret with welded roof and the circular lateral and driver's hatches identify for certain a Churchill Mk VII. The stronger new tracks were introduced shortly prior the Mk VII development, and would progressively equip all other models. Less conspicuous progress is the increase in front armour thickness to 152mm.
(Tank Museum 1775/D2)

box was altered to match the weight increase. Actually, the added armour made the Churchill one ton heavier (to 40 tons), and speed was reduced to 12¹/₂ miles per hour, whilst strengthened bogies made up for the added weight. At last, the tank commander had at his disposal a real cupola with eight episcopes, which were re-

trofitted on earlier models. Armed with a 95-mm howitzer, the Mark VII became the Close Support version Mark VIII. Although the exact production figures are not known, more than 1200 Mk VIIs and Mk VIIIs were probably built. In addition to the cupola, earlier Churchill models were modernized through added armour plates, and were later renamed Mark IX, X and XI.

The Churchill tank, allotted to Tank Brigades, was first used in combat by the Canadians at Dieppe, in August 1942, without much success eventually since the conditions were hardly favourable. Some units were equipped with Churchills in Tunisia and Italy, but it was truly during the campaign in North-West Europe that it showed what it was capable of. Mk VII and Mk VIII models were available in small numbers, especially within 6th Guards and 34th Tank Brigades, but the eight regiments fighting in Normandy were mainly equipped with Mk IVs, armed with 6 pounder or 75-mm guns, as well as Mk VIs (Close Support versions were limited to 10% of the total strength, whilst the 6 pounder gun was retained for its better antitank capacity). The Churchill revealed itself to be a comparatively reliable and comfortable tank, offering good protection that was appreciated by the crews, with good automotive qualities in spite of limited speed: it was endowed with excellent cross-country capacities, and was able to climb high-gradient slopes. Its armament was however too weak and the view of the driver was restricted on account of the high tracks. The Churchill was used as a basic for many conversions: AVRE, Ark, Scissors, ARV, Crocodile, and so on.

The Churchill Mk VIII was just an Mk VII with a 95-mm howitzer for close support. The turret was better designed on Mk VIIs and VIIIs, with two armoured cheeks on each side of the barrel, concealing and protecting the recessed gun mounting. The 11-bogies running gear guaranteed excellent off-road capabilities.
(Tank Museum 1774/A4)

An M3A1 tested by the Americans in a winter setting: the turret inherited from the M3 looks even smaller with the commander in the cupola; this was however unchanged until the M3A3 and M5A1. Despite its age, the Stuart III still equipped several units in Normandy (including 33rd Arm.Brig. and 31st Tk.Brig.) *(Tank Museum 2738/C2)*

# LIGHT TANK STUART

**T**HE M3 L**IGHT** T**ANK**, successor of the pre-war M2A1, was developed from November 1940 onwards in order to modernise the American armoured forces by learning the lessons from the recent fighting in Europe. When it entered production in March 1941, the M3 was already obsolete compared with the most modern German, Russian and even French tanks, those which had lost the battle in 1940.

With its 37-mm gun, it could on the other hand be compared with the British tanks, but had less armour than most of the latter. The M3 family was however to serve during the whole war thanks to its speed and mechanical reliability, but also because it was available in great numbers, and because there was nothing better at that time... With a four-man crew, the M3 was powered by the excellent Continental W-670 radial engine deriving from an aircraft engine. It first saw action during Operation, *Crusader* in November 1941, with the British who named it Stuart to differentiate it from the M3 Lee/Grant tank. In spite of real shortcomings, the British appreciated the M3 so much that it was nicknamed Honey. Modified to fulfil the needs of desert warfare, it was also progressively improved in the USA by fitting more solid vision blocks, changing the interior layout, deleting the lateral fixed machine-guns...

These modifications were retained on the M3A1, 4621 of which were produced between May 1942 and February 1943. The M3 successor was a stop-gap solution until a really new model was de-signed. It introduced a new welded turret including a Westinghouse gyro-stabilizer for the 37-mm gun allowing it to fire on the move, as well as a radio intercom. An Oilgear powered rotating system was installed in the turret, involving the fitting of a turret basket including the gunner and commander's seats. Each of the latter had a peris-cope, the commander's could rotate while the gunner's one was coupled with the M23 mount and could so operate to any elevation. The cupola which the British had criticized was replaced with two hatches on the turret roof. During production, two fuel tanks that could be jettisoned were added on the engine deck sides to double the tank's range (from 65 to 130 miles). A partly welded hull was substituted for the original riveted version, and 211 examples were produced of a variant equipped with a Guiberson T-1020 diesel en-gine. Weighing 14 tons in combat order, the M3A1 was armed with the M6 37-mm gun (with a 106-round supply), and with three .30 machine-guns including a coaxial one. With a top speed of 35 mph, it outclassed the performances of the best British Cruiser tanks.

With the front, rear and side sloped armour, the M3A3 was 50 cm longer and also slightly larger than the M3. Its modern and fluid silhouette, although spoiled by the small turret, is still enhanced here by the mudguards, which were often lost or removed in combat. *(Tank Museum 2739/C4)*

*Above.* **The sloped front but vertical side armour is typical of the M5 chassis. The antiaircraft machine-gun armour on the turret left identifies a late production M5A1. Although it appeared as early as November 1942, the M5A1 was delivered belatedly to the British, who for a long time had to make do with M3A3s or even old M3A1s.** *(Tank Museum 3022/B5)*

Its armour was unfortunately too weak: 44mm for the cast transmission housing, 3mm at the front, and only 25mm on the sides, so that it was even vulnerable to the German 37-mm gun. Through Lend-Lease, 1594 M3A1s referred to as Stuart III and IV (diesel engine) were supplied to the British.

In April 1942, the US armoured forces requested that the M3A1 be improved by using the new chassis developed for the M5 and its Cadillac engine. The hull was distinguished by a 40° front glacis plate offering more inner space, but the armour of which was only 29mm thick. To keep the weight within reasonable limits, this thickness was further reduced to 2 mm on the new M3A3 tank. On the improved and lengthened hull (by 50cm), the driver and machine-gunner each had a hatch and a rotating periscope at their disposal.

Unlike the M5, the hull sides and rear were also sloped at an angle of 20°, allowing two fuel tanks and the air filters to be accommodated. A new turret was designed with a rear bustle to house the radio set following the British practice. The hatches were enlarged, and that of the commander included a rotating periscope. The M44 gun mount was designed with tighter tolerances for a better sighting, and included an M54 telescope for the gunner (the elevation was still -10° to +20°). A 250-round ammunition box for the .30 coaxial machine-gun was substituted for the previous 100-round box. Weighing 16 tons, the M3A3 was heavier than its predecessor, and slower (30 mph at the best), but it carried 174 37-mm rounds instead of 106. Two pilot models were ready in late 1942 and the M3A3 production by American Car & Foundry Company really started in January 1943 to end in September after 3427 examples had been built. 2047 of them were supplied to the British under the Stuart V designation. The M3A3 was reserved for training in the USA, or else it was delivered to the Allies (French, Canadians, etc.)

In order to make up for the lack of Continental radial engines, kept in priority for the aviation, it was proposed in June 1941 to design an M3 version powered by two Cadillac car engines, and equipped with a Hydramatic transmission. The new power plant was tested on the pilot model M3E2 without turret armament, and results were excellent since performances were similar to those of the M3 despite a 2.5-ton weight increase. It was moreover less noisy and its transmission was less cumbersome. The M4 designation it was given was soon changed to M5, in order to avoid any confusion with the M4 Sherman. The hull was radically altered by adopting a sloped front glacis plate, as we have seen for the M3A3. The side walls were still vertical but the engine deck was raised to accommodate the cooling system. For the same reason, the tank was 30cm longer than the M3, the second bogie unit and the idler wheel being further apart. Initially, the glacis plate included besides the driver a fixed .30 that was soon deleted. The next prototype M3E3 was fitted with a M3A1 turret equipped with a M4 sighting periscope coupled with the M23 mount. New glacis and turret typified the M5 of which 2074 were produced from April 1942 onwards; it was not delivered to the British Army.

The M5 was successful, but the turret inherited from the M3A1

It is easy to recognize a Stuart VI (M5A1) on this photograph thanks to the raised engine deck housing the Cadillac engine, and the turret inspired from the M3A3's. The two turret hatches at last offered practical bale-out exits for the crew. This early production M5A1 has no rear basket and no machine-gun armoured shield. *(Tank Museum 3021/E3)*

was too small: a similar turret to that of the M3A3 which had just been designed was thus developed and accepted in September 1942, entering production in November. The M5A1 was the version produced in greatest numbers (6810 examples) until May 1944, by Cadillac, General Motors and Massey Harris. The antiaircraft machine-gun mount, similar to that of the M5, was modified in the course of production to be repositioned on the turret right side, and was later protected by an armoured shield. With a top speed of 35 mph per hour, the M5A1 recovered the M3A1 performances, but with a range of only 100 miles, and with a 147-round 37-mm ammo supply. 1131 examples of the new Stuart VI were delivered to the British, but it was far from having replaced the earlier marks in Normandy, and was only found at first in a few units such as the Guards Arm.Div.

The Stuart was issued to every British armoured unit, whatever the main tank model: the Recce Squadron in armoured regiments were given 11, and 30 were supplied to the Recce Regiment of each armoured division. Useless as combat tank in 1944, the Stuart

was also inferior in terms of manoeuvrability and speed to the first-rate armoured cars produced by the British. From July onwards, the latter began to remove the turret from most of their Stuarts, in order to get rid of the now superfluous 37-mm gun, to save weight and so gain speed, and to keep a lower silhouette more suited to reconnaissance tasks. Various .30 and .50 machine-guns arrangements were fitted for the light tank's defence. Some Stuarts were also converted by REME workshops into ammo or personnel carriers, ambulances or artillery tractors.

*Left.* **In addition to the stowage box, it was on the M3A3 that the rear stowage basket was first introduced (it was later adopted in various shapes on the M5A1). Unlike the Sherman, the Stuart was hardly modified for the British Army service, and only some clasps and ties were changed or added on the engine deck.**
*(Tank Museum 2739/C3)*

**Following the practice adopted by the British in the desert, and then by the Canadians in Italy, many Stuarts (sawn-off Stuarts) had their turret removed in Normandy as the 37-mm gun had become almost useless. Armour plates, of which several conversion sets were more or less standardized, are here welded by mechanics onto an M3A3 which benefits from a powerful armament: three .30 machine-guns at least in addition to the hull one.** *(RR)*

One of the first M10 produced, still in US registration: the running gear is no longer that of the M3 but of the M4, although the turret counterweights are absent and replaced with the grousers, which were used to improve the track grip on frozen ground. The look confirms reality: the turret was unbalanced without these counterweights. *(Tank Museum 2875/E1)*

# TANK DESTROYER M10 WOLVERINE

**F**OR A LONG PERIOD, the Tank Destroyer M10 remained the only operational tank hunter at the British Army's disposal, before the Achilles (which only was an M10 variant) and later the Archer arrived. Following the idea that tanks were mainly intended for infantry support, the principles for the use of armour in effect in the USA in 1940 said that enemy tanks had to be fought with antitank, and if possible self-propelled, guns.

The Gun Motor Carriage, armed with a more powerful weapon than the tanks, did not need thick armour but great mobility. The first US Tank Destroyer was improvised on a half-tracked chassis. However, in September 1941, the T24 was designed on a M3 tank chassis and armed with an antiaircraft 3 inch gun in the open-top tank hull, original armour remaining nearly unchanged. But a lower silhouette, better crew protection and 360° traverse were requested: the T35 thus appeared in November 1941 on an M4A1 then M4A2 chassis, and mounting a T12 3-inch gun in a open-rear turret.

The first combats in the Philippines revealed that sloped armour was advantageous, and it was adopted for the T35E1 in January 1942, with a single front armour plate obliging the hull machine-gun to be deleted. The vehicle developed by Fisher Tank Div. included a circular, sloped-sided and partially open-top turret. Trials at the Aberdeen APG showed that sloped armour was more efficient, but the unsatisfactory cast turret was replaced with another six - then five- sided welded model. The weight increase however necessitated reducing armour thickness on the whole vehicle: it was only 38mm on the glacis, 57mm at the front and 25mm on the sides. The one-piece armoured transmission housing was later used on all other Shermans. Standardized as "3 inch Gun Motor Carriage M10" in June 1942, the vehicle was also equipped with an additional hatch for the radio-operator, driver's periscope, and bosses for additional armour plates which were never fitted. The M5 mount of the M7 gun was simplified for production, with the new possibility of adapting the 105-mm howitzer or the British 17 pounder gun.

M10 production started at Fisher in September 1942, and continued up until December 1943 for a total of 4993 examples; to these must be added 1713 M10A1s using an M4A3 chassis, but most of them remained in the USA for training. With its GM 6046 12-cylinder diesel engine, the M10 could reach a top speed of 31 mph although weighing 33 tons, for a 200 km range. Manned by a crew of five, it was equipped with a .50 turret-mounted machine-gun, firing rearwards, as only auxiliary armament, and carried fifty four 3 inch rounds including 6 in turret ready racks. The first

Like the Achilles some time later, the M10 was fitted with a rudimentary gun crutch to relieve the mount from the weight of the 3 inch gun. This particular vehicle has part of its Deep Wading Equipment fitted under the rear armour rim: another bent part was connected to the trunk evacuating the exhaust gas.
*(Tank Museum 2997/D5)*

trials of the series production model showed only one major failing: the turret was unbalanced by the gun, and stowing the track grousers on its rear did not compensate for the 3 inch barrel weight. Rectangular counterweights were first improvised, and were soon replaced by two triangular 1800 kg pieces. The turret was always manually rotated, although tests were belatedly undertaken with a hydraulic system. The direct vision sight was replaced in March 1943 by indirect fire equipment and a M70G telescope. The turret rear was modified on late production M10s to give more room inside, and the counterweights then took on a duckbill shape. At the same period, the bosses for additional armour gradually disappeared from the hull and turret sides.

The crew's protection remained the main M10 shortcoming, and this was only partially solved later through improvised roofs.

**In its late version, the M10 had a more balanced silhouette thanks to the duckbill counterweights to the turret rear. The grousers were now stowed in hull side racks. Most M10s seen in Normandy retained this earlier, rounded version of the transmission armoured housing.**

**A close-up of the final production turret reveals that the counterweights were hollowed-out and could be used for stowage. One can also notice that the sides were really thin, and that the open turret was very vulnerable to enemy fire, particularly to artillery shells, mortar bombs or grenades.** *(RR)*

Otherwise, it was a reliable machine, with a precise, powerful gun (at least in its early career) which was more efficient than the 75-mm, but inferior to the German long 75-mm and 88-mm guns. The armour was on the other hand too thin, restricting the use of M10s to ambushes or covering missions. The front hatches were also ill designed for the driver and radio-operator baling-out. The M10 first saw action in Tunisia in early 1943. The British were supplied some through the Lend-Lease agreement from mid-1943 onwards, and received a total of 1648 examples, representing more than a third of the production. It was mainly issued to antitank units in infantry and armoured divisions, at the rate of 12 to 24 SPGs per regiment, before the Achilles was gradually introduced in greater numbers, but the latter never completely superseded the M10. It was also issued to independent antitank regiments attached to armies or army corps.

*(Tank Museum 2997/D3)*

# 17 PDR M10 SP CHILLES

The long gun barrel of the 17 pounder did not alter the Achilles' silhouette, which remained very similar to the basic M10. This self-propelled gun seems to have retained its full equipment, including the six spare track links in common with every Sherman-based vehicle, but the .50 machine-gun mount is in the wrong place, just in front of the driver's hatch!
*(Tank Museum 2999/F6)*

**I**N 1944, THE M10 TANK DESTROYER equipped with the 3 inch M3 or M7 gun was the standard US Army antitank self-propelled weapon, but the British Army too was equipped with it ever since early 1943 through the Lend-Lease agreement. With the approaching invasion of France, doubts began to emerge in the British Army about the relative weakness of the 3 inch gun, and a decision was taken in late 1943 to adapt the excellent 17 pounder Mk V antitank gun on the M10.

This gun was a variant of the Mk II towed version, and the most powerful antitank weapon of the Anglo-American arsenal, with equal or even better performances than its German 75-mm (long) or 88-mm counterparts. The conversion was facilitated thanks to the M10 turret mounting having been designed to accept guns other than the 3 inch. Changing two lugs enabled fitting to be carried out without any major modification of the 17 pounder breech block and barrel. However, the outer diameter of the gun being smaller, a special casting had to be fitted between the barrel and the mantlet: the thick connec-

*Next page.* **This close view of the 17 pounder breech shows how little space was left for the crew, hence the necessity to use the second turret style which was wider at the rear. The inner turret seems really dark coloured: following the conversion to Achilles standards, the original US Olive Drab colour may have been left on the inside when the vehicle was repainted.**
*(Tank Museum 3000/A4)*

ting washer also acted as a counterweight, since its heavy breech put the gun out of balance. Another counterweight in two parts, fitted just aft of the muzzle brake, helped to balance the gun. The opening for the visor on the left was enlarged, so that a new direct sight telescope could be used, the negative result being that the front turret armour was weakened. The secondary armament was still limited to one .50 heavy machine-gun fitted on a socket at the rear of the turret.

Other modifications were made to the inner turret stowage, to accommodate the new weapon, leaving room around the breech for the five crewmen. The 17 pounder ammunition being more bulky, only 50 shells were carried in the Achilles instead of 54 in the M10 (6 in ready racks in the turret, and 44 in the sponsons above the running gear). Elevation was a bit more limited than for the 3 inch gun, from +20 to -5 degrees, but remained sufficient as the weapon was only to be used in the antitank role. First studies made on middle production M10s with the early style turret were known as Achilles Ic (the letter C standing for the 17 pounder gun), but for production the conversion was only made on late models, equipped with the longer turret and duckbill counterweights. This turret shape afforded more room for the gun recoil. The first production vehicles were equipped with the early cast transmission armour, but most of them were fitted with the more pointed late model. The bolts for additional armour were deleted from the flanks of the superstructure.

The Achilles IIc was available just before operation Overlord, and was used for the first time in Normandy, from June 1944 onwards. Normal equipment was one or two batteries (12 to 24 self-propelled guns) for every antitank regiment in British (and Canadian) armoured and infantry divisions, and in Royal Artillery independent units under

**This Achilles IIc is representative of the latest version that just appeared at the end of the Normandy campaign: it was no longer equipped with the bolted fittings for the additional armour. These would also disappear from the glacis on the last converted models.** *(Tank Museum 2999/E1)*

control of armies or army corps. The new weapon was immediately successful thanks to its technical reliability (inherited from the M10, with similar performances), and its firepower. Furthermore, the British Army had developed appropriate tactics for this kind of vehicle: instead of being used as real tank destroyers in an offensive role to chase and eliminate enemy tanks, according to the American doctrine (the US motto being Seek, Strike and Destroy), their mission in the British Army was flank protection and reinforcement of the antitank defence of armoured and infantry units. This method made good use of the long range of the 17 pounder, and was a way to avoid direct confrontation with Panzers, thus sparing the Achilles' thin armour, the major failing on every M10 version.

Most of Achilles IIcs were equipped with a handle to help climbing aboard the vehicle, welded to the bolts for the additional armour on the front armour plate, but this handle was frequently lost in combat or was hidden by the crew's impedimenta carried on the glacis. The elongated aperture for the telescope can be clearly seen, but the hole on the right is only a flaw in the photograph.
(Tank Museum 2999/F2)

When on the move, it was prescribed to turn the turret to the 6 o'clock position so that the heavy 17 pounder barrel could lie on the rear gun clamp, and so relieve the mounting and keep the visor adjustment. The .50 machine-gun was then pointing forward and could be used for close or anti-aircraft defence.

(Tank Museum 3000/A2)

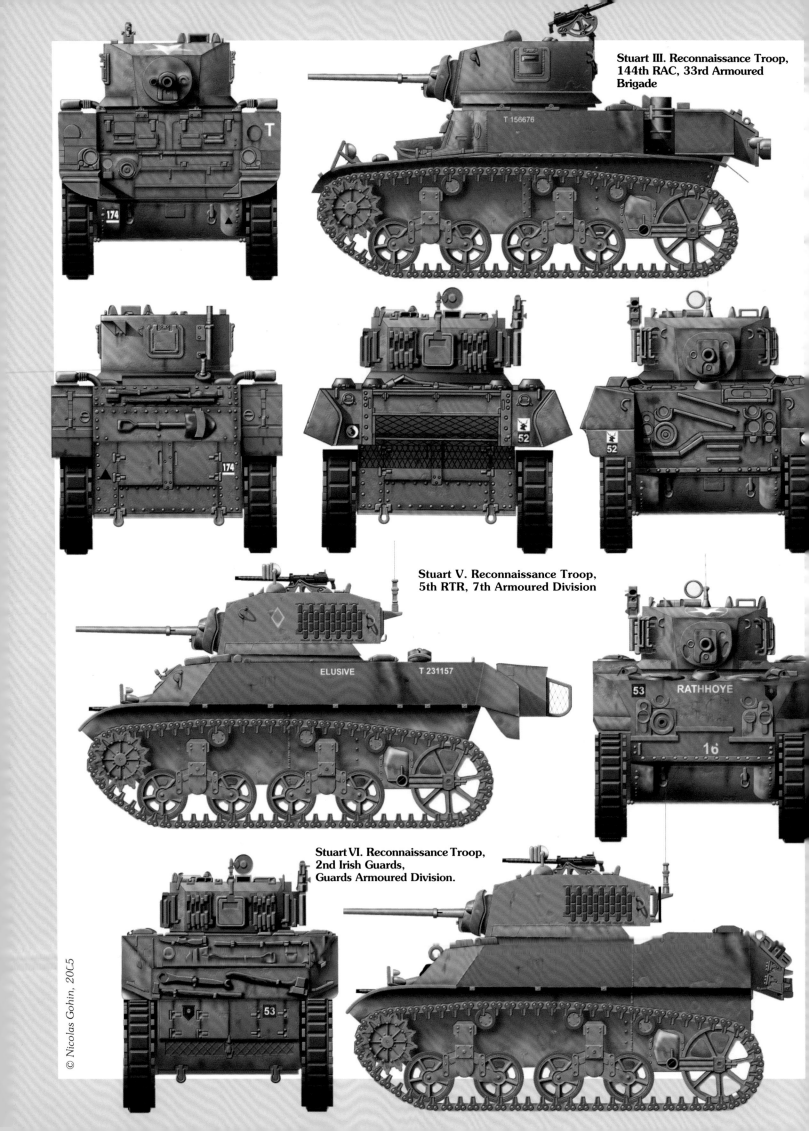

Stuart III. Reconnaissance Troop,
144th RAC, 33rd Armoured
Brigade

Stuart V. Reconnaissance Troop,
5th RTR, 7th Armoured Division

Stuart VI. Reconnaissance Troop,
2nd Irish Guards,
Guards Armoured Division.

# PRIEST AND SEXTON SELF-PROPELLED GUNS

The M7 Priest in its most common form was rather improved compared with earlier vehicles: the side armour was heightened, hinged plates were added, and the three-pieces bolted transmission housing was replaced with the late production one-piece cast one. *(Tank Museum 2741/A1)*

**U**P TO 1944, the British Army relied upon the USA for its self-propelled artillery. Its own trials, such as the Bishop on Valentine chassis, were rather inconclusive despite the great quality of the 25 pounder gun. Most of the armoured and infantry units landing in Normandy were thus equipped with the M7 Priest. In late 1941, the US Army had initiated the project of a self-propelled gun using its excellent M2A1 105-mm howitzer on an M3 medium tank chassis. Two T32 prototypes were soon after presented by Locomotive Works: the howitzer was mounted in a boxlike open-top armoured superstructure fitted on the M3 chassis.

During trials at the Aberdeen Proving Ground, a door was added to the rear to ease weapon maintenance and ammunition loading. Trials went on at Fort Knox in February 1942, and few modifications were adopted before the vehicle was standardized in April 1942 as "105-mm Howitzer Gun Motor Carriage M7". The changes affected the ammunition load, increased from 57 to 69 rounds through the removal of 4 crew seats out of 7, and the addition of a overhanging circular mount on the howitzer's right, for the .50 machine-gun, which was previously mounted on a rear pedestal or on a side swivel. The howitzer could be elevated from -5° to +35° (instead of +65° on the towed weapon), for a 15° left and 30° right traverse. The elevation was reduced to keep a lower silhouette, but was to raise problems in combat, and it would be sometimes necessary to build sloped platforms in order to obtain greater firing angles.

Manned by a crew of seven, the 25-ton M7 could reach a maximum speed of 20 miles per hour for a 123 miles range. The driver was positioned on the howitzer's left and was the only crewman to have a vision block in his front hatch, which could be fitted with a removable windscreen when opened. The transmission housing armour was the same as on the gun tank, i.e. 107mm, but was only 12,7mm on the superstructure, and only protected from small arms fire. American Locomotive Co. continued to build the M7 until August 1943, for a grand total of 2814 examples. Improvements introduced during the production mainly affected the chassis: the three-part bolted transmission armour was replaced with the Sherman cast housing, and the M3 bolted hull was later welded, as on the M4. The bogie with central return roller was substituted for the strengthened suspension with rear mounted return rollers. The British were the first users of the M7 at El Alamein, and they nicknamed it Priest because of the circular machine-gun mount resembling a pulpit. It was a welcome substitute of the T19 on half-tracked chassis.

Combat experience led to further improve the M7 in late 1943: hinged armoured plates then protected the vulnerable ammo stowage racks; the 105-mm howitzer was equipped with a new travelling lock; and more generally the modifications introduced on the Sherman were applied: suspension, idler wheel, mudguards, and so on. So modified, 500 M7s were produced between March and October 1944, with Federal Machine and Welder Co. building 176 examples from March 1945 onwards. The M4A3 chassis and its Ford engine were also used by Pressed Steel Car Co. to build 826 M7B1 up to February 1945. The Priest was issued to one or two batteries in the two Field Artillery Regiments of British armoured or infantry divisions, at the rate of four vehicles per Troop, for a total of 24 SPGs.

In June 1942, the Americans were informed that a requirement

*Left.* An early production Priest (see the bogies with central return rollers) reveals its inner arrangement. The fighting compartment seems roomy enough, but it was to accommodate seven crew members! The crew was often six actually, and the fuses adjustment and shells preparation took place on the engine deck or on the ground. *(Tank Museum 2741/C5)*

*Next page, top to bottom.*
The Canadian tracks with their particular sprocket wheel gradually appeared on the Sexton. This SPG is duly equipped with the battery and generator at the rear, but the lights are still fixed on the transmission housing and not on the glacis plate: it is thus an early production Sexton II. *(Tank Museum 2078/A5)*

Unlike the M7, the Sexton's driving compartment was located on the right as on any Commonwealth vehicle, and the gun was then shifted to the left.
By comparison with the view of the Priest's interior, the gunner seemed to be better protected here by the higher armour, and he had a seat. *(Tank Museum 346/D5)*

*Right.*
On this M7 interior view can be seen, from left to right, the driving compartment, the 105-mm howitzer breech and its mount, the .50 machine-gun pulpit, and two rudimentary crew seats on each side. A gun crutch at the extremity of the recoil rail maintained the howitzer while travelling. *(Tank Museum 2742/B6)*

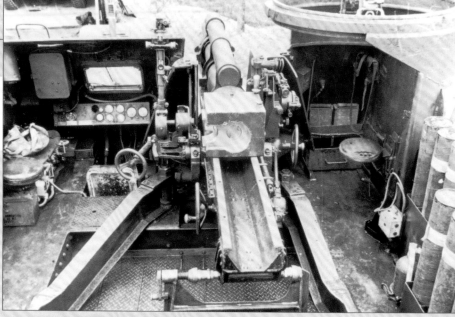

*Below.*
The first Sextons could be identified by the early production Ram running gear derived from the M3, with central return roller on the bogie, and by the bolted transmission housing (this vehicle probably is the prototype lacking a muzzle brake on the gun barrel).
It was the most common type in Normandy, where the Sexton saw service for the first time.
*(Tank Museum 2078/C1)*

existed to adapt a 25 pounder gun on a self-propelled chassis. They just took the second T32 prototype for the M7, fitted it out with the British gun through simple adapters, and proposed the "25 pounder GMC T51". Trials were however rapidly abandoned since the Canadians had just designed their own version on a Ram tank chassis (the latter being derived from the M3/M4). Actually, the British Army officially put the Canadian Department of National Defence in 1942 in charge of the development of a 25 pounder self-propelled gun on Ram chassis. The main concern was to stan-

dardize the ammunition supply within Royal Artillery regiments. The prototype was ready in late 1942 and was obviously inspired from the Priest without being a copy. After conclusive trials, the "*Tracked Self Propelled 25 pounder Sexton*" was produced from early 1943 onwards by Montreal Locomotive Works. The Sexton's nickname was in the lineage of religious terms initiated with the Bishop and Priest.

In the open-top superstructure, the gun was mounted on the left with the driver on the right, of course (he was also provided with a vision hatch). The +40° to -9° elevation was better

than on the Priest, but traverse was smaller (25° on the left, 15° on the right). The recoil was reduced to increase elevation; 112 high-explosive, armour-piercing and smoke rounds were carried. The arrangement was similar to that of the Priest, but the frontal superstructure armour was a bit thicker (19mm), the sides and rear remaining at 12,7mm. There was no auxiliary armament before the 147th Sexton was produced: a coupled Bren mounting was fitted later on. As for the Priest, the modifications introduced on the Ram were passed on to the Sexton: stronger bogies with rear mounted return roller, one-piece transmission housing. The Canadian track and its 17 teeth sprocket (instead of 13 on the Sherman) was very soon adopted. Performances were close to the M7's, although the new SPG was heavier (28 tons). The first 124 examples were renamed Sexton I when the Sexton II appeared, the main differences between them being the relocation of the lights to the glacis sides, and the addition of a battery and a generator on the rear hull. Manned by six crewmen and produced in 2150 examples, the Sexton first saw combat in Normandy where it gradually replaced the M7 Priest and equipped the Field Artillery Regiments at the same rate of four per Troop.

# ARMOURED RECOVERY VEHICLES AND BRIDGELAYERS

THE BRITISH ARMY ENTERED THE WAR WITH EXCELLENT recovery tractors, which could be used even for the heaviest armoured vehicles, but the need to recover a damaged tank on the battleground, under enemy fire, meant that special armoured recovery vehicles had to be developed for that purpose.

And the best solution was to use the chassis of the machine to be recovered, to create its recovery tractor. Thus, Armoured Recovery Vehicles (ARV) were made using the Covenanter and Crusader as a basis, but they were quickly abandoned, or at least reserved for training, because of their lack of power and their mechanical fragility. On the other hand, the Churchill ARV Mark I, available in 1942, was the first effective armoured recovery vehicle. Introducing a method that was to be also adopted for its successors, it consisted of a turretless Churchill chassis, and equipped with a simple jib crane on a boom at the front, and with additional equipment for recovery and repair. It was to be followed in 1943 by the Churchill ARV II, modified with a fixed turret and a dummy gun to make it less conspicuous, and improved internal stowage as well. This version was also fitted with a powerful two-speed winch, missing on the first ARV: it was therefore more powerful and multifunctional. Churchill ARVs were often converted from tanks returning for repairs, they were not in widespread use and

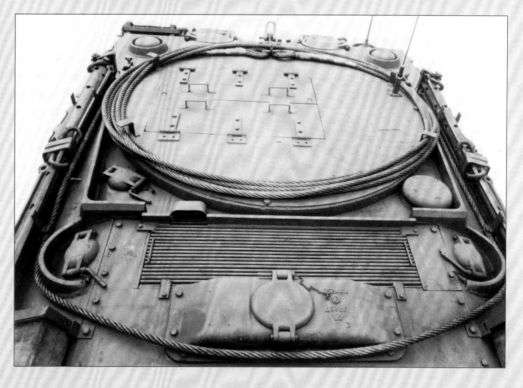

were rather seldom seen overseas: photographs of these vehicles in Normandy are scarce. Actually, in action, some Tank Brigades were equipped with Sherman ARVs instead.

In fact, the Sherman tank was used as the main basis for developing armoured recovery vehicles. The US Army had already designed its own version: the M32 had even been preceded in September 1942 by the M31 on a M3 Grant chassis. The M32 would be delivered in small number to the British Army, who was developing its own equipment to better suit its needs. The Sherman ARV Mark I was built in 1943 and again used the principle of a turretless combat tank: the turret ring aperture was plugged by an armour plate including a double rectangular hatch. The hull machine-gun was retained, and a twin-Bren mount could be fitted for close and antiaircraft defence. Both

flanks of the hull were festooned with stowed equipment, including the booms of a jib crane with a maximum 3360kg lifting capacity, which could be installed at the front. This crane was used to lift major assemblies such as power trains and engines, but not for recovery. For the latter task, the Sherman ARV I had a rear swivelling type connector, together with towing eyes for tow bars adapted to different types of vehicles. No winch was provided, a failing to be corrected on the Sherman ARV II, which was also equipped with a fixed turret and a dummy gun, and with a broad spade at the rear to increase the towing capabilities of the jib crane fitted on the rear engine deck. This crane was more powerful than the front one which was nevertheless retained. However, the Mark II appeared rather late in the fighting units, and does not seem to have been available in Normandy.

(Tank Museum 2785/D2)

In spite of the Sherman ARV being successful, and in order first, to standardize the recovery vehicles with the tanks they were to work with, and second, to ease the management of spare parts, an ARV was developed on the Centaur, and particularly on the Cromwell chassis. As usual, the turret was removed, and the standard jib crane on booms could be installed on the front. Either because its qualities as recovery vehicle were questionable, or because the production of Sherman ARVs was sufficient, the Cromwell ARV was rarely delivered to Cromwell-equipped units (such as 7th Arm.Div.) witness wartime photographs. The number of ARVs really present in fighting units is very difficult to ascertain, since although they were always crewed by the Royal Electrical and Mechanical Engineers, they were distributed according to the decision of the officer in command, among infantry or armoured brigades workshops, and even, as shown by the tactical signs seen on wartime photographs, among Light Aid Detachments or armoured regiments. The different armoured recovery vehicles never saw as widespread use in the Commonwealth Armies as in the US Army for example, for excellent British-made Scammel tractors, or even similar American heavy trucks (such as the Ward La France) were preferred.

An armoured vehicle to transport a Scissors bridge was designed from 1939 onwards on Mk V Light Tank, then A10 chassis, but production was finally scheduled on the more recent Covenanter The Scissors bridge, made up of two linked and folded halves, wa installed on a turretless chassis, one tip being fastened at the tank front. A long threaded axle, instead of the usual hydraulic device was used to first raise the bridge vertically, and then to unfold both spans before laying them down on the ground. The tank engine provided the power required via a transmission axle and an auxi liary gear box. Moreover, the bridge could be easily recovered and put back on the tank, when fixed crossing means were available The crewmen remained under shelter while the bridge was laid, bu they had to come out to recover it. The 5-ton bridging capacity of the Mk V was increased to 24 tons, with a total span of 7,90m From 1941, the Valentine was rapidly substituted for the Cove nanter chassis to install the conversion sets produced by Southern Railway near Southampton: choosing a new tank was surprising at that time, but was later justified when the Valentine was decla

**The recovery variant of the Cromwell was more "confidential" than its Sherman counterpart, the reason being probably the relative rarity of the basic tank (five regiments in Normandy), but also the less powerful Merlin engine, at least for a machine intended to tow another armoured vehicle The silhouette was on the other hand very low without the turret. (Tan Museum 473/B4**

*Left.*
The look of the Sherman ARV Mk II was much more "professional", with carefully planned stowage racks and fittings. The dummy gun was fitted to make the enemy believe that the recovery tank was more dangerous than it seemed: only the hull machine-gun was retained, unlike the American M32 which was also armed with a mortar.
*(Tank Museum 2785/D2)*

*Right.* The Valentine Scissors was a light and compact bridgelayer, yet with a crossing capacity rated at 9m. It was most often used within the leading units to set up the required crossing sites as fast as possible. The roller that can be seen at the front rested on the ground when the bridge was unfolded. *(DR)*

*Bottom.* The bridge carried by the Churchill Bridgelayer was more efficient than the Valentine Scissors, since it enabled the crossing of class 40 tanks (thus of the Churchill), and suppressed the weak point resulting from the central connection. The system was further improved, and two minutes were just enough to set up a strong bridge on a 10m-wide ditch.
*(Tank Museum 342/H3)*

...red obsolete, as the chassis then became available in large numbers. The final bridging capacities reached a maximum of 9 meters (crossing) and 30 tons, thus making it possible to take almost every tank, including Shermans, but not the Churchill. First used successfully in Italy, the Valentine Scissors bridge was in service in every British, as well as Polish and Canadian, armoured unit for the Normandy campaign. The three bridgelayers normally assigned to the armoured brigade HQ were often dispatched in forward units depending on needs, in order to provide fast and light bridging equipment.

In spite of its 30-ton capacity, the Valentine Scissors was still a light bridge. Late in 1942, the Experimental Bridging Establishment at Christchurch developed a bridgelayer prototype using a Churchill turretless chassis. The Churchill was chosen for its off-road automotive qualities and because it was the longest and heaviest tank in the British arsenal. On top of the hull it carried a N°2 bridge, 11,15m long and rated at 40-ton capacity, and was consequently lightened, by reducing the armour for instance. A boom was fixed to the middle of the bridge on one side, and to the tank front on the other side. One extre-

mity was fitted with two wheels resting on the ground during the launching cycle, which was performed through a hydraulic mechanism, linked to the Churchill's engine, and operating an enormous jack. The launching cycle took only one minute and 35 seconds, and it was hardly longer to pick up the bridge if necessary. Nicknamed Jumbo, the Churchill Bridgelayer had a crew of three (tank commander, driver and radio operator). 200 were required in 1943, but production was limited to 64 machines by mid-1944. Regarded as Royal Armoured Corps, and not Royal Engineers, equipment, it was delivered on a three-tank basis per armoured brigade, as a priority to Churchill-equipped units.

The Churchill Ark was not really a bridgelayer: it was a bridge on itself... The Octopus was its ancestor, which was intended for crossing minefields and consisted of two ramps fitted out as tracks extensions on a worn-out and turretless Churchill chassis. The tank had to drive among mines until it blew up on one of them and so came to a standstill: it then released the ramps, and a second Octopus climbed on top of, and over, it, riding on the ramps and tracks, to go on further until it met the same fate as the first vehicle, and so on. In addition to the fact that the system was hazardous

115

and very difficult to work with, the Octopus was above all an obvious danger for the crew, even with added armour plates, since an immobilized tank was an easy prey for antitank guns. It was logically abandoned, but was later diverted for another use in Italy, where crossing equipments were required to fill up the many antitank ditches of the successive German lines of defence. Renamed Ark, for its remote likeness to the Ark Royal aircraft carrier, this specialized tank was developed by local workshops. Yet, similar equipment had already been experimented with in Great-Britain before the war.

With the approaching invasion of France, 79th Arm.Div. adopted the idea and designed its own Ark I: very similar to its Italian cousin, it featured passages on the tracks, and also carried a fascine because it was intended for crossing the high seawalls. The technique was to drop a fascine at the wall base, to use it to reach the top of the wall with the upper ramps, and then to release the lower ramps. Another tank then climbed up on the ramps and the passages fitted with transversal slats above the tracks, and crossed the wall. Fifty Churchill Mk II and IV chassis were converted in 1943-44 by the Royal and Electrical Mechanical Engineers (REME) and MG Car Company, the superstructures being manufactured by TC Jones & Co.

After the landings on the beaches, where the Churchill Ark I had proved useful, needs changed in the course of the campaign: wide bomb craters or antitank ditches had now to be crossed. On the Ark II prototype designed by 79th Arm.Div., the ramps were thus lengthened to 3,80m each, and those on the left side were also widened so that they could take lighter or unarmoured vehicles. Crossing capacity was now 14,33m, instead of 8,30m for the Ark I. Once again, 50 conversions were ordered from a firm in Bolton, and were rapidly fitted by the REME in units. Some vehicles were thus available soon after the Normandy landings, and their use, although

**A Churchill Ark II is negotiating a bend on a leafy lane in Normandy: obviously, adding longer ramps to the front and rear dramatically increased the Churchill Ark's crossing capacities, but the vehicle also became very cumbersome and difficult to drive. The inner extension for light vehicles can be seen on the right ramps.** *(Tank Museum 2118/B4)*

**The Churchill Ark I in the course of development by 79th Arm.Div.: resting on a fascine, the vehicle is climbing up along the wall that had to be crossed and will stop at a sufficient angle to enable the following tank to mount on the ramps above the tracks. However, this variant was to be improved, since the rear ramps were obviously too short.** *(Tank Museum 350/B4)*

frequent, seems to have been completely satisfactory, since almost no commentary on the Churchill Ark I or II was kept in the division's war diary: it must be said that this kind of vehicle was put at the disposal of the units who asked for it, and was not used on a Squadron or even Troop basis.

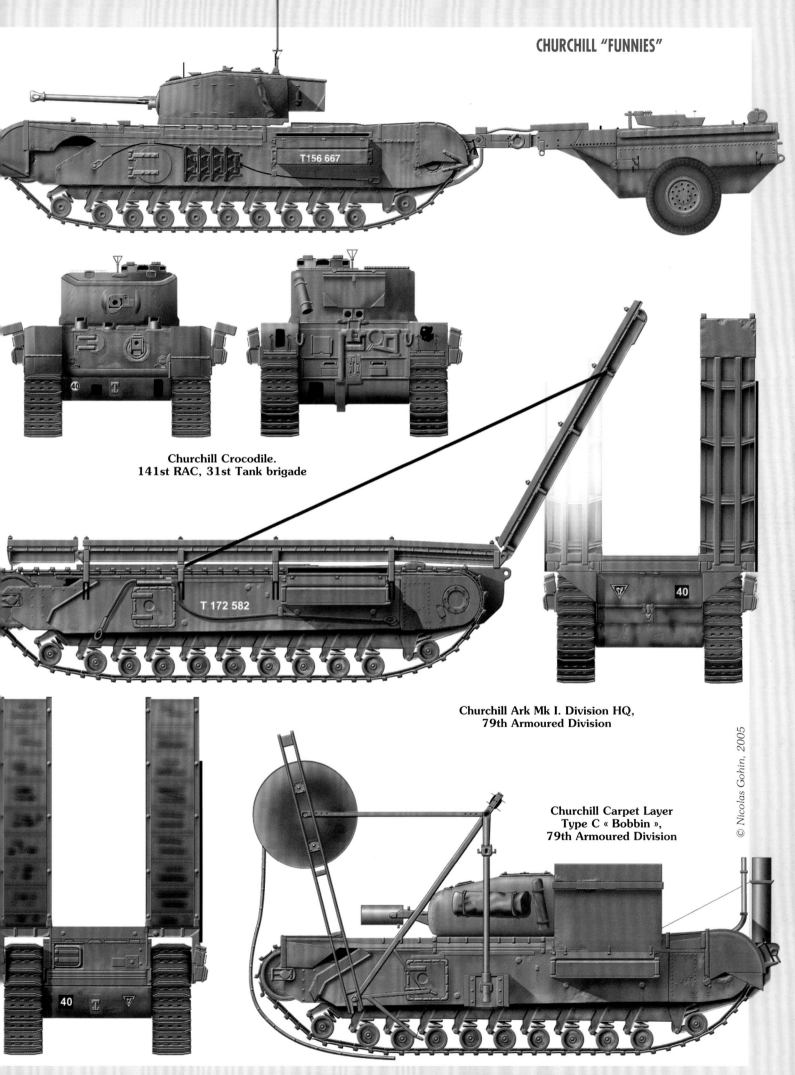

T156 667

Churchill Crocodile.
141st RAC, 31st Tank brigade

T 172 582

Churchill Ark Mk I. Division HQ,
79th Armoured Division

Churchill Carpet Layer
Type C « Bobbin »,
79th Armoured Division

© Nicolas Gohin, 2005

# ANTI-AIRCRAFT TANKS

**I**N SEPTEMBER 1941, **the Royal Artillery asked for a self-propelled anti-aircraft gun consisting of a 40-mm Bofors on a tank chassis.**

The first prototype designed by Morris Motors used an early production Crusader chassis, and was composed of the 40-mm gun simply mounted on the top of the tank, and protected by thin armour plates forming a complex superstructure. Expected protection was limited, and during tests in March 1943, the assembly turned out to be too fragile, for it fell to pieces when the vehicle was used off-road. The Department of Tank Design corrected this flaw in July 1943 on a second prototype, on which armour was reduced and simplified to limit weight, and which consisted now of a open-top, four-sided truncated structure directly mounted on the turret ring. The Crusader III AA Mk I on Crusader Mk III chassis soon entered production. It used a hydraulic mechanism for elevation and rotation, powered by a 2-cylinder 250 cc Enfield engine. The three-man crew just included driver, tank commander/gunner and loader/radio operator; 150 high-explosive and 40 armour-piercing rounds were carried. The vehicle proved to be unsatisfactory, the gun being unable to rotate rapidly enough to follow low flying and moving targets. Moreover, rotating the turret was impossible on uneven ground. An order was nevertheless put in for 250 vehicles, most of them being assigned to Royal Artillery anti-aircraft units, but the Crusader III AA Mk I was seldom seen on the battlefield.

In 1942, the Royal Armoured Corps was also interested in an anti-aircraft tank, and Morris Motors was also entrusted with its development. Vickers Mk VI Light Tanks armed with four .303 machine-guns already existed, but they were too tiny and their armament lacked power and range. The Oerlikon 20-mm gun with its high rate of fire of 450 rounds per minute seemed to be the right candidate for an anti-aircraft weapon. In June 1943, Morris Motors delivered the first Crusader III AA Mk II prototype, which included a low profile multisided turret sheltering two Oerlikon 20-mm guns fed with 60 rounds drum-magazines, and mounted on the Crusader turret ring. The four crew members (driver, two loaders, and commander/gunner) were a bit cramped, especially in the turret. Six hundred rounds of ammunition were carried, but the limited room allowed only five or six drum-magazines to be stored inside the tank, and they had to be re-loaded by hand when empty... The turret featured a very rapid elevation and rotation system, coupled to the tank engine. A bit too rapid actually, for the tests revealed that the rotating turret overshot the moving targets, requiring limitation of the rotating speed to 10 degrees per second.

A slightly larger turret was adopted for the Crusader III AA Mk III, which offered in addition better protection for the gunner. A little more room was also saved by moving the N°19 radio set from the turret to the driver's left, this crewman thus becoming radio-operator. The rotation system working with the tank engine power meant that the latter had to be kept running, but firing on the move was out of the question: aiming became even less accurate, and the Mk II inherited from its predecessor a marked difficulty in rotating the turret when the vehicle was on uneven ground. In spite of a questionable efficiency in combat, about 600 Crusaders III Mk II/III were built and delivered to armoured units, at the rate of two vehicles per armoured division HQ, two per armoured brigade HQ, and six per armoured regiment HQ (that mean 22 for a division and 20 for a brigade, all the same). This AFV was

*Above.* **The Crusader III AA Mk II was equipped with a better protected turret including raised armour for the gunner. Photographed soon after D-Day, this tank belonged to Staffordshire Yeomanry (27th Arm.Brig.): the sea-horse, which was the unit insignia, is visible on the right stowage box, and the tactical sign 52 is present on the antenna socket.** *(Tank Museum 1843/B6)*

*Left.* **The first turret model, identifying a Crusader III AA Mk II, was rather simple but afforded little protection for the gunner (acting as tank commander) in combat. The large insignia of Camp Lulworth indicates that this tank is undergoing trials (probably firing tests).** *(Tank Museum 1843/B3)*

*Below.*
**Only the more modern chassis, of which the hull machine-gun hole is plugged, distinguished the Centaur AA Mk II from its Crusader predecessor, the turret remaining unchanged. The shifted position of the two guns is clearly visible on this view: one of the Oerlikon is in full recoil position, because the guns fired in turn and not together.** *(Tank Museum 1843/A2)*

used for the first time in Normandy, mainly in the Mk III version, but progressively disappeared when the anti-aircraft units were disbanded from July 1944 onwards, because of the air-supremacy and the need to make good the losses in tank crews. The Crusader III Mk II/III still appeared in the 1945 organization charts, proving that some were retained in units: they were sometimes used as artillery observation vehicles, or successfully against ground targets.

Mention must be made of other similar anti-aircraft tanks on the Centaur chassis: Centaur AA Mk I (with the Crusader AA Mk II turret), and Mk II (with the Crusader Mk III turret). But production figures are unknown, and they do not seem to have been used in combat in Normandy, if wartime photographs can be considered as proof. Little is known, bar a photograph, about the triple-mount of superposed Oerlikon guns fitted on a simple platform on the top of a turretless Crusader chassis

*(Tank Museum 1843/A2)*

# SHERMAN CRAB

**T**HE NEED FOR A MINE-CLEARING TANK appeared urgent during the battles in North Africa, where the Germans had laid immense minefields: the mine was a passive and invisible weapon, which could be unearthed and defused by hand only.

Major Du Toit, a South African officer, took part with AEC in the development of the Flail, a rotating drum fitted with heavy chains which enabled mines to be detonated from an armoured vehicle. This system required an auxiliary engine often located on the side of a Matilda tank, as on the Scorpion or Baron. With the prospect of the Allied landings in France, the army required a less bulky machine that could be shipped in an LCT tank transporter. Choosing a Sherman V as basis, Samuel Butler Ltd suppressed the auxiliary engine by taking the power to rotate the flail directly from the sprocket wheels. The Pram Scorpion prototype was ready in May 1943, but it was very heavy (4.5 tons more than the gun tank) and its rotating system was complicated and fragile: linked to each sprocket, it suffered from the different track speeds in turns, and the drum had to be halved.

Another project in development used the Scorpion system on a Sherman V, the engine replacing the turret: the arms supporting the drum were fitted with hydraulic jacks allowing the flail to be raised in order to provide clearance in front of the vehicle and make it less cumbersome. The Marquis prototype was soon after tested, but was rejected for want of main armament. AEC resumed the Pram Scorpion development, retained the hydraulic arms of the Marquis, and completed in September 1943 the Sherman Crab design: the rotation was now directly coupled with the tank engine through cogwheels, a Cardan joint and a transmission shaft fastened to the hull right side. After trials, the arms were strengthened for the mass production of the Sherman Crab Mk I from October 1943 onwards, and the drum ends were equipped with wire-cutters against barbed wire. A 300-example order was initiated in November, to be completed by March 1944. Several accessories were introduced during

*This Crab is ready to take action and shows the 43 heavy chains, their ends fitted with a weight to increase the centrifugal effect and impact on the ground. Under the drum, and behind a tube which was part of the system's framework, can be seen a sheet metal plate which protected the tank's front from stones and splinters. (RR)*

production: a gyroscope and a compass were fitted in the turret, to help the tank commander find his way through the dust raised by the flail. The vehicles following the Crab in action were helped by guiding lights fitted to poles at the tank's rear. Finally, the track cleared of mines was delimited with flags or lights on markers which were automatically laid down by a system located in a box on each side of the rear hull.

Tests went on with the first models and revealed that mine clearing was less effective on very uneven terrain, the mines being hidden by the ground relief. A system of floating arms, with counterweights and an upper blocking device so that the drum was not raised too high, was tested on a Sherman Marquis: it appeared that at constant speed, the mine-clearing height (about 1,30m) naturally adapted to the ground relief, thanks to the double effect of the rotating drum and the chains' impact. 90% of the mines, instead of 60% with fixed arms, could be destroyed. This modification gave birth to the Crab Mk II which was produced from March 1944 onwards. However, a difficulty remained on high-gradient slopes: the flail rotating speed decreased with that of the engine when climbing up, and increased when going down, thus provoking more mine-clearing failures. The problem was solved by AEC through the fitting of an intermediate transmission box between the engine and the flail, allowing a constant rotating speed. Unfortunately, this device was not available in Normandy, and was only series-produced in February 1945,

In action, the Sherman Crab had to advance in first gear at a constant speed (about 1 1/2 per hour), all hatches closed down and turret to the rear. Clearing a 2,75m-wide path, it was often used in pairs with a second Flail following in a staggered position to get a

*Right. In action, the Crabs projected dirt, dust and stones all around them. This photograph has been taken during trials, for in combat it was prescribed to set the drum in motion with the turret rotated to the rear, otherwise the flying debris could shatter the periscope glass, damage the gun sight or else obstruct the barrel. (Tank Museum 2121/C5)*

passable track for any vehicle. The flail lost efficiency on soft or very hard ground. The Crab was moreover only valuable to clear already identified minefields, not to search for them: it was too slow, and destroyed the ground surface, damaging its own equipment. Actually, as clearing went by, the 43 chains were destroyed one after the other with each explosion, and the Crab was less and less effective: its work often ended when it blew up on a mine itself! The three regiments of 30th Arm.Brig. (79th Arm.Div.) were issued with Crabs for the Normandy campaign, and they saw action as early as D-Day. They were thereafter in constant demand for every offensive, on account of their effectiveness. The Crab could furthermore be used as gun tank when its flail was damaged since it retained its 75-mm gun, only the .30 hull machine-gun being deleted.

*Top.* **Part of the system of jacks, cogwheels and transmission shafts setting the drum in motion thanks to the tank engine power. The apparatus seems both sophisticated, considering the great number of mechanical parts, and rudimentary: it had to be particularly strong to stand the mines destructive power.**
*(Tank Museum 2121/B4)*

*Right.* **Close view on the flail extremity: the chains are in travelling position, wound around the drum. The wire-cutter is clearly visible, as well as the skirt under the supporting arm which was there to prevent dirt and stones from being thrown up to the tank top or to the running gear and sprocket wheels.**
*(Tank Museum 2121/B3)*

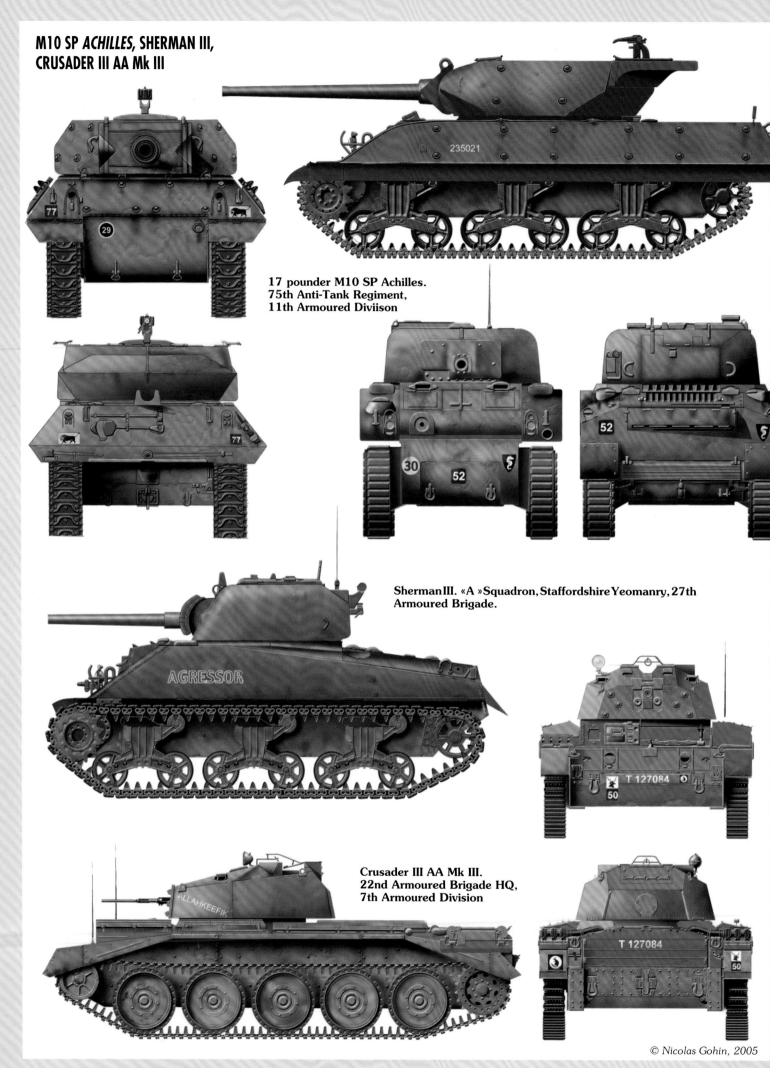

# M10 SP *ACHILLES,* SHERMAN III, CRUSADER III AA Mk III

17 pounder M10 SP Achilles.
75th Anti-Tank Regiment,
11th Armoured Diviison

Sherman III. «A »Squadron, Staffordshire Yeomanry, 27th
Armoured Brigade.

Crusader III AA Mk III.
22nd Armoured Brigade HQ,
7th Armoured Division

© Nicolas Gohin, 2005

Duplex Drive on Sherman V chassis (see the spaced bogies): even folded down, the flotation screen was cumbersome, but allowed the turret armament (75-mm gun and coaxial machine-gun) to be used quickly.
The rod on the turret is part of the platform and was used as a handle by the tank commander when steering the vehicle.
*(RR)*

# SHERMAN DUPLEX DRIVE

**W**HEN THE PLANS TO INVADE NORTH-WEST EUROPE became more precise, a crucial question was raised: how could armour support be brought to the first assault waves to land? The landings in North Africa, Sicily and Italy had shown that the Landing Craft Tank could carry nine tanks indeed, but was heavy and offered a huge target.

Moreover, if the first tank in the row was hit, it prevented any other tank from getting ashore. One solution would have been to use LCMs in great number, but they could only take a single tank at anyone time. The problem was solved by making these tanks float... Nicholas Straussler, a Hungarian by birth, had designed a simple system of inflatable canvas skirts and metal framework which allowed a tank to float, according to the Archimedes principle: first tested on a Tetrarch light tank, it was then successfully adjusted to a 16-ton Valentine. Nicknamed Duplex Drive (for it also used a screw to swim), it was series-produced from March 1943 onwards, and began to be issued to 27th Arm. Brig. The first trials were encouraging, the flotation screen withstood small arms fire, and a device named Belch, vaporizing water against flamethrower jets, was not even necessary since the tank could swim through flames without difficulty when immersed.

However, when the 79th Arm.Div. was created to regroup all specialised armoured vehicles under development, its commander, General Hobart, deemed that the Valentine was obsolete and poorly armed, and consequently asked for the Duplex Dive system to be designed for the most available combat tank, the Sherman. But this medium tank weighed 30 tons, twice as much as the Valentine. The Straussler system was nevertheless adapted successfully by heightening the screen: the water displacement

**The DD's height out of water was impressive: nearly 4 meters! A ladder was indispensable to climb in the tank, but in general the screen was inflated in the LCT, when the crew was aboard. Note the typical idler wheel, which is however devoid here of its usual sprocket plates, similar to the front sprocket wheels.**
*(Tank Museum 2198/B5)*

(Tank Museum 2198/A3)

*Above.* **The most perilous stage in the use of the Sherman DD probably was the launching: it was essential not to take too much water in, and to work smoothly in order not to damage the flotation screen. Once in water, only a meter of canvas or so revealed the presence of the DD, which became a very difficult target to hit.**

*Left.* **On this rear view may be seen, behind the turret, the platform on which the tank commander stood to steer the Duplex Drive when afloat. The barely visible running gear indicates that it is a Sherman II or III conversion. The propellers are in the raised position.** (Tank Museum 2198/A3)

*Bottom.* **A close view on the propulsion system shows the two three-bladed screws allowing the DD to swim in water, but which could be raised once on the ground. Part of the steering system can also be seen, as well as one valve of the flotation screen.** (Tank Museum 342/E3)

was then greater, and the vehicle was even more stable in water. Propulsion was by means of two three-bladed screws, which were folded up when the tank was on the ground, and which were linked to the rear idler wheel through a transmission shaft. The maximum speed was only 5,5 miles per hour on water, and the machine was driven by the tank commander standing on a small platform fitted to the turret, and operating a simple removable tiller on the engine deck.

The rubberized canvas screen was three times thicker on the lower sections, and was fastened on steel decking around the tank hull. It was composed of 36 tubular airtight pillars, made rigid by three horizontal frames, an internal metal framework,

and 13 hinged struts. A hydraulic device enabled the struts to be disconnected to fold down the screen. Two forward compressed air cylinders provided the inflation, and an electric bilge pump was fitted to deal with possible leakages. The system was light, not too cumbersome, but did not allow the hull machinegun to be used: it was often cut out after use, the steel decking even being twisted to fit the .30 back. When the screen was inflated, the height reached 3,96m off the ground, but only about 1meter in water. To get ashore on a beach, the method was to first fold down the screen at the front, to free the turret field of fire, while the rear was partly raised to protect the engine deck from the coming tide.

The training on Sherman DD tanks was particularly intensive, with a total of 30 000 launches from beaches or landing craft. The crews were also trained to use the rudimentary submarine apparatus they were issued with in case of capsizing. A successful demonstration of the Sherman DD capabilities was undertaken in January 1944 in the presence of Eisenhower, who requested a production increase. The capacities in Great-Britain being limited, production was quickly initiated in the USA too. Five British, as well as two Canadian and three American armoured regiments were converted to Sherman DDs. The British Army put an informal order for 500 examples, but the exact production figures are unknown. The British used mainly M4A4 and M4A1 chassis (Sherman V and II), but also some M4A2. The Sherman DD equipped two out of three regiments in the two first-wave armoured brigades on D-Day (8th and 27th Arm.Brig.), but these regiments were also operating standard 75-mm Shermans, and Fireflies, which landed normally thanks to LCTs once the beaches were seized.

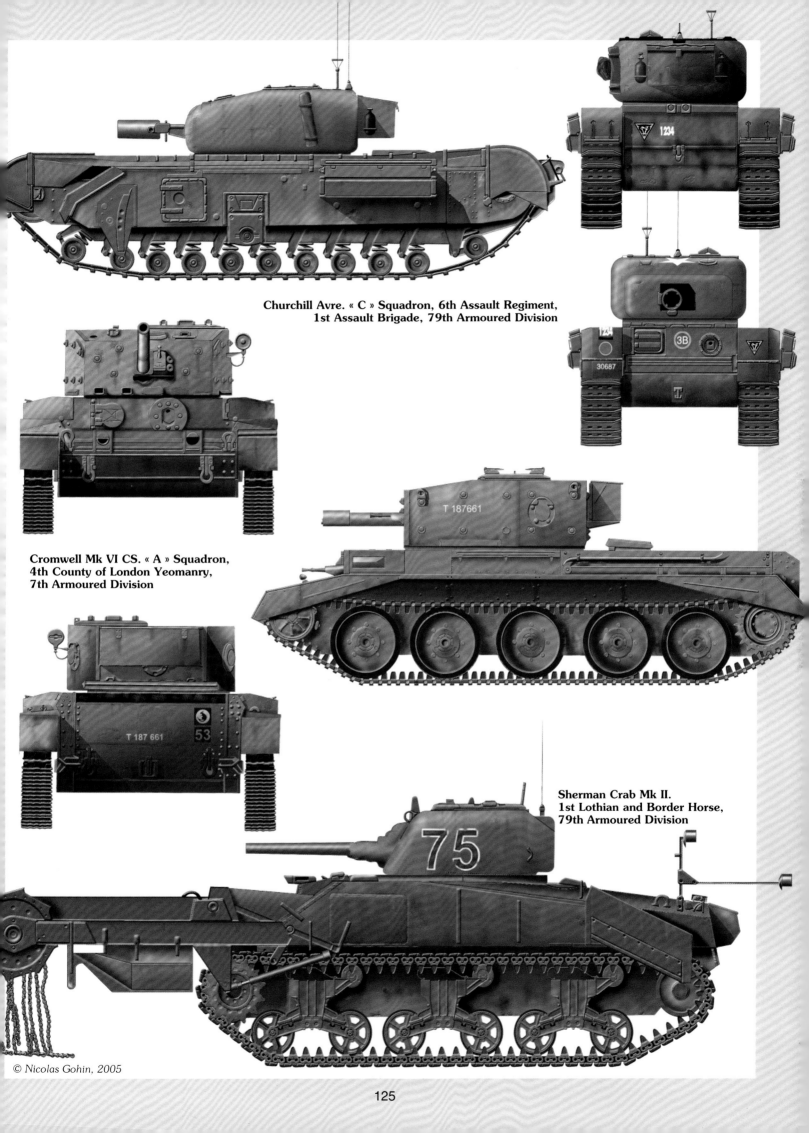

Churchill Avre. « C » Squadron, 6th Assault Regiment,
1st Assault Brigade, 79th Armoured Division

Cromwell Mk VI CS. « A » Squadron,
4th County of London Yeomanry,
7th Armoured Division

T 187661

T 187 661   53

Sherman Crab Mk II.
1st Lothian and Border Horse,
79th Armoured Division

75

1234

3B

30687

© Nicolas Gohin, 2005

# CHURCHILL AVRE

**F**OLLOWING THE RAID ON DIEPPE IN AUGUST 1942, the British Army noticed that the Canadian Churchill tanks brought onto the beaches in support of the assault force had been unable to find a way inland, for they had been blocked by ditches and antitank walls.

A Royal Canadian Engineers officer, Lieutenant Denovan, who was working for the "special equipment" branch of the Department of Tank Design, suggested that an engineer's tank on the Churchill basis should be developed. The latter was chosen for particular qualities: it was heavily armoured and equipped with lateral hatches, also featuring sufficient inner room to accommodate a lot of special equipment, and good cross-country capabilities. Thus, a prototype was proposed by the 1st Canadian Mechanical Engineers Company by the end of 1942.

During the same period, the Royal Armoured Corps asked for a tank for the Engineers, as standard equipment in every armoured unit. No main armament was deemed necessary, but trials soon revealed that a single tank offered insufficient protection to the engineers if they had to work outside, laying demolition charges by hand for instance. From Colonel Blacker, inventor of the Spigot mortar for the Home Guard, was ordered a lightened version of this weapon to fit in the Churchill turret. After many tests, he proposed the calibre 290-mm Petard, firing a 13kg explosive or smoke charge, the whole ammunition weighing 20kg. The recoil problem was solved by mounting a very strong spring, also used to cock the mortar for the next shot. The charge was nicknamed "Flying Dustbin" because of its shape, and had a maximum range of 200m, but the effective range did not exceed 50m. In return, its effect was devastating. The major flaw was that the weapon could only be loaded from the outside of the tank: it was "broken" like a shotgun but by pivoting upwards. The radio-operator then had to do the job, through a special sliding hatch above his seat, under enemy fire. Twenty-six rounds were carried for the Petard, and the two Besa machine-guns were retained for close defence.

One of the first converted Churchill AVRE photographed in England is still equipped with the early track pattern, rarely seen in combat. Spare track links are fastened on the hull front and turret sides, again an unusual practice. *(Tank Museum)*

When the development of all the special armoured vehicles to be used for the Normandy landings was entrusted to the 79th Arm.Div. in 1943, this unit merged the two projects to create the AVRE (Armoured Vehicle, Royal Engineers). Churchill Mk Is and IVs with cast turret, and a few Mk IIIs with welded turret, were used by the Royal Electrical and Mechanical Engineers and then MG Cars in Abington to produce the 700 conversions that had been ordered. The fighting compartment was entirely rearranged to accommodate demolition charges and accessories, as well as a crew of five or six, depending on the missions. The AVRE weighed 38 tons and had a maximum speed of 16 miles per hour, for a range of about 11,5 miles. It was a very adaptable machine, for it was fitted, on each side of the hull, with universal supports that could receive a number of special devices.

Indeed, although the AVRE was a very powerful demolition machine by itself, thanks to its Petard, it was mainly used to create variants adapted to the Engineers' missions. Thus in particular, several devices were studied to carry explosives charges intended for destroying antitank walls or beaches obstacles, on frames of various shapes at the front of the tank. Carrot, Onion and Goat variants were thoroughly tested, but do not seem to have been used in combat. On the other hand, one of the first operational conversions was very simple: the AVRE Fascine carried one of these rolls of wood stakes, previously used in 1917, which made it possible to fill up a trench, a ditch or a crater. In its modern version, the fascine was strengthened with metal pipe sections and carried on an angled framework attached to the front of the tank (placing it on the rear would have been much more practical, but the wood caught fire when touching the exhaust pipes). A quick-release mechanism was used from the inside to drop the fascine. The problem with this huge bundle of sticks was that it totally obscured the view of the entire crew, so that the commander had to stand on the top of the turret, and even clutch the fascine, to direct the driver from there!

Bridge laying tanks already existed in the British Army's arsenal, but they were sophisticated, costly, and scattered among the armoured units. The 79th Arm.Div. needed simpler crossing means which could

*Above.* **The rear of the same vehicle shows the turret stowage box with asymmetrical bevelled indentations and the spare bogies carried on top of the rear mudguards: the first AVREs that landed on D-Day were equipped in this way, but the latter arrangement seems to have been abandoned later.** *(Tank Museum)*

*Right to left.* **A close-up of the Petard reveals the simplicity of construction: the short barrel was fitted with four inner rails to guide the explosive charge. The fact that the weapon was loaded from the radio operator hatch involved that the turret had to be in 12 o'clock position for this operation, thus slowing down the rate of fire.** *(Tank Museum 124/C5)*

*Below.* **The reinforcing pipe sections lightening the fascine can be seen on this AVRE in training. The bust of the tank commander can also be made out just above the huge bundle of sticks, he is directing the driver, who is almost blinded by the fascine and its releasing system, by intercom.** *(Tank Museum 334/F6)*

**The rudimentary charge for the Petard weighed 20kg, and reloading required a good deal of physical strength from the radio/machine-gunner who had to lift it by hand from his hatch, then slip it into the barrel, the whole operation taking often place under enemy fire!** *(Tank Museum124/C6)*

be left in place for a long time, and so would not require any launching and recovery system. The choice fell on a shortened version (9,15m instead of 10,35m) of the Small Box Girder Bridge that had been developed before the war. This bridge was a rather crude assembly of pipes, steel sections and planks, but it was relatively light and very strongly built. It was carried at an angle of about 45 to 60 degrees to the front of the AVRE, thanks to two front fastening points, and cables leading via a boom to a frame on the rear engine deck, which included a small winch and a quick-release device. The bridge was just dropped on the obstacle to be crossed, but putting it in the right place was not so easy. The AVRE SBG was particularly difficult to steer and drive, the front bogies suffered from the added weight,

A lovely illustration of the bulkiness of an SBG bridge when it was transported on an LCT: the handling of the so-equipped AVRE was very awkward on the ground too. On this photographed taken some months prior to D-Day, the tank turret is still only armed with a Besa machine-gun. *(Tank Museum 444/E2)*

and uneven ground was to be avoided. It was also hated by the Navy since the long span of the bridge offered a large area to the wind, and threw the LCTs that were transporting them off balance. The SBG was however successfully used on D-Day, and remained operational for many weeks without problem.

A last variant of the AVRE was designed in a hurry a few weeks before D-Day, when large patches of very loose blue clay were located on the beaches. The Carpet Device, from which a makeshift model had been already used for the Dieppe landing, was fitted at the front of the AVRE and included a large framework supporting a large roll holding a carpet made of coir matting and strengthened with scaffolding tubes. The end of the carpet was tucked under the tracks, and it was reeled off as the AVRE advanced. The carpet was prone to crumple and retract very rapidly, and this problem was partly solved by fitting spring-balanced extensions. Named AVRE Bobbin, this device enabled a track strong enough for a few vehicles and tanks to set be up, even if it did not stand up to a lot of toing and froing and tides.

The AVREs exclusively equipped the three assault regiments of 1st Assault Brigade Royal Engineers, within 79th Arm.Div., and had great success from D-Day onwards, helping British and Canadians pass through the beach obstacles: the distribution of specialised armour in balanced teams, adapted to the missions, was often the key to success. As unit commanders discovered the AVREs' qualities, they demanded them for every operation, and the Squadrons were scattered all along the front, with negative consequences: the situation reduced their efficiency, hampered their control, and exhausted the crews as much as the vehicles. Major General Hobart had to display all his influence and persuasion to limit these nuisances and impose strict regulations on use.

*Left.*
**An AVRE Bobbin is demonstrating the simple method of laying its carpet on the soft sand of a beach. Three models at least of this specialised armoured vehicle existed, depending on the roll size and the fitting of teeth on it to align the carpet with the tracks: the Bobbin seen here is a Mk II.**
*(Tank Museum 413/G3)*

If it were not for the presence of the very compact flame-thrower replacing the hull machine-gun, the front of the Crocodile would be identical to the Churchill Mk VII's: it retained its main and auxiliary turret armament (75-mm gun and coaxial Besa), and could thus go on fighting as gun tank once its trailer was empty or destroyed.
*(Tank Museum 2247/D4)*

# CHURCHILL CROCODILE

THE FIRST REQUESTS BY THE BRITISH ARMY general staff for a flame-throwing tank dated back to 1938, but nothing was undertaken for several years. It was only in 1942 that the project was resumed, first on a Valentine tank chassis using a pressurized nitrogen flame-thrower.

From March 1942 onwards, the Petroleum Warfare Department and the Ministry of Supply controlled the design of a first prototype on Churchill chassis. Three examples of a provisional model, the Churchill Oke, were ready to take part in the Dieppe landing in August, but they proved unsatisfactory, and the development of a mass-produced flame-throwing tank went on. Attempts to include the large fuel tanks and the propellant

bottles inside the vehicle failed, and it was reluctantly decided to use a trailer, as on the Valentine-based tank. The first prototype on a Churchill Mk II chassis was ready at the end of the year and the first tests already showed a maximum range of 180m that was not even hoped for. New tests in early 1943 led to the conversion of six Churchill Mk IVs.

The flame nozzle was located at the front, replacing the Besa hull machine-gun, and the arrangement was advantageous in retaining the main armament (6 pounder or-75 mm gun). The projection mechanism, the tanks and the gas bottles were carried in a large two-wheel trailer, the sides of which were only lightly armoured (14mm) despite its dangerous load, since the added weight of a thicker armour would have limited its manoeuvrability.

**The hinge link between the trailer and the Crocodile was quite sophisticated for it included the pipes bringing the propellant gas and the flammable liquid, but yet it had to be able to stand cross-country movement without the risk of seeing the trailer turn over or jam. The team was then rather cumbersome and tricky to manoeuvre.**
*(Tank Museum 2247/E5)*

As it was designed, the trailer did not hinder too much the tank's movements, even across-country, and could be jettisoned if necessary, when empty or damaged. The load of flammable material and propellant gas allowed for 80 one-second spurts with a practical range of 70 to 110m. The projection mechanism being located in the trailer, only the pipes ran from it and under the tank hull to reach the front compartment. The inflammable liquid was set on fire electrically, and thanks to its consistency, stuck to every object it hit and then penetrated through every chink.

Because of the great success of the new vehicle, an urgent order for 250 examples was put in August 1943, initially on

**A demonstration of the Crocodile's firepower which speaks for itself: it could throw a flaming liquid that stuck to anything it touched up to 110m, and slipped into the slightest crack or flaw of a building or a vehicle. In general, the fate of the men hit by this weapon was death.**
*(RR)*

Churchill Mk VI chassis: as the Crocodile became a priority, it was decided to produce all the new Churchill A22Fs (Mk VII and VIII) with the required arrangements for their conversion to flame-throwing tank by the units workshops. Actually, it was first planned to issue every Churchill-equipped unit with a certain number of Crocodiles. Finally, the flame-throwing tank was only used in special regiments, of which just one was available in Normandy: the 141st Battalion Royal Armoured Corps from 31st Tank Brigade, which would later be incorporated into 79th Arm.Div. On 6 June, only six Crocodiles were to land with the first wave, dispatched in two LCTs one of which was unable to put its load of tanks ashore. Out of the three landed vehicles, one fell into a water hole: there were only two operational Crocodiles left, but no report exists about their use on the beaches.

The Crocodile was not faultless: it was prone to gas and fuel leakages, needing careful control and filling-up of the bottles before each action. With use, the trailer proved vulnerable, with disastrous effects on the tank (and its neighbourhood) when directly hit. Crocodiles also brewed up when hit near the flame nozzle itself, on the hull front. But it was a terrifying, formidable and effective weapon: vehicles, tanks, buildings, bunkers were all vulnerable to its flaming jets, and the soldiers' death was dreadful. It was therefore an important means of dissuasion and persuasion, and many surrenders occurred after a simple demonstration of the Crocodile's firepower. On the other hand, the vehicle was hated by the enemy and with experience the Germans took them as primary targets, especially trying to hit the trailer. It has also been reported that Crocodile crews were executed on the spot after their capture, with at least one confirmed occurrence: that of Lieutenant Harvey and his men from A Squadron, The Buffs, on the Caen – Tilly-sur-Seulles road in mid-July 1944.

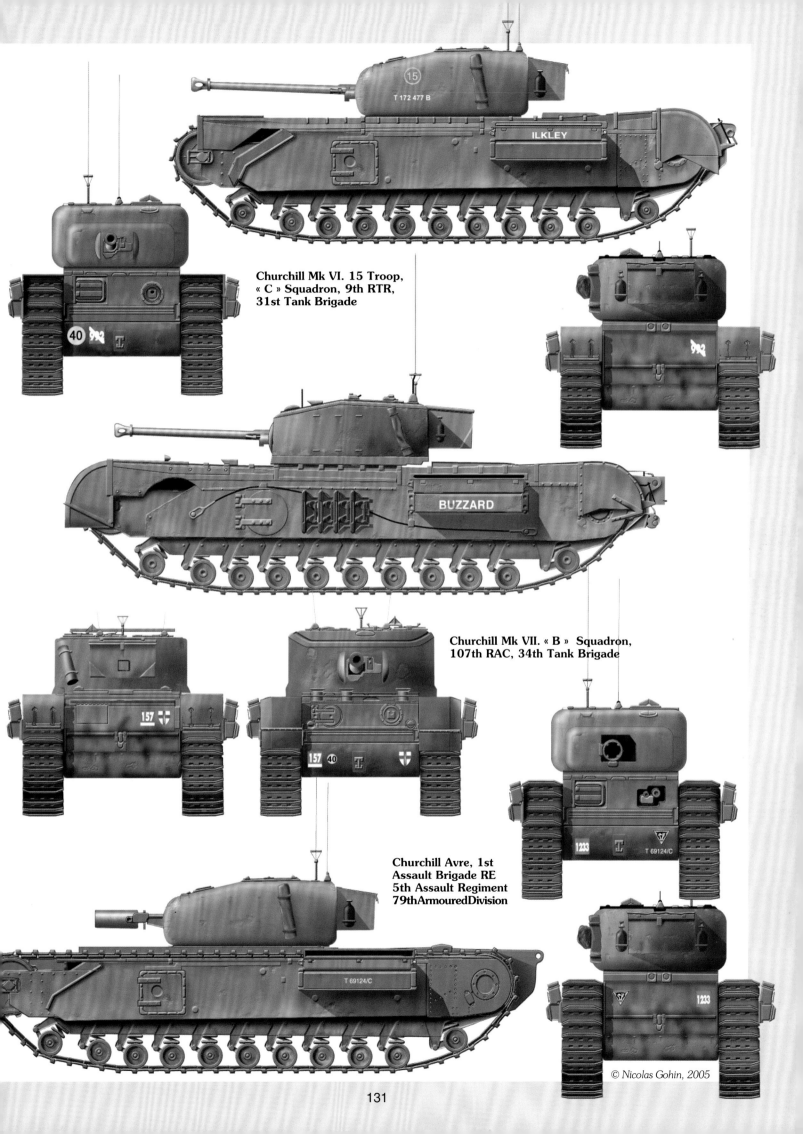

Churchill Mk VI. 15 Troop,
« C » Squadron, 9th RTR,
31st Tank Brigade

Churchill Mk VII. « B » Squadron,
107th RAC, 34th Tank Brigade

Churchill Avre, 1st
Assault Brigade RE
5th Assault Regiment
79thArmouredDivision

© Nicolas Gohin, 2005

# Tactics, organisation, results

High hedgerows, small fields, orchards: the Norman bocage was a nasty surprise for the British tank crews. On 4 August, Sherman II DDs are advancing near Ondefontaine; they belong to 8th Arm.Brig., which was the only unit to be still equipped with DDs after the disbandment of 27th Arm.Brig. Note the circle of a C Squadron on the turret left front, with an almost erased number 2 in its centre. (IWM B8588)

**T**HE BRITISH ARMOURED FORCES landed in Normandy with a long past of won or lost battles since 1939.

If the Battle of France had not been distinguished by the massive use of armour on the British side, the fighting in North Africa had in return allowed, and prescribed, radical modifications in the tactics regarding the use of tanks. Great-Britain entering the war still retained the concept inherited from the First World War of Infantry tanks and Cruiser tanks. This distinct separation between the two roles had given birth to many tanks of which very few were successful: Covenanter, Crusader, Valentine… The warfare experience against the Afrika Korps, which had made use of the Blitzkrieg by adapting to the very particular desert terrain, had reduced but not suppressed the difference between Infantry and Cruiser tanks. In spite of massive deliveries of American Shermans from 1942 onwards, which represented at that time a good compromise between mobility, armament and armour so that it was suitable for both missions, the British had continued to develop more specialised tanks, of which the last representatives were well present in Normandy: the Churchill and the Cromwell. The Churchill tank, very well protected but slow, had seen its armament progressively improved up to the 75-mm gun, while the Cromwell, the last of the Cruisers, had become heavier because of improved armour but without losing its mobility.

The distribution of Churchills, Cromwells and Shermans in infantry support, reconnaissance or more "general-use" units could have conferred a positive tactical advantage to the British, if the pre-war theories had still been really valid. Unfortunately, the Second World War had seen the development of a multipurpose and universal tank concept that David Fletcher has perfectly analysed in his book "The Universal Tank". Sherman and Panzer IV, the most widespread medium tanks in the Allied and German armies, were fit for infantry support as well as for antitank fighting, in attack as well as in defence. Besides these important nuances regarding the tank's use and nature, the British armoured forces had generalized, if not in theory, at least in practice, tactics that had been learnt during three years of desert warfare. But the tank fighting in North Africa had been characterized by speed, fluidity, and the importance of by-passing, encircling and large-scale movements. Even in the participants' opinion, desert warfare rather seemed like a naval battle, because of its vast movement and far-reaching field of vision.

The campaigns in Sicily and Italy had brought little change to this conception: Sicily, and to a lesser extent the south of Italy, recalled certain aspects of the desert, but the country was closer, hillier, and the many towns and villages should have implemented the tactical changes to be forecast. However, the battles in Sicily and Italy, up to early-1944, had been above all an infantry and artillery affair, and defence had been very scattered. The tanks had only played a minor part, often in infantry support, for the very reason that the Germans on their side had not had many armoured units in this area. Things had really begun to change in Italy with the Anzio landings, where the tanks could have played a great part in the breakthrough to Rome. But the British had only put a single armoured regiment ashore at Anzio, and the fighting had soon turned into trench warfare: no lesson had thus been learnt from the face-to-face with Tigers and Panthers prior to D-Day.

## Often untried units

In other respects, most of the British armoured units which landed in Normandy had seen no action before: three out of four

# Tanks and infantry

Epsom was an operation implying close cooperation between tanks and infantry: on 26 June, a Sherman belonging to 4th Arm.Brig. or 11th Arm.Div. is supporting infantrymen from 15th Inf.Div. *(IWM B5979)*

The bocage could be more open but then often became more wooded. Two antiaircraft Crusaders are sheltered behind a hedgerow near Cheux on 26 June, during Operation *Epsom*. The wartime caption indicates that they belong to 31st Tk.Brig., of which two Churchills can be seen in the background. The Crusaders seem to have spoke wheels, but it is more probably due to oil stains from the greasing points. *(IWM B5978)*

Cooperation between tanks and infantry was essential for the war in Normandy, and we have seen that the British only mastered it progressively. But what was the relationship between these two service branches?

Infantrymen and tank crewmen knew that they closely depended on each other, but they were often dissatisfied during their common operations: the infantry deemed that the tanks were seldom there when needed, and had a regrettable tendency to reveal their own positions and attract enemy fire, even though the tank crews themselves were protected from machine-gun and mortar fire. Furthermore, they used to withdraw at night to leaguer, just when their presence would have been welcome.

In return, the infantry also admitted that tanks were indispensable to suppress enemy machine-gun nests, artillery and fortified positions. They offered shelter, protection, and were often encouraging when the time came to attack.

The complaints of tank crews about the infantry were also varied: infantrymen too often requested useless support, an armoured intervention on impassable terrain, or just asked for the armour to do their job. Infantrymen did not follow the tanks' swift progression, dug in too early, and did not protect them from tank-killer teams. The latter was actually the main service done by the tank-accompanying infantry: they pointed out the presence of antitank guns, eliminated snipers and enemy soldiers armed with Panzerfausts or Panzerschrecks.

This hate-love and interdependent relationship was however essential on the battlefield, and the men knew it well. In spite of outward contempt, there was real mutual esteem, and infantrymen and tank crewmen would not have traded their places for anything in the world: the first refused to be locked up in a steel box which had every chance of becoming their coffin, with no freedom of movement and no possibility to hide behind a wall, a tree, a rock, or to quickly dig in into the always welcoming and protective ground.

The second were sorry for their comrades who were obliged to walk in the mud, under the rain, at the mercy of shrapnel or machine-gun bullets, even though themselves were relatively protected and could hope to spend their night elsewhere than in a frontline trench.

divisions and five out of seven brigades had never fought as organized unit. Even though one regiment in one or another unit (such as 3rd RTR in 11th Arm.Div.) already had a good experience of combat, and even though some of their officers or NCOs were veterans, the fact remains that these units arrived in Normandy with a mainly theoretical vision of war, which was only very gradually revised. Operation *Goodwood* was the perfect illustration: right up to the highest command levels, the plain of Caen was considered as good "tank country", since it was similar to Salisbury Plain where every British armoured unit had trained. But the first fighting experience in Normandy should have been sufficient to demonstrate that the enormous advantage enjoyed by the Germans thanks to the calibre and long range of their tank and antitank guns, made this country excellent "anti-tank country". In comparison, the close bocage so much hated by the Allied tank crews was much more favourable, for it reduced or even suppressed this enemy advantage. In return, it hampered or even forbade some cross-movements and good observation, but on that point Germans and Allies were in the same situation.

## Improving cooperation between infantry and tanks

Desert warfare, where the armour had acted with great autonomy in its relations with the infantry, had also been the cause of another British Army flaw: good infantry/tank cooperation, although this aspect had been emphasized during training. Armoured divisions were however better balanced than in 1942, with both a tank and an infantry brigade, and the additional asset of a half-tracked Motor Battalion which could follow the tank pace with a minimum of protection. Tank and Armoured Brigades had likewise intensively trained with infantry. Nevertheless, the high command ignored the relationship and affinities which had appeared between these units, and scattered them in different sectors of the front according to the needs. The reasons were various: the distance between units, the mid-June storm which prevented the planned formations from arriving, the concern about moving units as less as possible, or else

The plain around Caen is vast and even, a so-called "tank country" that was actually very favourable for the German defence. In an already high wheat field, a Churchill from 31st Tk.Brig. is moving up towards St-Manvieu with an infantry unit, probably from 15th Inf. Div., on 26 June, first day of Operation *Epsom*. *(IWM B5956)*

# War Diary

In addition to many official documents (birth registers, parish census inventories, military service records...), the Public Record Office in London keeps every War Diary of any unit having taken part in World War II. These documents, of which the PRO can also provide photocopies, are an inexhaustible source of information, although studying them seems difficult and unattractive at first sight. The War Diary, written at division, brigade and regiment level by an officer assigned to this task, relates the day by day troop movements, the name of officers in post or at rest, the official visits, the attachment to other units, and of course the fighting, which is often detailed in annexes. They are variously written, by hand or type-writer, and much depend on the officer's personality, on his talents as a narrator and writer. Some war diaries are laconic, with an event report limited to the minimum (34th Tk.Brig.); some are bristling with abbreviations and short cuts (13/18th Hussars, 31st Tk.Brig.); others are written with real care for script and narration, and are the most valuable when studying particular battles: it is the case with the East Riding Yeomanry, 1st Northamptonshire Yeomanry or 144th RAC war diaries.

However, two of the features missing in many war diaries are the list of human and materiel losses, and the claims for the number of enemy tanks, guns and vehicles destroyed: when they are present, they mention exaggerated claims for Tigers and 88s, mainly in the early campaign. In return, although the war diary was in principle reserved for purely factual reports, it happens that personal opinion or feelings show through by the way of comments about troop weariness, air-support deficiency, results of an ill-prepared operation, etc.

ted them to the Squadron commander, who himself passed them on to the Troops involved. These liaisons took precious time, and were sometimes improved when the HQ Squadron command tank was directly operating with the leading tanks. Better still, telephones were fitted to the rear of Troop commander tanks, and the infantry officer could then communicate directly with the commander of the supporting tanks. Unfortunately, these telephones were only supplied progressively, and were difficult to use because of the din of the battle on top of the engine and exhaust noise. The good old method was then the only solution: the infantry officer climbed onto the tank and knocked on the turret hatch to talk with the tank commander, both taking enormous risks.

## Rigidity or improvisation?

The lack of initiative left to the units' commanders, even senior officers, was also detrimental to infantry/tank cooperation. Thus, it was not until Operation *Bluecoat* that the 11th and Guards Arm. Div. commanders were able to arrange their units as they wanted, by associating them in regimental groups very similar to the successful Combat Commands in the US Army and the 2nd French Arm.Div., with good results immediately. The belated integration of armoured car regiments into the armoured divisions actually allowed the Cromwell-equipped reconnaissance regiment to be freed, and to form four combat groups associating the four armoured regiments with the three infantry brigade's regiments and the Motor Battalion.

The rigidity of hierarchy and line of command in general was significantly harmful to the efficiency of armoured units in Normandy. These had essentially to fight on the move and to grasp any oppor-

to spare the energy of those which had just seen action. The fact remains that all that had been so carefully acquired (habits, reactions, and personal relationships between officers) had been spoiled, and that everything had to be hastily rebuilt, in the confusion of the fighting.

On the other hand, communication between infantrymen and tank crews was not easy on the battleground. Squadron and regiment command tanks were indeed equipped with N°38 radio sets of the type used by the infantry, but the command links were complex: the command tank received infantry requests, transmit-

**The 6th Guards Tk.Brig. was first committed during *Bluecoat* with 15th Inf Div., but its tanks are here carrying Guards Arm. Div. infantrymen round about 10 August, probably in the area of Chênedollé. A bogie is missing on the right front of the first Churchill, but its running gear is so well equipped (11 bogies on each side) that it is able to go on moving.**
*(Tank Museum 4799/B4)*

# Administrative Order, Operation Order and Operation Instruction

The Administrative Orders are annexed to the War Diary and are also accessible through the Public Record Office. Without fixed periodicity, they were issued by the high command and included both the usual working regulations, and those to be applied within a specific operation. Thus, Administrative Orders usually planned any aspect of the tank crews' life: they could cover food distribution methods, access to water cisterns or ammunition supplies, as well as saluting insignia-wearing regulations, setting up latrines, opening hours for the officers' mess (and which equipment it sold), burying the dead (both friend and foe), behaviour towards the civilian population... up to how to resole officer's boots! This latter topic is explained in 22 text lines in Administrative Order n°6 of 30 June 1944 (codified as secret!) for 27th Arm.Brig. The Administrative Orders issued before each important operation were more essential: they planned the general movements of every unit committed, fuel, ammunition and rations supplies, medical installations, and so on.

The planned development of the major operations prepared in advance was described in the tiniest detail in the Operation Orders and Operation Instructions, which were delivered to every unit involved. The maps, directions, timetables, codenames, signals to be used, as well as the assembly, attack, withdrawal and infantry-meeting areas..., everything was specified, explained, referenced. For instance, Operation Order n°2 of 6 July 1944 for Operation *Charnwood* not only specified the number and type of specialised AFVs from 79th Arm.Div. that were assigned to every assault unit, but foresaw their employment too: paragraph 6 planned for two AVRE Fascines to move up with B Squadron, Staffordshire Yeomanry, and use their fascines for the crossing of the Natural Obstacle only (the obstacle referred to here seems to be a stream running through Biéville).

If they proved to be useless, the fascines were to be unloaded from the AVREs and stored apart.

Complementary maps were also provided showing the enemy positions and armament, the expected movements, the attack axis, the landscape features. Some opposition was expected, and the instructions then specified who was to take over from the assaulting unit or to come up as reinforcement, how the resistance positions were to be bypassed, and where the limit progression was. Other enemy reactions were also envisaged: desertion, flight, strong or weak resistance. Of course, the artillery and aerial support, the various timetables, the name of the observation and liaison officers, the enemy units involved which were probably present or liable to intervene, were also mentioned. The codenames chosen for the radio communications were predominant, and were intended for units, vehicle types and places: thus, for Operation *Goodwood*, a tank was codenamed Box, a Flail = Whip, a Crocodile = Lizard, an AVRE = Fort, field artillery = Meadow and infantry = Locusts. It can be noticed that these codenames were vaguely related to what they designated. On the other hand, those given to places were very different: for *Goodwood*, they were chosen both among dog breeds and diseases! If Bretteville-le-Rabet = Labrador, Moult = Corgi, Danneville = Boxer and Cauvicourt = Setter, St-Aignan-de-Crasmenil became Cancer, Morteaux-Couliboeuf = Pneumonia, Jort = Typhoïd and Falaise = Gastritis!

Operation Orders and Operation Instructions were even more precise at regimental level, notably when timing was concerned. For instance, the Regimental Operation Order n°1 of 13/18th Hussars for *Goodwood* naturally gave the departure hour (16.45) and that of the preliminary bombardment, but also the exact hour planned for every passage point and for the reliefs, as well as the speed expected. This extremely close timing, the various instructions, the multiple codenames must have represented a real brainteaser for the senior and junior officers already busy with commanding their troops on the battlefield.

On 28 June, Major Taylor (Royal Artillery), Lieutenant Colonel Delacombe (8th Royal Scots) and Lieutenant Colonel Gainsford from 7th RTR are installed on the top of a Churchill Mk III from the latter regiment, organizing future actions. Too great rigidity in the battle plans often led to failures, in spite of the improving collaboration **between the various branches of the service.** *(IWM B6113)*

certain flexibility in the armoured units' movements recorded, made easier, as a matter of fact, by the German withdrawal. But the very distinct improvements were slow to appear and were paid for at full price.

The over-strict management also applied to junior officers: the Squadron and Troop commanders had little freedom of movement, between the direct orders of the hierarchy and the very precise directives of the Operation Orders and Instructions (see boxed text). An initiative such as Michael Wittmann's, taking alone or nearly alone the lead in an improvised counterattack which eventually stopped the whole 7th Arm.Div. in Villers-Bocage, would have been exceptional in the British armoured forces. Culture, tradition and training, as well as many senior officers, often opposed that kind of idea. Over-strict instructions to the units proved that the high command imagined and planned the battle development, without taking enough into account what could happen, and anything could hap-

*(IWM B9187)*

tunity to breakthrough the frontline and disrupt, bypass, encircle the enemy. But studying the battles conducted by the 2nd British Army shows that the senior officers too often stuck to the plan and neglected the opportunities for outflanking movements. Attacks were developed according to the textbook, with in the early campaign a feeling of superiority which was the cause of much harm, like the 7th Arm.Div.'s failure in Villers-Bocage. There were no general officers such as Patton or Leclerc, who kept up the cavalry spirit, to lead the great British armoured units, with the possible exception of General Roberts from 11th Arm.Div. Only in early August was a

*Ci-contre.* **Near Estry, infantrymen from 4th KSLI are taking a rest in the shade of a 2nd Fife and Forfar Yeomanry Sherman V. A bit too perfect illustration of tank/infantry cooperation, but which shows the success of 11th Arm.Div. in this domain, a success that was to be confirmed from *Bluecoat* onwards.**

pen in Normandy: weather, hazardous air bombardments, unexpected enemy defence, natural obstacles, etc. Because of the desire to foresee and control everything, it was often forgotten that uncertainty played an enormous role on the battlefield, and obliged officers to react, to think rapidly, to adapt, to change the tactics, to improvise.

## Inferior equipment

The heaviness of the hierarchy, of its instructions, of the theory taught in training, partly explains a certain timidity and a lack of energy in offensive operations, particularly early in the campaign after the first failures. But another element is essential for analyzing the behaviour of British armoured divisions in Normandy: the crews were constantly issued with equipment of lesser quality than that of the Germans, or barely equal in the case of the Panzer IV. This materiel inferiority had not been considered enough when Operation *Overlord* had been prepared, notably because some American or British experts and senior officers had asserted that the Allies' tanks could match the Germans'. More seriously, this lie was repeated after the fighting had demonstrated the Panzer's superiority: Montgomery, in a report handed over to Churchill in early July, went on asserting that the Sherman and Cromwell could at least equal their counterparts if they were used properly. The Prime Minister himself made use of this report before the House of Commons, and these arguments were published in the press. Whatever the reason was, reassuring public opinion, defending national honour or regaining the crews' confidence, these declarations had deplorable results.

Actually, from the very first days, the mainly Sherman- or Cromwell- equipped British crews realised that their tanks had less armour and less effective guns than the enemy's. Shooting tests on the first captured Panthers showed that even at point blank range, their frontal armour was impervious to the shells of the 75-mm gun arming most of the tanks in service. It was the same for the Tiger, and for the Jagdpanther which was fortunately seldom met. Their own tanks were in return vulnerable even at long range to the German 88 and 75-mm guns, including the Panzer IV's 75-mm L/48 equivalent to the PaK 40. The better armoured Churchills had a better reputation than the medium tanks, but only their frontal

The wreck of a Sherman I Hybrid probably belonging to 11th Arm.Div. lies in front of Fontenay-le-Pesnel on 27 June. The adversary who brewed it up and made several holes in its frontal armour could be the Panther in the background: one more testimony of the superiority of German equipment over Allied armour. *(IWM B6043)*

armour, particularly on the Mk VII and Mk VIII versions, offered real protection. Moreover, only eight Churchill regiments at best were present in Normandy.

Thus British crews daily faced Panzers and antitank guns that pierced their armour, and set them on fire with disheartening regularity, while their own shells bounced off the Panthers' and Tigers' armour. Only the Firefly, with its powerful 17-pounder gun, could defeat these dreadful opponents, but its armour was that of the standard Sherman, and it was thus very vulnerable. In the high command spheres, experts had established that it was possible, without running the risk of being short of equipment, to lose five to six tanks for every destroyed Panzer, thanks to existing stocks, to American supplies, and to the quality of repair workshops. But the human aspect had been totally ignored: four or five crewmen manned each of these tanks, and risked their lives. The vision of friendly tanks destroyed or brewed-up, the loss of their wounded, mutilated or killed comrades, the permanent threat upon them for even the smallest operation, had an often underestimated influence on the behaviour and the results of British armoured units in Normandy. And the additional danger of the individual antitank weapons such as the Panzerfaust and Panzerschreck did certainly not improve the situation. The survival rate was of course better in the tanks than in the infantry, and some crewmen lost their tank two or three times without being hurt. Nevertheless, the almost certainty that the first enemy shot would be lethal to their mount hardly encouraged the crews to boldness, especially since their almost continuous attacking position put them in unfavourable situations: it was generally admitted that the defender had a 1 to 3 advantage, i.e. that he only needed one tank to contain the assault of three enemy tanks.

## Manpower shortage and confidence crisis

If the losses during the early days were less than expected, the war of attrition conducted during 11 weeks on the Anglo-Canadian front caused a dangerous threat to the troop reinforcement system, which was in very bad condition in the fifth year of the conflict. Even though the situation was less serious for armour than for infantry, the manpower shortage made it necessary to disband the antiaircraft units, which were actually seldom needed thanks to the Allied air superiority, from late July onwards. The 27th Arm.Brig., which had not been expected to survive so long anyway, was also disbanded on 30 July, and its regiments were distributed among the most weakened units: the brigade was only an administrative unit, and this measure had little consequences. But it was more serious to disband the 24th Lancers and 153rd RAC (and amalgamate the 3rd and 4th CLY), because the British Army basic entity, the regiment, was affected. Although the chosen regiments were among the more junior ones, without deep-rooted traditions, their members' reactions were brisk and their resentment sometimes lasted well after they joined their new unit. One only has to see how much energy was shown by the senior officers of these regiments, appealing to the highest levels of the State (the Prime Minister and even he King) and trying to avoid the disbanding, to understand the traumatic experience generated by this decision, which eventually seems to have been necessary.

The high command had not always taken good decisions, by the way. The organisation of operations involving important armoured forces left much to be desired, and highlighted the shortcomings of many corps and division commanders, who notably underestimated the German defence, and misjudged the psychology of the combatants on both sides as well as the essential relationship that had to be established between the different services composing their formations. Between the giant offensives and the small inadequately planned and equipped attacks, it was rare for the decisive thrust to be delivered in the right place, at the right time and with the right forces. But it was only when these conditions were indeed fulfilled that an operation could have any chance to succeed.

*Epsom*, the first major offensive west of Caen, just managed to monopolize the German defence, but did not achieve the expected breakout. The British tanks, particularly those of the 11th Arm.Div., were knocked out from a distance by German antitank guns, whilst the delays and hesitations during the attack did not enable Hill 112 to be kept. *Goodwood*, which was launched from a bottlenecked start line with three armoured divisions against a narrow and heavily German-fortified front, sorely lacked infantry to hold and clear the terrain. Only Operation *Bluecoat* (and to a lesser extent Operation *Totalize*) almost responded to the expectations despite the hostile terrain, for the enemy defence had weakened. If the failure, or semi-failure, of these offensives disturbed the dissatisfied staffs, and caused the replacement of a handful of generals, the average soldiers in every service branch were the ones who mainly suffered the often fatal consequences. Tank crews were no exception, and they gradually lost their confidence in their officers, at the highest level. Squadron and regiment commanders were more often praised, with the exception of some difficult or incompetent individuals, but the higher brigade or division levels brought more doubts and suspicion.

## Organisation and tactics

With the introduction of Fireflies into the units, a few weeks prior to D-Day, most of the Sherman - or Cromwell - equipped armoured regiments had modified their organisation: from five three-tank Troops plus a two-tank HQ Troop in each Squadron, they changed to four four-tank Troops, including a Firefly, plus a three-tank HQ Troop. The average total remained 17 to 19 tanks per Squadron. There were exceptions still: the first wave regiments within 8th and 27th Arm.Brig. had thus grouped their Fireflies in the Squadron that was not DD-equipped (the Firefly could not be converted into DD because of its long gun). It seems too that these brigades had been issued with Fireflies in smaller numbers than other units, for the same reasons: they only had 22 and 29 17 pounder Shermans respectively on 30 June, instead of the normal issue of 36.

Two de-turreted Stuarts from 11th Arm.Div. have stopped near St-Martin's church and are stirring up the curiosity of the inhabitants of Laigle on 23 June. The British had known for a long time that their Stuarts were obsolete, and they had begun to remove their turrets in Italy, in 1943, to gain speed and discretion. The same modification only took place gradually in Normandy. *(IWM B9653)*

8th Arm.Brig. had only 22 Fireflies on 30 May 1944, and is a good example of the various types of organisation within regiments. The two leading DD-equipped Squadrons in Nottinghamshire Yeomanry were made of four three-tank Troops plus a four-tank HQ Troop, for a total of only 16: the other Shermans were assigned either to the regimental HQ Squadron, or to 24th Lancers. Actually, the latter regiment which landed with the second wave was organized in five three-tank Troops plus a four-tank HQ Troop, for a total

Major Holtby, commanding C Squadron of East Riding Yeomanry (27th Arm. Brig.) is conferring with his Troop commanders on 28 June. If the combatants had often doubts about their senior officers and the high command, they generally had greater confidence in the hierarchy just above them. *(Tank Museum 2719/A3)*

of 19 Shermans per Squadron. Whereas all regiments gradually adopted the organisation that was to become standard (one Firefly in each four-tank Troop), for a long time 24th Lancers retained its Fireflies gathered in a single Troop, the kind of distribution that was more often abandoned even prior to D-Day. But the use of Fireflies could be adapted to the needs of the moment: during Operation *Goodwood*, Major Close commanding 3rd RTR's A Squadron set his four Fireflies in a row, with a 40 yards gap interval, behind the rest of the Sherman Vs advancing towards the Caen – Troarn railway line.

The Tank Brigades that had not been issued with Fireflies retained the basic organisation of five three-tank Troops per Squadron, plus a two-tank HQ Troop. This older method was still adapted to infantry support which was the main task these units were intended for. Depending on each Tank Brigade, and on the equipment they were issued with, the 6 pounder-armed Churchills were distributed at the rate of one per Troop (as in the 4th Scots Guards), or else were gathered in one or two antitank-purposed Troops, since the 6 pounder gun was reputed to have better armour-penetration power.

**Sherman IIs and IVs from 11th Arm.Div. (or 4th Arm.Brig. which was assigned to the latter and was also equipped with Sherman IIs) are assembling on 25 June for Operation *Epsom*. Many other AFVs can be seen in the background: such a concentration of vehicles in the open was only possible with the almost absolute Allied air superiority.**
*(IWM B6018)*

**The Firefly was a most innovative element within the British armoured units, which allowed them to be almost on a par with the best German tanks, and the result was tactical and organisational changes. This Sherman Vc, belonging to 27th Arm.Brig. according to the tactical sign's position, has been photographed on 13 June while operating with South Lancashire Rgt (3rd Inf.Div.).**
*(IWM B5546)*

The organisation of progression in combat depended on the Norman countryside, on the objective assigned, and on the defence disposition. The formations taught in training (one-up, two-up), which were triangle-shaped, were used with success. Within a Cromwell or Sherman Troop, on open ground, the tanks generally advanced in arrow formation: a 75-mm tank at the front, the 17 pounder tank behind, and a 75-mm tank on each side. But the Norman countryside, and above all the Bocage, often obliged them to advance in column: if the expected frontal opposition was rather composed of infantry and antitank guns, a 75-mm tank led, followed by the other two, the Firefly being at the rear. Actually, the 75-mm gun fired a high-explosive shell which was very effective against unarmoured targets. If Panzers were expected, the leading 75-mm tank was immediately followed by the Firefly armed with the formidable 17 pounder to defeat any AFV, and by the two other 75-mm tanks. In any case, the first tank was sacrificed, for it would be hit by the first, often fatal, shells: a rotation was thus very often

One or two ARVs were often assigned to each Squadron, in addition to the Light Aid Detachment: here, the commander of a Sherman ARV is discussing with an MP in the middle of an 11th Arm. Div. column (see divisional insignia on the Bedford truck) south of Vire, on 2 August. In the foreground can be seen the shield of a 17 pounder antitank gun. *(IWM B8489)*

instituted in the units to lead the column, so that the leading crew was not always the same and had a chance to get through...

In spite of trials to make the Firefly lead the column, since it was better suited to deal with a tank or an SPG, the Squadron leaders soon understood that these precious tanks had to be spared since their 17 pounder gun was the only chance to knock-out the enemy's Panther and Tiger heavy Panzers. All the more so as the Germans had also quickly learnt to recognize the long Firefly gun, and tried to destroy them as fast as possible. The usual tactic was to wait until the first tank was hit, hoping that the other tank commanders could detect where the shot came from and then eliminate the opponent: if it was a Panzer, the Firefly took an appropriate position to shoot while the other two 75-mm tanks pounded the enemy tank, without much chance of scoring a serious hit, but hoping to hinder its movements, the turret rotation or the gunner's aim. One of the 75-mm tanks frequently stayed close to the Firefly to observe the firing results, for the 17 pounder shooting cause so much smoke and such a flash that it was impossible for its commander to appreciate its effects.

For infantry support, the tanks most often moved along with them, one Troop being assigned to a particular platoon, for instance. But this tactic was often ill suited to Normandy: in hedged-off country like the Bocage, the tanks presence revealed that of the accompanying infantry, who should have enjoyed the cover of the vegetation, to the Germans who were then able to engage them from a distance with mortars, a weapon their perfectly mastered. There was more advantage to be gained by having an infantry unit nearby, which could point out an antitank gun or a Panzerfaust-armed soldier, and so help to eliminate any opposition. As early as 9 June, East Riding Yeomanry developed an infantry support tactic in contradiction with the textbook, but however very effective (or should I write: thus very effective?!) Instead of moving up with

A late production M10, maybe an Achilles, is heading southwards of Caumont-l'Eventé on 31 July. British TDs were skilfully used to support other units, and were responsible for the destruction of many Panzers. One of the crew members shows the advantage of the rear-facing .50 machine-gun on the M10, when the tank was travelling with the turret reversed. *(IWM B8083)*

the infantrymen, the Shermans chose covered positions offering them an excellent view of the terrain, and with their sustained gun and machine-gun fire, they really "shot in the infantry". This method was successfully used in support of 3rd, 51st and 59th Inf.Div. from Operation *Charnwood* onwards, and was more or less to spread in other units as their experience built up. Actually, the textbook lessons were very soon arranged or even forgotten to adapt to the various combat situations.

When the whole regiment could proceed over open ground, it generally also adopted a triangular organisation inherited from the desert combats: one Squadron led, followed by the HQ Squadron flanked on the right and left by the other two Squadrons. It must be noted that the British made very successful use of the M10 and Achilles Tank Destroyers: they were not considered as tank-hunters, in an offensive role, but as antitank reinforcement for infantry and tanks, or as flank protection for armoured units. Depending on the speed of progression and the expected opposition, the Recce

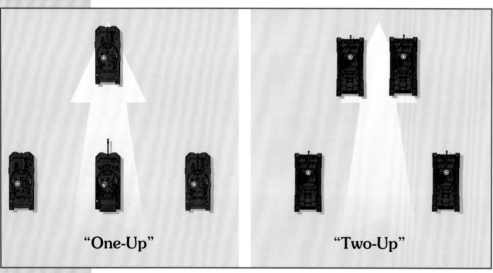

"One-Up"     "Two-Up"

Having not been issued with Fireflies, the Tank Brigades retained the organisation of five three-tank Troops per Squadron. A Troop of Churchills from 31st Tk.Brig., with an accompanying Bren Carrier, is getting ready in the Odon valley, early in the morning of 15 July, during Operation *Jupiter*. The tank in the foreground is a Churchill Mk II armed with a 6 pounder gun. *(IWM B7433)*

*Next page, top.* The British artillery power was also present within armoured units, thanks to the Sextons which replaced the earlier Priests: the 25 pounder self propelled gun could move up with the tanks at the same speed and on the same terrain. The threat of an artillery or mortar stonk is here a reality, since the crew members of this Sexton in action are all wearing steel helmets. *(Tank Museum 2079/B5)*

Squadron was top of the league, or on the contrary brought up the rear to spare its light tanks. As always, exceptions were frequent: for instance, the 13/18th Hussars during *Goodwood* moved up in line and according to the following organisation: A Squadron, B Squadron, Rgt HQ, C Squadron, Recce Troop, A1 Echelon. The A Echelon identified the transports immediately following the assault force and mainly loaded with ammunition, rations and fuel (generally for one day), which often included the Light Aid Detachment with one or two ARVs and some replacement crews. B Echelon followed behind, also bringing ammunition and fuel together with warm food, crews' personal equipment (bags, bedrolls, covers, tents) and what was needed for a temporary encampment. A Echelon was sometimes divided in A2 and A1 Echelons, the latter almost moving up with the tanks if a rapid progression was expected. F Echelon was strictly composed of the fighting vehicles and their crews, occasionally supplemented with ammunition and fuel trucks

It was however rare for a regiment to be entirely committed, and with the exception of some major offensives such as *Goodwood* and *Totalize*, the Squadron formed the basic unit. Organisation was then always the same: one or two Troops leading, HQ Squadron behind, often with the reconnaissance Stuarts and the antiaircraft Crusaders, the other two Troops on each side, the last Troop in the rearmost position if necessary, when it was not in the lead. Tank Brigades were here again exceptions to the rule: Churchills were rather committed in Troops, and only Operations *Epsom*, and to a lesser extent *Bluecoat*, saw an organisation based on Squadrons. By operating closer to the infantry, the Churchills most often gave each other mutual support, like infantrymen: one tank would advance up to a sheltered position, with the cover of the other two, and when it had reached it, one of the other tanks overtook the first two and progressed a little farther, up to a new sheltered position, and so on. It must be remembered however that the great offensives were only high points during the battle of Normandy, most of the fighting, in particular for Tank Brigades, taking place on a day to day basis, in a reduced area, in support of small units and against limited attacks. The terrain and the enemy more generally dictated the organisation and tactics that were used.

## Some special cases

One of the main characteristics of the tactics employed by the British in Normandy was the massive use of the 79th Arm.Div.'s specialised armour, as early as on 6 June. D-Day had demonstrated the huge possibilities of the AVREs, Crabs and other Crocodiles, so

they were called on for major operations as well as for daily fighting, and this was not without causing premature equipment wear and excessive weariness for the crews. AVRE Petards were used to destroy fortified positions, too well-defended houses, but also to cut exits through the Norman hedges, jointly with Sherman Dozers or Bulldozers, and prior to the Cullin Hedgerow Cutters developed by the Americans being available in late July. The Fascine and Bridgelayer versions were often required to cross streams, wide craters, and antitank ditches. Crabs used to precede every progression if the Germans were suspected of having laid down minefields in the attack area, but they also cleared roads, verges, fields where laagers were set up. Crocodiles, more often kept for the great offensives, were occasionally called on in support against a fortified position or an enemy detachment which had to be persuaded to surrender…

Antiaircraft Crusaders had not much to do since the Luftwaffe was almost absent from the Norman skies, especially by day. But they were not left unemployed: before their units were disbanded to become replacements, they often reinforced the Recce Troop's Stuarts, and were also used for liaison and escort missions, and even in direct infantry support. For instance, just prior to *Goodwood*, Sergeant Caswell from B Squadron, 5th RTR (11th Arm. Div.) was escorting two reinforcing Shermans towards the front with his Crusader: during a break to relieve himself, he suddenly spotted a German infantry group busy with installing an antitank gun 80 yards from where he stood. They were routed by firing the Oerlikon 20-mm guns and the Shermans' .50 machine-guns, but one of the latter tanks was destroyed by the antitank gun. And on 30 July, Churchills from the 4th Grenadier Guards (6th Guards Tk.Brig.) were escorted with Crusader Mk IIIs from the regimental AA Troop to support infantry towards Sept-Vents.

## Irregular performance of armoured divisions

On account of the numerous elements influencing the development of the fighting, analyzing the results of the British armoured units in Normandy is not an easy task. Nevertheless, among the largest formations, 11th Arm.Div. was undeniably the most successful. Even though its baptism of fire during Operation *Epsom* was costly and none too glorious, it was the one which carried out most of the breakout during *Goodwood*, and it was also successful during

Operation *Bluecoat* in seizing a bridge essential to the progression on the River Souleuvre. It was successful as well in liberating Vassy and Flers, and in pursuing the Germans up to the River Seine. By the way, these successes and those to follow led Lieutenant General Dempsey, commanding the 2nd British Army, to declare after the war that he had never met a better division than the 11th Arm. There were several reasons for this effectiveness, the first being a very varied and extremely thorough three years' training, in the early days under the aegis of Major General Hobart, which welded the different divisional units together. When another capable commander, Major General Pip Roberts (who, after having superbly proved himself in the desert, was at 37 the youngest divisional commander in this campaign), was appointed, it was possible to put into practice tactics involving regimental groups and close cooperation with infantry very early, which were lacking in most other units, while retaining the initiative and speed of the cavalry. The regiments who had not seen action were mostly commanded by veterans, and benefited from the 3rd RTR combat experience gained on all fronts since 1939: this balance between the junior regiments' spirit and lack of concern, and the competence and wisdom of the 3rd RTR and veterans was essential for morale and esprit de corps.

Even though it was sometimes inadequately used, 79th Arm.Div. was the other large formation to enjoy very satisfying results, in a quite different domain: actually, it was never used as a whole unit but was scattered around depending on requirements. Its success was due as much to the quality of its specialised armour, to its members' competence (tank crews, engineers and technical personnel) and to its innovative spirit, as to the authority of its commander, Major General Hobart. We have seen that this Royal Engineers officer during the Great War, who was born in 1885 and had already commanded 11th Arm.Div., had also been commander of the 7th Arm.Div. when it was created in 1938, and had previously taken part in the formation of the 1st Tk.Brig. The influence on the definition of the principles governing the use of British armour of this rather unknown General, who was eclipsed by more media-covered personalities such as Montgomery, was considerable. Convinced of the importance of tanks in future wars, in the same vein as General Estienne in France, Hobart had often openly expressed his opinion during the interwar period, maybe too loudly, for this caused him (apart from real health problems) to be kept away from any command in 1940, to end up as

*Above.*

**Specialised armour from the 79th Arm.Div. proved so useful that it was committed in almost every offensive, whether important or not. On 18 July, Crabs are moving up with an infantry unit mounted on a Sherman Squadron for Operation *Goodwood*. Note in the background an M5 or M9 US half-track displaying a huge Red Cross, and a Firefly.** *(IWM B7521)*

*Right.*

**Preceded by Shermans, two Crabs from 1st Lothian and Border Horse Yeomanry (see 79th Arm.Div. divisional insignia and tactical sign 52) are moving up with infantry from 3rd Inf.Div. south of Escoville: these specialised AFVs used to pave the way for the attacks, but tactics were progressively arranged and these Flails were only to intervene if the assaulting force met a mine-field.**
*(Tank Museum 2241/B2)*

Lance-Corporal in the Home Guard! Cleverly recalled by Churchill in 1941, Hobart thus brought his experience, enthusiasm, energy and creativity to three of the four armoured divisions committed in Normandy. Supporter of the most rigorous training, he could have adopted this maxim often repeated in the German Army: *Sweat spares blood*".

The Guards Arm.Div., which arrived later in Normandy, was not at first very convincing: its first commitment during *Goodwood* was far from spectacular, and it was not before *Bluecoat* that Major General Adair was able to reform the tactical groups he had often practiced in training, and give back the division its effectiveness. A traditional unit par excellence, renowned for its discipline and drill qualities, the Guards Arm.Div. may also have suffered from

some kind of rigidity and lack of initiative in the chain of command, detrimental to the flexibility needed for an armoured formation. In any case, the Guards did not lack courage: the divisional history and lists of losses, particularly in officers and NCOs, show that the Guards displayed gallantry, and even temerity. The glorious memory of their predecessors and the respective regimental traditions, sometimes dating back three centuries, played a predominant part in the Guards' behaviour.

Having suffered a terrible mauling in June at Villers-Bocage, during the Normandy campaign the 7th Arm.Div. never recovered its fighting virtues so often demonstrated in North Africa. Its behaviour was actually rather similar to that of the 51st Inf.Div., another veteran unit that Montgomery had brought back, for their

*Above.*

**A Sherman Dozer and a Crusader AA Mk III from 2nd Fife and Forfarshire Yeomanry have been photographed near Eterville on 29 June. The Sherman Dozer proved very efficient to break lanes through the Bocage hedgerows, but the antiaircraft Crusader, which could not fulfil its normal task for lack of aerial targets, was restricted to escort and reconnaissance missions.** *(IWM B6187)*

*Below.*

**The Cullin Hedgerow Device developed by the Americans for Operation *Cobra* was also produced for the British, but often arrived too late to be put to good use. Only the first tank in this column is so equipped; the vehicles have probably been photographed in mid-August, soon after Operation *Bluecoat.***

*(Tank Museum 3581/C1)*

history was comparable. On paper, the 7th Arm.Div. was a capable and experienced unit, maybe too experienced. It may seem paradoxical, but it has been demonstrated that a unit continuously gains experience in combat, up to the moment when the losses endured and the time spent on the frontline have an inverse effect on its efficiency. *The Desert Rats*, who had fought almost relentlessly from 1939 onwards, felt that "*the same always did the job*". Their return to England to discover that two armoured divisions and several armoured brigades had been kept there for two or three years had certainly not changed this feeling. They arrived in Normandy blasé, resigned and cautious at the same time, with

# The role of the British Armoured Division

The Bovington Tank Museum preserves in its archives the Military Training Pamphlet n°41 titled "The tactical handling of the Armoured Division and its Components", dating from July 1943, which is enlightening for the role assigned to the British armoured units in general, at the time of the Normandy invasion. According to this manual, the primary missions of the armoured division were: envelopment; deep penetration; breakthrough; destruction and pursuit of the enemy. To this primary offensive role, which was directly inherited from the Blitzkrieg, were also annexed consolidation and clearing, while defending positions and pressing down the enemy were pushed into the background. It was specified that the armoured division was not to be committed "piecemeal", which sometimes happened however in Normandy. Night attack was emphasized, a rare occurrence in Normandy although it was effective when used, for instance during Operation *Totalize*.

The infantry in an armoured division took second place since it advanced more slowly, and mainly consolidated the ground gained, mopping up resistance pockets and preparing the launching positions for the next attack. Its protective role towards tanks only came next, even though it turned out to be crucial in Normandy: this theoretical shortcoming was probably one of the causes which led to the lack of tank/infantry cooperation. The artillery supported one or the other service branches, and proved essential: the experience gained during the First World War had convinced the British Army of the importance of artillery, which underwent a significant development in the interwar period, and became the most important service in the Army in that it regrouped 18% of the total fighting strength. The power, precision and excellent organisation of the British artillery supported the offensives effectively, and allowed many counterattacks in Normandy, even those led by Panzers, to be repelled. The other components (engineers, transports, signals, reconnaissance, etc) provided assistance to the chiefly offensive missions of the armoured division.

The second part of the pamphlet notably dealt with the organisation of the armoured regiment, emphasizing tank/infantry cooperation. Here again, the whole regiment, or even the whole brigade, was to be committed if possible, since concentration was required to obtain the right firepower and breakout opportunities. Attention was also given to flexibility, training and information. The paragraph about the cooperation with infantry is rather amusing for it underlined the fact that "*the British character is naturally not inquisitive enough*", and that the officers and soldiers "*tend to shirk inquiring into matters which they consider the business of other people*". In English, the word "inquisitive" can have the same pejorative meaning of "indiscreet" as the word "curieux" in French. The next sentence, "*it is the business of everybody to win the war*", came with a plea for the suppression of watertight compartments between the various branches and units.

The other chapters dealt with the various formations to be adopted in combat (see above), the great principles governing the employment of the armoured division (cooperation, concentration, surprise, protection), the Operation Orders and Instructions. Chapter V about the tactical handling is rich in lessons: it depicted the types of action that could be met, and underlined the necessity of adaptability and quick decision, which was sometimes lacking in Normandy. A paragraph described the hull down and turret down positions, another dealt with tank against tank actions, comparing them with some kind of hide-and-seek. The importance of reconnaissance, of map reading, of terrain study was underlined, and these are elements that are often evoked in the wartime memoirs of junior officers, who mastered these practices. In return, they seem to have sometimes failed at the highest command levels.

The paragraph about attacking enemy static positions is revealing: it recommended always carrying out single- or double-flank attacks, the frontal attack being only used in emergency or in the case of major operations, for it was "*likely to result in heavy casualties*". Actually, the frontal attack was too often used in Normandy, during both major offensives and local operations, with the above-mentioned consequences: exceedingly heavy losses. A paragraph underlined the skill of German combined forces (infantry, tanks, antitank artillery) in creating traps to attract enemy forces and destroy them. Despite these warnings, this strictly defensive tactic was still used successfully by the Germans in Normandy, for they had the perfect means to carry them out (camouflage, gun range, Panzer armour). Harbouring was included in the chapter about protection, and was particularly well studied with regard to its position, defence, and organisation.

Chapter VII about administration described the various Echelons (see above) as well as the fuel and ammo re-supplying procedures, and the organisation of cooking, of medical aid posts, of repairs and recovery, etc. The last chapter was about intercommunication, which, in addition to the radio, relied upon dispatch riders on motorcycle or on foot and upon liaison officers, and put an emphasis on the clarity of messages, on security, on the task of regimental signal officers, and on radio traffic.

a strong feeling of rebellion. The cases of desertion, which were also recorded within 51st Inf.Div., eventually proved that there was a morale crisis among the veterans. They had not really integrated the "rookies" that had been posted in England into their ranks, and the division lacked cohesion. Combat conditions were very different from those they had known in the desert or in Italy and contributed to their instability. The brutal and offhand manner Montgomery displayed when transferring several senior officers but also a hundred junior officers and other ranks after *Bluecoat*, although it was certainly necessary, did not make it possible to regain confidence and morale: the 7th Arm.Div. only became itself again after the Normandy campaign, even though the speed of its Cromwells allowed it to play a fair part in the pursuit to the River Seine.

## Efficient brigades

Naturally closer to the infantry divisions they had to support, the armoured and tank brigades were generally committed more often and for longer periods than the armoured divisions. By their daily presence beside the infantry, they proved globally efficient but with some nuances of course. The 4th Arm.Brig. had approximately the same history as the 7th Arm.Div., with which it shared common origins, but its commitment in Normandy was more progressive and this spared it the traumatism the *Desert Rats* went through. The fact remains that its early results were disappointing, and that Brigadier Carver dismissed several unit commanders after *Epsom*. The phase of pursuit after 15 August seemed to better suit the brigade, which then recovered its ability for speedy exploitation. The 8th Arm.Brig. was also a veteran unit, but had been rejuvenated by the arrival of new regiments providing a good balance between experience and spirit. It had refined the DD-tank tactics, and carried out its missions on D-Day perfectly. In spite of the 24th Lancers' disbanding and their replacement by 13/18th Hussars, the brigade remained fully operational all along the campaign, and benefited like the 4th Arm.Brig. from its Motor Battalion to ensure good infantry/tank cooperation.

The 27th Arm.Brig. landed and fought on D-Day, met immediate success and was almost constantly committed, with very good results. Having suffered heavy losses, it was unfortunately to be disbanded to provide reinforcements for other armoured units, but its former regiments continued to perform with gallantry. As for 8th Arm.Brig., the fact that its regiments had come under the temporary control of 79th Arm.Div. for training seems to have inspired it with a bit of the aggressive and innovative spirit of the latter. The 33rd Arm.Brig. was untried when it landed in Normandy, but it was committed in a major offensive three weeks after its arrival, and then had time to familiarize with the terrain. It performed remarkably during Operation *Totalize*, and once again was able to demonstrate its mobile qualities during the pursuit to the River Seine.

The 6th Guards Tk.Brig. arrived late in Normandy, its debuts were a bit difficult, but it recovered its efficiency when it was associated again with 15th Inf.Div., with which it had trained so well and for so long. The 31st and 34th Tk.Brig. were also Churchill-equipped, they did not achieve exploits but carried out their close support missions steadily: the infantry divisions were most often satisfied with their presence. More generally, tank and armoured brigades achieved good results when they were used in their primary role, and when the high command did not scatter them along the frontline. Their specialization (DD, infantry support) brought additional efficiency, while the ability for swift and outflanking movements of the more traditional units, emphasized in training, were confirmed when the front became more fluid and thus better suited to armoured warfare.

## An effective but costly strategy

The strategy adopted for the Normandy campaign is an essential element to explain the relative failure of British armour. The reality of Montgomery's strategy consisting in fixing the enemy

(IWM B6019)

was discussed a long time ago, some American writers having even asserted that the main part of the job had been done by the US Army while the British front stagnated. In July 1944, the American newspapers and some American generals had already mentioned the so-called British timidity in Normandy, and this criticism was relayed by part of the public opinion in Great-Britain. It is known today with certainty that very early during the planning of Operation *Overlord*, the Allied strategy had been to deliberately put the Anglo-Canadians in charge of fixing the Germans in the east, whilst the Americans in the west were first to seize Cherbourg to have a large harbour at their disposal, and then breakthrough out of the Cotentin peninsula. Repeated offensives in the east were necessary

Armour from 11th Arm.Div. is assembling on 26 June for Operation *Epsom*. This division certainly was the most successful in Normandy. In the left foreground can be seen a Humber Scout Car, and on the right a Sherman V command tank, as indicated by the multiple antennas and the steps welded at the front. The two vehicles belonged to the 29th Arm.Brig. HQ.

Thanks to its specialised armour and the competence of its crews, the 79th Arm.Div. made a handsome contribution to the success of the British campaign in Normandy. A column of Crabs from 1st Lothian and Border Horse Yeomanry (the tactical sign 52 is faintly visible on the right) is waiting for the launching of Operation *Goodwood* on 18 July, on the road to Escoville. *(IWM B7541)*

to maintain pressure on the Germans and prevent them from counterattacking.

From this point of view, the Allied strategy worked perfectly in Normandy: the Germans were never able to mount a counter-attack strong enough to threaten the beachhead, and the successive offensives, in the east or in the west, forced them to commit their precious Panzer-Divisionen piecemeal, as they progressively arrived on the invasion front. Operation *Lüttich*, launched on 7 August against the Avranches corridor after the American breakout of *Cobra*, was the only offensive involving several Panzer-Divisionen: it was far too late then, and this attack even hastened the fall of Normandy with the loss of many Panzers.

The 21st Army Group had thus scrupulously followed the strategy planned, but Montgomery's personal responsibility can nevertheless be seen in the partial failure of several operations: there is no reason to consider here tactical mistakes, which could have been made by others in similar situations, since the analysis would be too long

In Normandy, the 7th Arm. Div. did not recover the qualities it had displayed in North Africa and Italy. A column of Cromwells from a reconnaissance regiment, the tactical sign 45 of which can be seen on the left side of the first tank, is advancing on 18 July in the plain, south of Caen. Close examination of the cap badges confirms that the crews and their vehicles belong to 8th Hussars (7th Arm. Div.) *(IWM B7740)*

and beyond the scope of this book, anyway. It is rather through his definition of the objectives and through the importance of the resources committed that Montgomery revealed his hidden desire to accomplish a breakout on the British front, thus showing a great personal or national ambition. Actually, although it was essential to launch repeated offensives to attract the Germans' attention, it was not necessary to allot them objectives that were impossible to reach, or make them so large-scale.

In this respect, Operation *Goodwood* was highly revealing: three

146

These Churchill Mk VIIs of an unidentified independent brigade are gathered in the shelter of a terrain undulation,
before a probably important operation considering the number of tanks and the presence of a Churchill Ark and even of an SBG bridge in the background. All Tank Brigades provided much appreciated support for the British infantry divisions.
*(Tank Museum 4834/E1)*

armoured divisions, with many units from the other branches of service (artillery, heavy bombers and infantry) were committed on 18 July in the eastern outflanking of Caen. Montgomery had clearly specified to the officers in his orders that the final objective was the Bourguébus ridge located 6 miles south of the starting line, but he unofficially mentioned a breakout towards Falaise. Montgomery, whose troops had made difficult progress of a handful of kilometres in six weeks, thus expected them to break through over a distance of 6 miles against an enemy defensive line reputed to be very strong, in order to possibly reach a city 20 miles away. For the men who were

taking part in these offensives which were allocated huge resources, and who knew the German defensive power that they faced every day, determining such remote and obviously inaccessible objectives was demotivating, especially since they regularly saw small attacks fail for lack of sufficient means, for instance an infantry battalion or a tank Squadron.

## A formidable enemy

Nevertheless, it would be vain to evoke further British possible faults or shortcomings to explain their relative failure in the early Normandy campaign, since the chief reason for the stagnation on the Anglo-Canadian front was the Germans themselves! In Normandy, the Allies faced German units of uneven value, particularly when considering infantry, but they were also confronted with the Panzer-Divisionen elite: descending from a long Germanic war tradition, but also upkeepers of the more recent Blitzkrieg

A long row of Shermans
is ready to enter action on 28 July.
The wartime caption specifies
that these are tanks from 27th Arm.Brig., a very efficient unit
that was present from D-Day on,
but which was however disbanded
on 30 July. These tanks belong
to East Riding Yeomanry: the tactical sign 53
can be seen on the first tank's transmission housing beside
the sea-horse of the brigade.
*(IWM B6166)*

The 88 FlaK 36/37 gun, the greatest terror of British crews together with the Tiger, was even more powerful in its PaK 43/41 towed antitank version. This gun had been destroyed with its half-tracked tractor, probably a French Somua S 307, by the 1st Polish Arm.Div. during Operation *Totalize* in August 1944.
*(RR)*

tactics they had invented and in spite of the many setbacks suffered on the Eastern and Western fronts, these divisions maintained unequalled qualities. They enjoyed far superior materiel, very experienced officers, and combat practice which were missing on the Allied side. Despite the overwhelming Allied air superiority, which limited their movements and supplies, and the power of artillery which stopped most of their counterstrokes, they went on carrying out their mission in very difficult conditions.

The terrible experience gained on the Eastern front endowed them with a remarkable ability for defence, camouflage, counterattack and improvisation: the skill in recapturing just-lost positions or in forming ad-hoc Kampfgruppen in a hurry to counter an expected threat was often employed against the British. The oldest divisions (2. Pz-Div., 1. and 2.SS-Pz-Div.) just like the most recent ones (116. Pz-Div., 9., 10. and 12. SS-Pz-Div.) were composed around veterans and during training and fighting had gained a competence the British acknowledged. Reinforced with three Tiger battalions, they were the hard nucleus of the German defence, and were moreover supported by outstanding antitank artillery, and by mortars and Nebelwerfers which were the first cause of the Allied losses in Normandy. Actually, up to eight of the eleven Panzer-Divisionen committed in Normandy were concentrated on the Anglo-Canadian front, east of the beachhead. Consequently, little wonder that British armour met such great difficulty in progressing in June and July, whereas the Americans, on a front half the size, only advanced with terrible losses against units essentially composed of infantry and paratroopers! Only when the beachhead was noticeably broadened, when moving became easier and when the Germans were forced to withdraw, could the British armoured units give of their best: that was confirmed some weeks later by their dazzling advance towards northern France and Belgium

**Although formidable, Hitler's army could nevertheless be defeated in Normandy, and was actually defeated during one of the worst failures of his short history. On 10 July, Lance Corporal James and Sergeant Coe, crew members of a Sherman I Hybrid command tank (see the multiple antennas) from 27th Arm. Brig., proudly show to the photographer the Nazi flag they have just captured after Operation Charnwood.** (IWM B6904)

The legendary British phlegm "in action", hiding concentration under apparent nonchalance: three pipe-smoking tank crewmen, probably belonging to 3rd RTR, are waiting the order to move on to Argentan, while attentively observing the road from the turret of their Sherman, on 21 August. The track links protecting the turret side have been taken from a Panther.

*(IWM B9538)*

## Traditional qualities

In spite of a long military and colonial past, Great-Britain in 1939 was no longer a warlike nation, but maybe more than the other European democracies she maintained the pride of her history and her traditions. The country no longer intended to commit troops on the continent, and considered its role more like that of a policeman of the world. It however ended up alone facing Nazi Germany in 1940, to defend its freedom, indeed with the support of a strong and densely populated Commonwealth, rich in raw material and present in all areas of the world. The power of Great-Britain of course relied upon the Navy, but also upon the Army split between Regular, Territorial and Reserve Army, allowing it to quickly mobilize large and valuable forces. In fact, the qualities of the British soldier are renowned from long ago and are undisputed: obedience, organisation, courage, stoicism, rigour and tenacity. He probably lacks the aggressiveness and professionalism of the German soldier, or else the "furia francese" sometimes demonstrated by the French soldier, and these shortcomings were harmful to his results in attack. In return, the British soldier is pugnacious and stubborn in defence, and the Germans themselves acknowledged that it was almost impossible to drive out a British unit installed on its defensive positions.

As such, tank crews were not different from infantrymen, artillerymen or engineers; they possessed the same qualities and shortcomings: sometimes hesitant in attack, often unshakeable in defence.

The Germans thus noticed that the Allied tank crews seldom showed an aggressive attitude, preferring slow advances in easy stages to fast rides or deep breakthroughs. They used to consolidate their positions like infantry, and often adopted very effective hedgehog defence. In return, the reconnaissance units were considered much more enterprising, almost intrepid, a behaviour which caused them heavy casualties, above all when they fought in more vulnerable armoured cars or light tanks. Of course these are only general cases, and the history of armoured divisions and brigades in the first part of the present book shows that some officers knew how to lead their Troop or Squadron with a fighting, go-ahead spirit, in keeping with the traditions of armoured cavalry.

On the other hand, the German noticed that the Allied crews were very sensitive to antitank fire, and used to stop as soon as their tank was hit, without hesitating to bale out. They used to immediately call for artillery or Typhoons to clear the terrain before resuming the advance. This attitude might have been surprising for the Germans who had well armoured and armed Panzers, but was quite understandable when considering the inferiority of Allied, including British, equipment. The British crews were also aware that their side mostly had the battleground under control, and that their mount could be recovered and repaired: for instance, out of the 300 tanks lost during Operation *Goodwood*, two thirds were recovered and refurbished. In conclusion, if the British armoured units probably revealed weaknesses and shortcomings during the Normandy campaign, mainly in the first weeks, they were far from bearing the whole responsibility for this, and in any case their men's courage cannot be questioned. These units gained costly but valuable experience for the future, which they were to put into practice to pursue the Germans up to the Seine then to the Somme, to Belgium and to Holland, in order to bring the war onto German soil.

# Daily Life in Normandy

After the confusion of the fighting, the units on the British beaches get organised: two AVREs from 79th Arm.Div. keep close to a half-track and a Sherman in front of a damaged house in Lion-sur-Mer, on 6 June. The front of the tank on the right is still equipped with an unknown apparatus, maybe an explosive charge-placing device. *(Tank Museum 5871/F6)*

OPERATION *OVERLORD* HAD BEEN PREPARED down to the tiniest details, and the armoured units had not been left out of this thorough organisation: the crews of DD tanks from 8th and 27th Arm.Brig. and of specialised armour from 79th Arm.Div. landing on 6 June knew exactly what they had to do, for they had rehearsed again and again for several months.

After having spent two or three days on the quays or at sea in the ships, because of the delay caused by the bad weather, the assault force began a long crossing of the Channel on 5 June, on a very rough sea and in the rain. The memories of the tank crew members are similar to those of other participants: they tell of fear, anguish, waiting, and some kind of excitement. Most of them were seasick, and the nausea was not really calmed by the tablets distributed before they set sail. It must be said that most of them travelled on flat-bottomed landing ships that were not intended for high seas, and which rolled heavily. Some men arrived literally exhausted on the Norman beaches, but for others the seasickness was almost an encouragement: they would rather have faced enemy fire than have continued to endure that nausea! Those who were lucky enough to be good sailors, and to travel on American ships, could enjoy a warm welcome and rich and abundant food, delicious for them who in Great-Britain had suffered from the privations of four years of war.

Action soon outshone fear, when the ships came in sight of the Norman coast pounded by aircraft and naval artillery. Amidst the clashes of explosions, the DD tanks were launched from their landing ships, generally much closer to the shore than had been planned since the sea was too rough: with the edge of their in-

flated screen barely emerging above the water surface, some were drowned by the waves with part of their crew, but most made it to the beach. The LCTs had in the meantime put the 79th Arm.Div. specialised armour ashore, trying to stay away from the obstacles that had not all been cleared by the engineers: AVREs and Crabs thus were often the first AFVs to land. The confusion of the fighting did not leave them much time to look around and think: all opposition having got through the bombardments had to be suppressed, and beach exits had to be opened as soon as possible. The mission was fulfilled, specialised armour proving particularly effective in spite of high losses sometimes.

The testimony of Lieutenant Ian Hammerton, tank commander in B Squadron, 22nd Dragoons, is a good illustration of how the initial combats developed: his Flail was in third position in the LCT; the two first Crabs in his Troop came down in shallow water, and he followed them, striking a booby-trapped tetrahedra, but continued on his way without damage. Once the most cumbersome parts of his waterproofing had been released, the Flail worked its way on the beach, then tackled an Element C with high-explosive shells, and so cleared a ramp immediately climbed over by AVREs: the first one tipped over on its side, and then the second one blew up on a mine. Hammerton and his crew dismounted to tow the Element C wreckage out of the path by attaching the tow ropes under enemy fire. Once the passage had been cleared, he ordered to one of the other Crabs to go up the ramp, but in the meantime his driver warned him that he had water up to the knees, and the engine was soon flooded. The crew baled out and managed to save enough food and armament to hold until the beach was cleared.

Sherman DD n°43 from B Squadron, 13/18th Hussars, is seen supporting infantry from 3rd Inf.Div. or rather Commandos, judging by the Bergam bag of the central soldier. The tank seems to be carrying a canvas panel with four large contrasted-colour squares on the rear, probably an identification sign. On account of its poor quality, this view may have been taken from a film.
(Tank Museum 2241/B1)

*Bottom.*
Soon after the DDs, the Navy put standard Shermans ashore: besides an armoured bulldozer in action, LCT 1076 is disembarking vehicles from 8th Arm.Brig., the insignia of which can be seen on the tank still in the ship. "Aberdeen", a Sherman from an A Squadron (see the triangle on the turret) is still fitted with its Deep Wading Equipment, and is already climbing up the beach.
(Tank Museum 440/F3)

# Early hours

As seen from the sea, the apparent confusion reigning in the landing area struck those who arrived first on the beach, but was actually soon dispersed: the engineers cleared the mines and obstacles, opened up passable tracks, while the Beach masters were efficiently organising the exits for vehicles and men. The wreckages were cleared up in a matter of hours, and even the corpses of infantrymen, who littered the beach, were gathered and covered with blankets near the dunes or the antitank walls when the second wave units, such as 7th Arm.Div., landed. While the Mulberry artificial harbours were being installed, the landing went on uninterrupted, but the big LSTs could not approach the shore: the vehicles they transported were transferred on Rhino Ferries which grounded onto the sand and pulled off rearwards, immediately or with the next tide. Even

though the beaches were in principle secured, it was impossible to avoid accidents owing to an unfilled shell crater or a forgotten mine. The formidable armada of several thousands of ships, as well as the obvious aerial supremacy, impressed and reassured the armoured units' personnel who pushed on inland to reach the assembly area: only the two armoured brigades of the first wave were committed on 6 June, the other formations entering combat only later.

Some of them (11th Arm.Div.; Guards Arm.Div.; 34th Tk.Brig.) even remained several weeks in the beachhead before their first action: their members then had a chance to meet the comrades who had already fought, to share their experiences. They were also able to visit the battlefield, and the discovery of the first Tigers and Panthers was none too comforting: all were impressed by the size, armour and barrel length of these mastodons. The 75-mm or 6

As early as 7 June, the landings took place in a calmer atmosphere: at low tide on Gold Beach, a Cromwell from 4th CLY (7th Arm.Div.) is going ashore from a large LST, carrying a section of infantry taking advantage to land with dry feet. The canvas cover protecting the gun mantle and Besa can be clearly seen, as well as the shipping stencils.
*(IWM B5128)*

pounder gun of their own tank seemed then rather puny, and the first doubts about the quality of Allied equipment, that they had been told was superior or at least equal to that of the Germans, began to beset them. These doubts would unfortunately be confirmed in the following days.

When reaching the landing area, the tank men were often a bit disappointed: after so many weeks spent in doing, undoing, and doing again the waterproofing on the tanks, planned for a depth of 6 feet, most of them landed in a few inches of water! Moreover, de-waterproofing was not trouble-free, for the watertight joints had to be removed by setting off small explosive charges slipped into the Bostik. When he was put ashore in Normandy in early July, Trooper Digweed, the driver of the Churchill "Buzzard" from B Squadron, 107th RAC (34th Tk.Brig.), inadvertently pressed the switch detonating these charges and was seriously wounded in the hands: except for the first wave units, the waterproofing was only to be removed on order, and in any case once the assembly area had been reached (only the metal engine trunks were released earlier).

## The disillusioning Sherman

The first actions carried out by the British armoured units were not very successful, the most serious reverse being suffered by the 7th Arm.Div. at Villers-Bocage on 13 June. The Allies' apparent superiority, which had reassured the crews when they landed, had paradoxically induced some of them to feel exaggeratedly unconcerned and confident, but this feeling soon vanished when they first confronted the Germans. The campaign which was beginning was not to be child's play, and the opposition promised to be fierce and stubborn. The crews soon realized that the enemy enjoyed greatly superior equipment: the Panther and then the Tiger, which had already highly impressed them by their size and their gun, confirmed their qualities in combat. Moreover, the shooting trials against captured Panzers were disastrous, the 75-mm shells desperately kept bouncing off the armour of enemy heavy tanks even at short range: only the 17 pounder, and to a lesser extent the 6 pounder gun with the new discarding sabot ammunition and from cer-

tain angles of fire, could defeat these thick carapaces at reasonable distances. The German antitank artillery was as powerful and precise, and the clashes always ended up in the loss of several tanks: even the Churchills could not resist the 88 shells despite their thick armour. The Cromwell was not armoured enough, the Stuart was completely obsolete and under-armed, hence the decision to remove the turret to make it more inconspicuous and fast, at least.

The Sherman was a serious disappointment: its propensity to catch fire as soon as hit earned it the nickname of "*Ronson*" (from a brand of cigarette lighter) by the Anglo-Canadians, or Tommy Cooker by the Germans. The crews suspected that the fuel tanks were responsible for these fires on the Sherman, and because of this they preferred the M4A2 diesel engine. Actually, the losses statistics do not show that one model was more vulnerable than another. On the other hand, it seems that the frequency of fires was less in the 32nd Guards Arm.Brig. (Guards Arm.Div.), and it would be due to the better discipline of the Guards units, the crews of which did not carry additional ammunition stowed anywhere: the veterans' testimonies actually mention the usual practice of carrying rounds on the tank floor, in the turret basket, or even in crates on the engine deck (this habit was even more widespread among the Americans, who also suffered heavy losses).

In a letter to the author dated 7 April 2003, Robert Boscawen M.C., Lieutenant and Troop commander in the N°2 Squadron of the 1st Coldstream Guards (Guards Arm.Div.) in June 1944, clearly explained his feelings about the Sherman V: "*We, who were serving and fighting in the American-built Shermans (...), did not hold them in high regard. Against the German Mark IV and Panther Mark V, let alone the Tiger, they were really pretty useless, especially the majority which only had a 75-mm gun. They were mechanically reliable and kept going, but caught fire very readily and we lost a great many casualties from their «brewing up» as we called it. I had four Shermans knocked out under me, one of which blew up, and we lost very many wonderful men.*" Brew up was a typical expression of British humour, employing the same word to signify "*preparing tea*"... One of the worst experiences of the British tank crewmen was in this way compared with a typical moment of the daily life.

## An often hostile land

Although the Norman countryside is quite similar to some English landscapes, the British crews, who had trained so long or

the Salis bury plains, were disturbed by the close Bocage they met from the beginning.

The high and dense hedgerows, often rising above thick stone walls, compartmentalized a country made of small fields and meadows, criss-crossed with a net of narrow, embanked and rather tortuous lanes, where visibility was nil. Ideal for the defender, this terrain was only a series of traps for the attacker, and the hull-down position, so appreciated by the British, could not be used since the hedgerow top was higher than the turret roof. The tank commander could only observe the country by standing on the turret, and he then became very vulnerable to snipers.

The Bocage presented other risks of shooting mistakes: faced with an unidentified target, it was usual to shoot first and then ask questions… Actually, the very nature of the landscape, devoid of landmarks and badly represented on the military maps, made that some units could advance faster than others unwittingly, and then end up in the aiming sight of friendly tank or antitank guns. The AVREs, thanks to their powerful Petard mortar, were first used to break through the thick hedges; bulldozers were employed for the same task, but they did not have much armour or even not at all and were thus too vulnerable.

The situation improved when the first Sherman Dozers arrived, since they retained their armament, but it was not until late July (and even on 11 August for the Guards Arm.Div.) that the American-developed "Cullin Hedgerow Devices", or "Rhino Prongs", were fitted to a few Shermans and Cromwells: this device was made up of beach obstacles pieces (tetrahedras) that were recovered, cut with a blowtorch, assem-

*Top.*
**On 20 June, in ruined Lingèvres, a burnt-out and trackless Sherman from 4/7th Dragoon Guards (8th Arm.Brig.) stands as a testimony of the violent fighting on the 14th. No less than five impacts having easily penetrated can be seen on the transmission housing, the most armoured part of a Sherman. C Squadron had been surprised by Panthers from the Panzer-Lehr, and this Sherman was destroyed, but a single Firefly succeeded in immobilizing five Panzers.**
*(IWM B5783)*

*Right.*
**Here is a much dangerous situation for a tank trying to pass through a Norman hedgerow: this Churchill is showing its very vulnerable ventral armour, and the crew has absolutely no possibility of seeing where it is going. Actually, the hedges in Normandy, several centuries old, are heightened and strengthened at their base by the piling-up of all the stones recovered when the fields are ploughed.**
*(Tank Museum 4834/F6)*

On 17 June, the crew of this Cromwell from 4th CLY (7th Arm.Div.) is preparing its meal on a Primus stove: main ingredients probably come from a Compo Pack, maybe supplemented with eggs from a nearby farm. A metal rod, welded between the tank's two light protectors, make it possible to stow a spare wheel.
*(Tank Museum 3579/A6)*

**A crate of Type D Compo ration and some of its contents**
*(Photo P. Charbonnier, courtesy J. Bouchery, © H & C)*

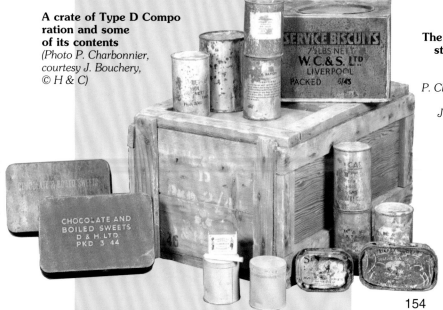

**The collective stove ready for use.**
*(Photo P. Charbonnier, courtesy J. Bouchery, © H & C)*

bled to form a multi-pointed plough, and then welded to the front of a standard combat tank.

The landscape of the plain of Caen, considered as "tank country" for its similarity with Salisbury Plain and with the wide expanses of the North African desert, turned out to be murderous for the British crews and their tanks: the cavalry charges they dreamt about were stopped by the 75-mm and 88-mm German guns, which could knock out a Sherman or a Cromwell at 1,500m or even 2,000m range. Operations *Goodwood, Totalize* and *Tractable* showed that against such a skilled, superiorly equipped adversary, who was moreover entrenched in strongly fortified villages, the plain was no more favourable than any other terrain.

Fighting again in the Bocage during the late campaign, from Operation *Bluecoat* onwards, brought the same difficulties as in June, but the German defence fortunately began to weaken in mid-August. On the other hand, fighting in orchards revealed an unexpected threat: the apple trees were covered with unripe fruits and the tank commanders who were up in their turret were hit in the face by the low branches, while the apples bombarded them and piled up in the bottom of the tanks... These clashes also caused sometimes the open hatch to be suddenly unlocked, the doors then falling back violently on the head or the fingers of the one who was not fast enough... Actually, the danger with apples was met as early as on 10 June by the East Riding Yeomanry (27th Arm.Brig.): on that day, near Anisy, the driver of a B squadron Sherman signalled that his "throttle pedal was sticking", but the fitters discovered that it was simply jammed by apples piled up and crushed behind it... A similar adventure happened on 25 August to Ken Tout, Lance Corporal in 1st Northamptonshire Yeomanry (33rd Arm.Brig.): then, the apples had rained into the tank from the upper hatch and ended up jamming the turret.

## Eating and drinking

After sleep, which he never had enough of, the things a soldier is most interested in are food and drink (and sex, but that is another story...) The British tank men were no exception and used to attach a great deal of importance to these elements when they arrived in Normandy, more than the Americans or the Canadians for instance. It is worth remembering that as early as 1940, Great-Britain had had to institute a strict rationing on drink and food, mainly on account of the German blockade which cut her off both from European and Commonwealth supplies. The British lived through difficult days, nearly as much as the peoples in occupied territories, and more than the Germans who were able to enjoy the riches of

the countries they were occupying. Upon their arrival in Normandy, the British soldiers thus began to search for anything which could improve their rather monotonous standard fare.

The British tank crewmen used to land with one or two "24-Hour Ration Packs" per man, which, as their name indicates, were conceived to provide food for one day: they consisted of food dehydrated (meat, tea) or with great energizing qualities (porridge, chocolate, sugar) in a small volume. But these individual rations were to be opened in emergencies only, the standard fare or "Field Service Ration" being normally supplied by the mobile field kitchens, which could serve hot meals based on fresh, congealed or dehydrated products, as well as bread. However, in Normandy, because of the necessity to secure a beachhead rapidly and to keep up with the rhythm of the fighting, priority was given to reinforcements, equipment, ammunition and fuel. The mobile kitchens were thus seldom supplied with the required food-stuffs, and did not have food preservation and storage means during the first weeks.

The soldiers had thus to rely upon the "Compo Ration Pack", a box of collective rations including the meals for 14 men for a day. Whereas the distribution was rather easy in infantry units, it was always difficult to divide 14 rations up between four of five tank crewmen... since the Compo Pack could include seven different tinned menus, marked from A to G on the package, and everybody would have liked to choose his meal: mutton stew, pork and vegetable, ox-tail with beans, and so on. But each box contained 14 times the same menu, so every man was likely to eat the same meal two or three times in succession. The Compo Pack also included tinned vegetable and fruits, biscuits, cigarettes, powdered soup, sugar, sweets, toilet paper (84 sheets!)... The crews were thus mainly supplied with Compo Packs, except when they were withdrawn from the front, well away from the battlefield, where mobile kitchens could be installed.

To prepare hot meals themselves, the tank crewmen had a Primus gas-operated stove as standard issue in each vehicle. It was however common to use a makeshift method which had proved itself in the desert: in the cut-out bottom of a 4-gallon can or a large biscuit box, sand was poured and then impregnated with petrol. Once on fire, an almost unnoticeable flame produced enough heat to warm up a meal or some tea. Let's not forget the famous self-heating soup cans, which included a simple candle in the middle of the can enabling the contents to be warmed up. According to the veterans' memoirs, this much appreciated product was available in the early days, but was only seldom delivered during the rest of the Normandy campaign.

The Invasion money which had been distributed before landing having no value for the Normans, the British tank crewmen relied

## Snipers

For the tank commander, if the hatches were closed, observation from the Sherman, Cromwell and Churchill turret was only possible through two periscopes on the rotating cupola, which had to be turned continuously without providing a global vision (it was even less practical on the Stuart). Since the fighting in the desert, the tank commanders were used to command their crew by observing from the open turret hatch, even in the middle of combat: losses were high, but there was no other solution. But the situation worsened in Normandy since the Germans used to install sharpshooters along the front line, concealed in high places (trees, houses, church towers). When they withdrew, they also left snipers behind them intended to delay the Allied advance and control of the ground. Officers were of course the favourite target of these snipers, and in order to escape this threat, it was not uncommon to see Allied infantry officers commanding their troops with all the signs of their rank and function (shoulder straps, insignia, binoculars) camouflaged, and carrying a rifle like a private.

This stratagem was not possible for the tank commanders, since their position in the turret naturally pointed them out to the snipers. Some units thus recommended wearing helmets (34th Tk.Brig., Guards Arm.Div.), which proved to be far from convenient in the cramped compartment of a tank. The helmet furthermore hampered observation and listening, and prevented the easy use of the intercom: the beret remained the most common headgear. The losses of tank commanders were thus very heavy all along the Normandy campaign, in spite of improvised solutions such as the fitting of armoured plates to the rear of the

cupola by the 6th Guards Tk.Brig. workshops in July. The crews also got into the habit of systematically machine-gunning, at the slightest suspicion, the snipers' possible hiding places. Finally, close cooperation with infantry, who could clear the terrain around them, was the best chance for the tank commanders to avoid sniper fire.

**Protected in this way by an armour plate added to the cupola's rear, by the hatch's doors and by his helmet, this tank commander of a Churchill from 6th Guards Tk.Brig. (the insignia of which can be seen on a vehicle in the background) did not fear the snipers anymore. Unfortunately, his field of vision was drastically reduced, and above all he could hardly hear what was happening around him.** *(Tank Museum 3581/A4)*

**On 30 June near Rauray, soldiers are digging a hole beside a Sherman I Hybrid (from 8th Arm.Brig. according to the wartime caption). Although they are infantrymen, the scene is evocative of the encampment conditions in armoured units: a shelter was most often dug, and the tank was sometimes parked on top of it to improve protection against mortars and Nebelwerfers.** *(IWM B6225)*

upon barter to obtain the fresh provisions and alcohol they needed: cigarettes were used as main exchange money, but also sweets, chocolate, tinned fruits, or even clothes, shoes, and blankets. They were bartered for eggs, potatoes, chickens, and specially cheese, cider and Calvados. Unfortunately, the British digestive system soon seemed quite unused to the farm cider that was drunk every day… As for the Calvados, it was much appreciated, but was often too strong for their throat: when it was too powerful, some even used it to fill their lighters! Camembert was also surprising for British taste, but some greatly liked it: Trooper Tony Matza, from 23rd Hussars (11th Arm.Div.), had obtained a number of these barely ripe cheeses, and stowed them in a blanket he forgot on his tank's rear deck. The combined action of the summer sun and the engine heat speeded up the Camemberts' ripening process, which soon signalled their presence through the revolting smell!

Drink remained a problem throughout the Normandy campaign: water had a foul taste, for it was automatically disinfected with chlorine tablets (and this was necessary on account of the streams, rivers and ground water being contaminated by the human and animal corpses, and the ensuing dysentery epidemic). Beer was only exceptionally issued, and there was not much wine left after the Germans had passed. The tea supplied in the rations was always mixed with powdered milk and sugar: the result was poor, and there was no possibility of changing the ingredient dosage. The best solution, according to John Stone from 9th RTR, was to heat it for 30 minutes, and then add three spoons of sugar per cup… Only milk was reasonably available, since the country was stocked with cows the

dead or evacuated owners of which could not take care of, and which were mooing from pain, waiting to be milked. It was also by putting a cow wounded during the fighting out of its misery, a frequent occurrence, that the British crews were able to get fresh meat. Finally, there was a particular alcoholic drink officially issued in units: the Regiment Quarter Master Sergeant had rum at his disposal, which he could only issue on order, in collective or individual rations. The cold was not a major concern in Normandy, so rum was sometimes distributed on the eve of an attack to warm up the troops' ardour (a reminiscence from the First World War, even though it was not intended then to make the soldiers totally drunk so that they could forget they were marching to death…) But there were other opportunities: thus, when the 24th Lancers were disbanded, the regiment's Colonel ordered the whole stock of rum to be broken out, and this led to a night of drunkenness appropriate for consoling the men for the bad news.

## Encampment and sleep

When evening came, the tanks used to withdraw just behind the front line to settle in a "*laager*" following a common but contested practice (their presence could be reassuring for the infantry). The word "*laager*" (modified into the verb "to leaguer") was inherited from the Boer War and designated a protected hedgehog encampment for better overall defence. In Normandy, each Squadron arranged some of its tanks around the soft-skinned or lightly armoured vehicles, to cover the four cardinal points. The other tanks were grouped in the middle, a rotation and regular patrols being organised to carry out the night guard in and around the laager. At regimental level, various states of alert were also maintained in rotation, so that a Squadron could be ready to intervene in 30 minutes, one hour or two hours. This involved the men on alert sleeping bit by bit, completely dressed in their tank.

The others could settle down more comfortably, but except during the rest periods far from the front, it was overoptimistic to expect peaceful and refreshing sleep... The summer nights were actually short and noisy, and reveille was sounded very early: there were at best four or five hours left for sleep. Almost totally chased out of the skies during the day, the Luftwaffe was very busy at night, harassing the resting Allied units with more or less hazardous bombardments, or even with strafing by fighters when the moon made this possible... and this caused the antiaircraft batteries to open fire, which was of no help in restoring silence! Moreover, by day or night, mortars, artillery and Nebelwerfers started sudden poundings that were called stonks by the British, causing heavy casualties and forcing the men to stay under shelter most of the time. It was out of the question to sleep in a tent or in the open: digging trenches was a gruelling task after a fighting day, but it proved indispensable. Most of the crews even drove their tank just over the trench to protect it completely. On the other hand, many others hesitated to sleep under the tank without digging a shelter, for the choice of the ground was then essential: the story was told of crews crushed by their tank because it had slipped or sunk during the night...

Practically, sleep was a coveted but seldom accessible luxury for all. The tank crews of the first assault wave had been kept awake trough the use of Benzedrine pills, but this stimulant had redoubtable side-effects, and could only be employed exceptionally: it could provoke hallucinations, uncontrolled fits of madness, and in the long term it inhibited the most vital reflexes. Stopping the treatment was moreover dangerous, and some officers were seen falling suddenly asleep because they had forgotten to take the medication once... The tank crewmen thus had to content themselves with little sleep, accumulating a weariness that was already increased by stress and fear. This chronic lack of sleep is in fact characteristic of every soldier at war, whatever the service branch or the country. Finally, there was also the bad luck to be billeted in areas impossible to live in: for instance, after Operation *Goodwood*, the *Coldstream Guards* (Guards Arm. Div.) were withdrawn from the front line but had to settle down near a field where a 5.5 inch gun battery was installed: the roar of the detonations prevented most of the men from sleeping, even though some were so dog-tired that they barely noticed it!

## Maintenance and supplies

There was a long period between laagering and sleep, during which the tank crews were kept very busy: unlike the infantrymen, who had limited daily upkeep of their weapons, the tank crewmen had to carry out maintenance of their tank almost every day: greasing, cleaning, adjustment, control, of the engine and transmission, of the gun and machine-guns, with their lot of dismantling and reassembling, bolts to be screwed and unscrewed, pieces to be changed. Some veterans still remember that it was necessary to regularly drain the recoil system on the 17 pounder gun to prevent the spent cases from jamming after shooting. The radio set, electrical system, sights, episcopes and periscopes also had to be maintained or replaced. Thus, from 6 to 16 August, the 9th RTR crews, after a swift advance on dirt tracks or across country, had to spend up to three hours every evening cleaning the sights, episcopes and armament of their Churchills (let alone the engine and ventilation), which otherwise would have been out of order because of the all-persuasive dust.

The crew members were also required to carry out refuelling and ammunition replenishment, these supplies being brought up by the RASC's trucks from A and B Echelons. Fuel was most often carried in 25-litre jerry-cans that had to be manhandled again and again (the fuel tanks of a Sherman held an average 790 litres, that is to say 31 jerry-cans...), not to mention the 75-mm, 95-mm or 17 pounder heavy shells, ammunition and ration boxes, and so on. These tasks often took the men up to midnight or more, thus shortening the night further.

*Above.* **The slightest lull was taken advantage of to read one's mail, and even answer it if the lull continued. On 10 June, two crew members of Sherman n°69 from 13/18th Hussars (27th Arm.Brig.) are writing letters, while others have a short nap. Note the regimental flash on the helmet and sleeve of both men on the right.** *(IWM B5425)*

*Below.* **Reading a newspaper was an occupation restricted to prolonged relaxing periods, far from the front: on 15 June, a tank man of 22nd Arm.Brig. HQ (7th Arm.Div.) is reading The Empire News besides a still sleeping comrade. The fact that these men have not dug any shelter for the night near their Cromwell is an additional indication of their position remote from the fighting area.** *(IWM B5598)*

33rd Arm.Brig. is preparing on 7 August
for Operation *Totalize*: in the foreground
can be seen a Sherman I Hybrid followed
by a Firefly and a line of 75-mm Shermans.
The welding seam joining the M4A1 cast front
with the M4 welded hull can be made out
across the additional armour plate.
The shelter in front of the tank may have
been that of a Priest crew, since it
is surrounded with 105-mm ammo boxes.
*(IWM B8805)*

## Recovery and repairs

The crew used to carry out the standard maintenance of the tank,
and it was also in charge of the simple repairs: changing a bogie
or a track link, for instance. More serious repairs as well as main
mechanical part changes were undertaken by the Royal Electrical
and Mechanical Engineers, at different unit levels depending on
their importance: the Light Aid Detachment assigned to the armoured regiment was only equipped with a few trucks, a wrecker and
a tank transporter, but had the basic equipment for urgent recovery,
fitting, adjustment, and replacement of single parts. The brigade
workshops (combined within the armoured divisions under the com-

*Above.* **On 7 August, for Operation *Totalize*, the crew of the Firefly
"Houghton" from C Squadron, 1st Northamptonshire Yeomanry
(33rd Arm.Brig.) is handling the heavy 17 pounder rounds to stow
them in the racks occupying the seat of the machine-gunner, which
can be reached only from the outside. Sergeant Ginns on the left is
oddly wearing the regimental cap badge on his belt, but also that of
the RTR, of which he may have been a former member?** *(IWM B8793)*

*Above, left.* **On 17 July, two tank men of the "Briton", from
34th Tk.Brig., are carefully checking the cartridge belts for their
Churchill's Besa machine-guns. Re-supplying the tank with
ammunition was not restricted to filling the magazines or boxes,
but the ammunition had also to be checked to avoid any jamming.**
*(Tank Museum 4835/C1)*

*Above, left and right.*

**A Sherman I Hybrid, from 27th Arm.Brig. according to the wartime caption, has blown up on a mine on 9 July, and two crew members are trying to recover the track links which are still driven into the ground with a sledgehammer. It is more probably a tank from 33rd Arm.Brig. taking part in Operation *Charnwood* in the same sector, since 27th Arm.Brig. was equipped with Sherman IIIs and DDs.** *(IWM B5423)*

**On 7 June, fitters helped by the crew of a Sherman Crab from the Westminster Dragoons (79th Arm.Div.) are replacing a wheel and a bogie half, probably destroyed by a mine judging from their look. The use of the jack is well illustrated here: it lifted the bogie, and not the whole tank, of course.** *(IWM B6747)*

mand of a REME HQ) enjoyed permanent installations, and could notably carry out the replacement of complete assemblies (engine, transmission). In return, the 3rd and 4th echelon repairs required heavy materiel and could only be undertaken in rear area workshops: replacement of entire armour plates, of the turret of the gun, refurbishing of burned-out or badly damaged tanks and so on.

*Below.* **The engine of this Cromwell is requiring intensive care the rear deck has been completely removed, and two mechanics stripped to the waist are immersed in the tank's bowels. Note al around the men several spanners, and a box filled with nuts and bolts that will have to be put back in their places.** *(Tank Museum 3581/A1*

A Sherman V ARV is travelling through Bourguébus on 9 August, towing a Sherman with all hatches open. This recovery tank probably belongs to 144th RAC from 33rd Arm.Brig., for it bears a large white T on the right front, the meaning of which is unknown, but which can be seen on a Stuart and a Sherman of this unit (see the chapter about 33rd Arm.Brig.) *(IWM B8910)*

*Below.*
On 9 August, in the workshops of 8th Arm.Brig., REME mechanics are replacing the Continental radial engine of a Stuart III (M3A1) named *"Shipley"*. The recovery truck used to lift the engine is probably a Ward-La France. *(IWM B8891)*

The fitters then did everything to put a tank back in running order, and they salvaged any part they could: soon after D-Day, the Cromwell of Sergeant Moat, named *"Defiant"*, had been hit by a shell which had destroyed the front running gear. This tank was adorned with a painting by Corporal Telford representing a lady in naughty clothing showing one of her legs. During *Goodwood*, the Sergeant's new Sherman Firefly exploded on a mine which holed the fuel tank. When being given another Firefly, Sergeant Moat's crew was amazed to see that one of its additional armour plates was still wearing the painting of the naughty lady that was previously on the Cromwell!

Towing was often the first task of the REME fitters, and the ARVs were generally assigned to the fighting units, at the rate of one per Squadron, to recover as fast as possible the combat-damaged tanks. The conditions in which the ARV crew carried out the recovery were then dangerous, since they often operated under enemy fire. It was not uncommon that this type of urgent recovery required the participation of one or two combat tanks, although it was not recommended using them for this job during which they were likely to be damaged. The case of Major Wormald, commanding A Squadron of 13th/18th Hussars, is interesting since he incited the ARV crews who were attached to his unit to bring along with them one or two replacement tanks usually kept at the rear: this initiative allowed very quickly a damaged or knocked-out tank to be replaced, and thus to keep up the impetus of the attack. The recovered tanks were transported towards the rear by tank transporters or heavy trucks (Scammel, Diamond T or Ward-LaFrance) which brought the wrecks back to the workshops, with the help of a trailer if necessary.

## Washing and the necessities of nature

Every tank crewman was issued with two battle-dresses, and sometimes Denim overalls: one of the uniforms was worn every day, the other one was kept for the days off or for great occasions. In combat, the same uniform was thus worn several days and often several weeks at a stretch, without being changed or washed, and it was not better for the underwear. Personal hygiene was then essential, but it was often neglected out of necessity: between the fighting, the movements, the multiple tasks that befell them, the

Once recovered by an ARV, the damaged tanks were transported to the REME workshops: here, the latter are settled down in a large meadow, and mechanics are working on the engine of a Sherman II DD while a Scammel is bringing a trackless Sherman on its trailer. It is an early production M4A2, judging by the shape of the metal skid supporting the track on top of the bogie. *(Tank Museum 6179/C6)*

On 31 July, a Sherman is passing the upturned wreck of a Humber armoured car from 15th Inf.Div., on the Caumont road. It could belong to 11th or Guards Arm.Div., which were both in action in the same 8th Corps sector. The cloud of dust raised by a single tank is impressive, and one can imagine the result of a column including a whole Squadron. (IWM B8272)

crews did not have enough time or means to regularly wash or shave. A billet near a stream or a river with more or less clean water was a godsend, but most of the time, particularly in combat, they had to content themselves with a mug of water on the face, and a shaving every two or three days (except the Guards, who shaved every day of course.)

Rest periods at the rear were all the more appreciated but they were scarce and short. Periodically, and more often for the armoured divisions than the armoured or tank brigades, it seems, the units were pulled out from the front to replace and maintain equipment, absorb reinforcements, reorganise, and above all have rest. But sometimes they had to wait a very long time for this: having landed on 7 June and having been committed almost continuously until then, the East Riding Yeomanry had to wait until 10 July before being billeted to the rear. There, it was much like paradise after hell for the combatants, since in spite of occasional mortar shelling or Luftwaffe's bombardments, they could relax, wash themselves thanks to hot bath units or at least showers, and give their uniform and underwear to the laundress. They also had regular and complete hot meals, sometimes billets in houses spared from destruction, or even real beds, a luxury they had not enjoyed since they had left the civilian life.

Rest was also the opportunity to bathe, sometimes in the sea, to organise sport competitions (mainly football and cricket), and to be entertained: cinema projections, ENSA musical shows, visits by stars and personalities. The men could quietly read their mail (even though it regularly reached the front line), and answer it at last. On the other hand, there were not many days out to expect, since most of the towns were devastated. At the very most the crews could go to the local café and try to speak with the civilians in spite of the different language, do a bit of barter and black market, or court some young women in the vicinity. In the latter case, the difference of language did not seem to be an obstacle, although the naturally modest British are very discreet in their memories about these passing romances… It is actually strange enough that the British were often surprised to see that the Normans did not speak a single word of English, although they themselves did not speak French either…

For bodily needs, collective latrines could seldom be arranged on the front line. It was thus usual in armoured units to go and dig an individual hole at a distance from the encampment, field kitchens and water resources, and to carefully fill in it again after use. But in combat, and under enemy harassing fire, it was not always possible to do so. Some ran the risk of crawling outside the tank, but most preferred to use a spent shell case to urinate in, or a helmet (a German one, if possible) for more consistent needs; all they had to do was then to throw everything through a hatch during a lull in the fighting. During an advance under enemy fire there is the example of a Troop from the East Riding Yeomanry who used to arrange its tanks in tight square, in order to protect the crew members who could then relieve themselves without being disturbed in the middle!

## Nuisances and little worries

War is only an enormous nuisance, but as in every military campaign, the Allies fighting in Normandy had to face a multitude of little worries that kept on complicating their already threatened existence. Since they were fighting and living in their closed vehicles, bad weather had less influence on tank crews than on infantry. Rain and cold in early June did not affect them, though they suffered comparatively more from the heat of August: fortunately, the Norman nights used to be cool. In return, rain was an indirect concern for its consequences on the terrain: for instance, the torrential rains which fell at the end of Operation *Goodwood* caused many vehicles to get bogged down, and thus represented a lot of additional work for the tank men who had to help the recovery engineers pull their tank from the mud, and then to clear it out. Ground humidity also presented the risk of getting stuck in the mud and being blocked in the middle of the battle, and in sight of the enemy. Finally digging more or less dry trenches became impossible, particularly in the valleys where a stream enlarged by the rain often flowed.

However, the tank crews would almost come to the point of regretting the rain when they had to progress across country or on a dirt track, raising huge clouds of dust in the process. Only the first in the column had a chance to avoid being blinded (in return their tank was a target offered to German guns and Panzers…) The others were covered with dust, especially the commander and the driver who had to travel with open hatches, and had to protect their face with a scarf and to wear goggles. They realized then that the British protective goggles were almost useless: they preferred

American models they had bartered, or even salvaged German goggles. Moreover, the dust raised by a vehicle speeding along used to provoke enemy fire, hence the signs reading "*Dust brings Shells*" or "*Dust means Death*" and marking the road sides; not to mention the cleaning that this all-pervading dust necessitated every evening, as we have already seen.

Operation *Totalize* is a good example of the damages that could be caused by dust, although common and apparently anodyne: in the night of 7 August, aerial and ground bombardments preceding the attack raised such a dust screen, mixed with the smoke from explosions, that it was impossible to see further than two metres, despite Very flares, lighting shells and tracers. The results were

collisions, direction mistakes, and vehicles falling into invisible craters (not to mention shooting mistakes, since many Canadian and British tanks would be recovered with shell holes in the rear of the hull or of the turret...). The movement and night march of three armoured divisions for *Goodwood* were also very eventful for the same reasons.

Noise was also omnipresent for the combatants in Normandy, and particularly for tank crews: locked up most of the time in a metal box, they endured the engine roar, the continuous messages on the intercom, and the din of explosions. All is noisy in a tank: the slamming breech, the machine-guns' staccato, the gun bang, the spent case falling on the metal floor, the various pieces of equipment and

## The British and the Normans

The relationship between the troops who landed from 6 June onwards and the Norman civilians they were supposed to liberate, were at first ambiguous. Pounded by the aviation and the naval artillery, their livestock decimated, their houses and farms in ruins, the Normans, who had sometimes lost one or several members of their family during the fighting, did not always welcome the Allied troops with warmth and kindness in the early days. The most understanding among the British soldiers, when observing the damage done to this rich country, excused this attitude. It was only in Bayeux, which had been spared the destructions, that the British were really and sincerely welcomed in early June. But the surrounding villages, in the middle of the combat zone for several weeks, were often given up by their inhabitants who took to the road under the bombs to seek refuge in more sheltered places. However, relationships began very soon to develop between civilian population and liberators, which were strengthened by a common hostility towards the Germans, a sure taste for democracy... and by exchanges of food-stuffs and goods.

It was mainly during the encirclement and pursuit phase, from early August onwards, that the British, in their faster progression, reached regions which were less affected by war, and where the delirious welcome of the population reassured and encouraged them. Up to the River Seine, the crowds of civilians came in succession to the liberated towns, even hindering the British pursuit of the Germans. The help of the Resistance, even though it was sometimes considered with caution when providing information about the enemy forces, was generally appreciated: the Resistance was given the guard of the increasingly numerous German prisoners after the closing of the Falaise pocket, and some reconnaissance units (such as the 11th Hussars from 7th Arm.Div.) took advantage and used it. The British were often shocked by the treatment reserved for the Collaborators and for the women accused of having slept with Germans, but they usually did not interfere in these more or less justified settling of scores (they had actually been ordered not to intervene, unless these events hindered their progression).

The understanding between liberators and civilians kept improving along the campaign, and the British were often moved by the care the Normans took over the burial of their comrades, when it was possible of course, with flowers being regularly laid on the graves: this attention was in strong contrast with the practices they observed every day on the battlefield. The Normandy's gratitude was to be obvious after the war, as much by the meticulous and respectful conservation of the Allied cemeteries, or the establishment of steles and plaques honouring the combatants, as by the frequent organisation of memorial ceremonies, which still take place regularly 60 years later.

On 7 August, in an unidentified village, the crew of a Churchill Mk VII (maybe from 6th Guards Tk.Brig.) is handing out its mess tins to two young girls so that they could pour milk or cider in. The wartime caption refers to an attack towards Mont Pinçon, but no Tank Brigade was committed for this operation, and this hill had already been captured the day before. *(IWM B8784)*

On 17 August, a Sherman V from 11th Arm.Div. is cheered by the population in a place named Cinq-Becs, in Flers-de-l'Orne. The town has just been liberated, the civilians warmly welcome the British in spite of the destructions inflicted to their houses: liberation was sometimes costly to the Normans, and they first experienced mixed feelings towards the Allies. *(IWM B9330)*

Two young ladies from Athis are shaking hands with the crew members of a Humber Scout Car from the Inns of Court: this armoured car regiment was assigned to 11th Arm.Div. from the end of the Normandy campaign. Women and children played an essential part to develop friendly relationships between Norman civilians and British soldiers.

*(IWM B8*

aide de camp of General Roberts is known, who had to be relieved from his post because of mosquito bites. The recrudescence of these insects was probably due to the presence of so many human beings and horses in such a restricted area (remember that the Wehrmacht was horse-drawn in all its infantry divisions), as well as to the many floods provoked by the Germans to hinder the Allied advance. But above all it was the dreadful numbers of human and animal dead bodies, left in the open under the summer sun, which attracted the parasites and caused infectious bites.

Death, which threatened the combatants every day, was omnipresent through these putrefying corpses, and the stink soon became the mark of the Normandy front: all veterans remember this smell of rotting, burned flesh, mixed with that of powder, fuel, human excrements, which increased all along the campaign. If the Allied soldiers' bodies were buried quite rapidly, those of the enemy remained in the open for a long time, and were added to the carcasses of the livestock killed by bombardments and bullets. Faced with the health danger threatening the air as well as the drinking water and the food, orders were hastily given from July onwards to bury all these dead bodies, human and animal mixed up, thanks to bulldozers, in common graves. Nevertheless, the stink of death was to float around for a long time over Normandy, and aircraft pilots

Panzerschreck and Panzerfaust: weapons which were light, discreet, easy to produce and to carry, but represented one of the greatest dangers for the British tank crews in Normandy.

objects clanging and clashing as soon as the tank moved… And during the fighting, it was not more silent outside! Pulling out from the front at nightfall then gave a sudden decrease in the sound intensity level, but the relative silence was soon disturbed by Luftwaffe bombardments, a salvo from antiaircraft guns, or as already mentioned, the thunder of a firing artillery unit in the next field.

A misunderstood nuisance, although omnipresent in the Normandy veterans' memories, was… mosquitoes! In the (sometimes) marshy area around the river Orne or later in the Bocage, the British crews like other Allied or German soldiers were assailed by mosquitoes, but also by horse-flies, wasps, flies. Every rainfall brought new assaults by myriads of insects, and some tank men were bitten so many times they could not see anymore, their face being so puffed up. Others were practically poisoned by the accumulated venom, and had to be sent to hospital for a few days! The example of the

flying over the territory at low altitude several weeks after the battle would state they were still sickened by the clinging stench emanating from this land which had been previously so lively.

## Mines, mortars and Panzerfausts

There were however much more dangerous nuisances than mosquitoes or dust: the minefields, which were not only present on the coast but also inland. The antitank Tellerminen did not inevitably represent a serious danger for the British tanks, as they most often caused a broken track or a destroyed bogie (they were more treacherous for light armour). A mine exploding just under the driving compartment could certainly wound or kill the driver or the machine-gunner, but it seldom involved the loss of a tank. The problem was that the Tellerminen were seldom alone

they were generally laid together with antipersonnel S-Minen (or Schu-Minen), small boxes full of steel balls which, once triggered off, jumped up three feet and exploded at belly height, causing awful and often fatal wounds. Examples are not rare of tank crewmen having blown up on a mine at the very moment when they were repairing the damages of a Tellermine on their tank. The Crabs were able to clear the ground of any kind of mine, but they could not be everywhere, and were in general used during offensives. Royal Engineers then had to clear most of the encampment areas with mine detectors.

And if there had been only German mines...: the congestion of the beachhead for several weeks and the relief of positions by successive units involved minefields being laid, but badly (or not) marked. When a change of sector occurred, the departing unit was supposed to hand over maps of the minefields it had laid to the following one, but after two or three reliefs, it became impossible to locate the successive minefields. The latter, like those of the Germans, were generally laid on passing points (water supply points, crossroads, embanked roads, or main streets of villages) but also around these spots, in order to hinder any attempt at bypassing. Thus, one of the first tanks lost by the 11th Arm.Div. was that of the commanding officer, General Roberts, which blew up on an unmarked Canadian mine.

The mortars, and the Nebelwerfers (nicknamed "Moaning Minnies" on account of their howling when they were fired), were the main cause of Allied casualties in Normandy, some sources even stating that they were responsible for nearly 50% of the killed and wounded. The Germans were past masters in using these weapons (usually 8cm and 12cm mortars, and 15cm and 21cm towed or self-propelled Nebelwerfers),

**Captured on 20 July near Troarn, a formidable 15cm Nebelwerfer 41, one of the weapons most feared by the Allied soldiers in Normandy, and whose rockets announced their arrival by a frightening howl. Fortunately, the quantity of smoke emitted during the firing made them easy to locate, and the batteries had to change position frequently.** *(RR)*

and their presence on the site had allowed them to spot key targets well before the Allies seized them. This knowledge offered them the opportunity to start very accurate shooting at will, as soon as an observation post revealed the presence of valuable objectives to them. Examples are numerous of Order Groups interrupted by a mortar or Nebelwerfer stonk, with nearly always heavy losses. And it was similar for the supplying or leaguering areas.

The British tank crews met the Panzerfaust and Panzerschreck very soon after the landings, but their number regularly increased afterwards, and they became really frequent in August. These light antitank weapons, shooting hollow-charge rockets, were one of the terrors of the tank men. On 7 June, the Sherman III "Bloody Mary" from B Squadron, 24th Lancers, had a narrow escape from destruction: in support of Royal Marines, the tank commander, Lieutenant Richard Leather, heard a hiss above his head and ordered the driver to move forward abruptly. He felt the blast of an explosion just after that, identified a shooting flash in a thicket, and so smashed the latter with a high explosive shell. Some minutes later, his driver reported that the engine was overheating, and when the tank stopped, the crew noticed that there was a small hole in the rear right hull: the engine seemed untouched, but the right ventilator fan had completely disappeared! Lieutenant Leather only unders-

tood later that this impact was due to a Panzerfaust or a Panzerschreck. Actually, he was to be seriously wounded on 12 June by a Panzerschreck rocket that he saw fired at him through his binoculars: the rest of the Sherman crew was killed.

The crews tried progressively to counter the threat of these weapons by welding track links (considered, probably wrongly, as being also effective against antitank shells) or by arranging sandbags on the front of the tank, but the best defence remained infantry support, since Panzerfausts and Panzerschrecks had a very limited range and had to be shot almost at point blank range.

## Fighting

When considering the time spent on journeys, encampment preparation, maintenance, washing, meals, sleep, rest at the rear, and waiting, the fighting in itself only took limited time in the life of a tank man in Normandy.

However, it was round the fighting that all other secondary activities revolved, as it was the main concern for all. Any amusement, any occupation was to prepare for war or to make one forget it, since fighting was unavoidable, despite the risk, or even near-certainty, of wounds or death.

Like any soldier, the British tank men were scared before the battle, even though the multiple tasks they were busy with allowed them to think about something else. One can hardly imagine the courage of these men who had to climb in their steel box and face a more powerful and better armed enemy... However, the veterans do not say much about courage, patriotism, glory, but about duty, responsibility towards the other crew members, refusal to give in to fear in the presence of comrades.

War was indeed less hazardous in armour than in infantry, which suffered much higher losses. And yet, the survival of a tank crew depended not only on each of its members, but also on its equipment, and the death they could meet was no better than that of the infantrymen.

The four or five men manning a tank depended on each other, one was the brain and the eyes (commander), another was the ears (radio operator), another still was the legs (driver)... They were locked up in their noisy machine, almost deaf and blind, and were at the mercy, in Normandy, of an antitank gun, a Tiger, a Panzerfaust, a mine, without being able to do much to avoid danger. In combat, the gunner and the commander were often the only ones to see the target, if that: many shells and cartridges were shot on potential targets, or ones so far away that they could not be made out.

*Top.* **On 26 June, a truck exploding in the middle of the assembly area of 11th Arm.Div. The photographs of real "in combat" tanks are scarce in the British archive: the position of a photographer accompanying an armour attack was particularly perilous, and the British seldom used reconstructions to supplement their newsreels, unlike the Germans and the Soviets.**
*(IWM B6017)*

*Left.*
**Posed photographs showing a falsely relaxed crew before combat, like the one here of a Churchill, were quite numerous on both sides, since they were there to reassure the families at home. The BBC or Army reporters seldom caught on film the moments of fear, feverishness and anguish preceding an attack.**
*(Tank Museum 4834/E4)*

*Right.* **Here is Sergeant Dring, on the left, posing on 30 June near Rauray with his crew on their Sherman named "Akilla". These men were said to have knocked-out two Tigers, a Panther and a Panzer IV in a single day: if it is true, it was a real exploit, which is in contradiction with the rule of *"five Shermans lost for every Panzer destroyed"*!** *(IWM B6222)*

The advantage of tank men over infantrymen was that they could busy their hands and brain with many essential tasks before the fighting. Four members of the *"Briton"* crew (34th Tk.Brig.) are gathered on their Churchill; Lieutenant Fathergill, the tank commander, is exposing the details of the next attack. Note the fine camouflage net enveloping the turret, to conceal its silhouette and fasten some foliage. *(RR)*

## Bale out!

The pattern of a fight in a Sherman, a Cromwell, a Stuart or a Churchill was unfortunately often the same: an attack or a reconnaissance had been decided, the Troop's tanks got organised, and then progressed towards the enemy lines, taking advantage of cover... On lucky days, the crew strafed machine-gun nests for the infantry, found a camouflaged antitank gun and shot some high-explosive shells at it, even managed to hit a Panzer IV or an SPG which had just fired on another tank, and succeeded in pulling back to its positions. Unlucky days were numerous, alas, when the tank was suddenly hit by an 88, which killed one or another of the crew members, and obliged them to leave the tank in emergency when someone shouted "Bale out!"

Fearing the regrettable tendency of their tank to catch fire (especially the Sherman, and the Cromwell to a lesser extent), the crews did not hesitate to bale out from their mount as fast as possible once it had been touched... even if they had to climb in again in the case of a false alarm!

Nonetheless, some were reluctant to leave their tank before it was inevitable: a Churchill from N°3 Squadron, 4th Grenadier Guards (6th Guards Tk.Brig.), commanded by Lance Sergeant Davies, bogged down on 3 August during Operation *Bluecoat*. Despite the water reaching the turret, and the enemy trying to open the hatches and sabotage the engine, the crew remained in the tank the whole night, shooting a shell or firing the Besa now and then, before being freed at dawn by the Royal Scots Fusiliers infantry. Moreover, for

A damaged and captured Tiger I has been photographed
on 27 June between Bretteville-l'Orgueilleuse
and Fontenay-le-Pesnel. The wartime caption states
that it had been knocked out by the crew of Sergeant Dring,
from A Squadron, Sherwood Rangers (8th Arm.Brig.),
but the sSS-PzAbt. 101, the only heavy tank unit in the sector,
reported that the Tiger lost on that day had been destroyed
by antitank guns: who is right? (see also previous page)
*(IWM B6047)*

## Tiger, the "*bête noire*"

If its mechanical reliability was never questioned, the crews had
very little confidence in their equipment, particularly in combat.
Repeated traumatic experiences of the losses or of the vision of
tanks exploding or brewing up caused a real psychosis, illustrated
by the terror inspired by the Panther, and above all the 88 gun
(PaK 43/44 or FlaK 18/36/37) and the Tiger: the crews saw them
everywhere as soon as they were under enemy fire, even though
there were perhaps only 75-mm self-propelled or towed antitank
guns, or Panzer IVs, which were nevertheless powerful enough
to cope successfully with Shermans and Cromwells. Thus, during
Operation *Charnwood*, the war diaries stated that the enemy front
was defended by dug-in Tigers: wartime photographs are here to
prove that they were Panzer IVs from Panzer-Regiment 22.

Despite the terror they inspired, the German heavy tanks were
far from being invincible, but overcoming them required boldness,
tenacity and skill, and often a bit of help from fate... Here are
some examples which turned to the British advantage, even if the

most of the men, baling-out was  only conceivable if the whole
crew could make it: on 9 June, whil supporting an infantry attack
at Cambes, the Sherman of Lieutenant Brooke, from A Squadron,
East Riding Yeomanry, was hit and its commander was killed.

Corporal Fellows, the driver, remained at the controls and continued to move backwards until the tank began to burn, then dragged
the wounded crew members out one after the other, and finally
brought them to safety at the rear: he was awarded the Military Me-
dal for this heroic feat, which was far from being an isolated case.

results were unfortunately most often in favour of the Germans. On 14 June, Lieutenant Walker was commanding Troop 5 from B Squadron, 1st RTR (7th Arm.Div.), in protection of 1/6th Queens near Amaye-sur-Seulles. He detected the muzzle brake of an enemy tank along a hedgerow, and sent an armour piercing shot at turret level with his Cromwell's 75-mm gun, while the tank of Sergeant White did the same. A third shot hit, but the tank continued to advance in the open, and Walker recognized the running gear with large interleaved wheels of a Tiger or Panther. The three Cromwells of the Troop kept on shooting, without stopping the Panzer, but the latter's crew baled out and found shelter in the hedgerow. As Troop 5 had no Firefly, Walker asked for one from another Troop: the Firefly fired three 17 pounder shots, and managed to stop the tank. Another Panzer appeared that Walker and White repelled with 75-mm fire: it would be soon after destroyed by C Squadron. The Lieutenant came back later to fire five 75-mm and three 17 pounder shots on the first Panzer, which still refused to catch fire! The tank was however left as destroyed. The only Tigers in this sector belonged to sSS-PzAbt. 501, which reported no loss on 14 June (the four losses on the 15th were due to bombardments). It is thus probable that the Panzers knocked-out by the 1st RTR were Panthers, maybe from 2.Pz.Div.

In a different style, Major Semken, commanding A Squadron from Sherwood Rangers Yeomanry (8th Arm.Brig.), emerged the winner of his encounter with a Tiger I on 26 June, during Operation *Epsom*: moving round a house corner in the main street of Fontenay, his tank found itself face to face with a Tiger, only 50m away. Before the Panzer could change position, the Sherman's gunner fired six 75-mm shots in a row, and one hit the turret ring, causing the crew to bale out: the Tiger was captured almost intact. Nevertheless, the victory went not to a tank crew but to an infantry unit: Company A from 5th Duke of Cornwall's Light Infantry, actually supported by B Squadron, 4/7th Dragoon Guards, entered Le Plessis Grimoult on 7 August, during the attack against Mont Pinçon. The infantrymen saw two Tiger IIs surrounded with vehicles supplying them with ammunition. Since the company had no more PIAT, Major Parker ordered all the available weapons to be fired, including the 2 inch mortars. Either by falling directly through the commander's hatch or in making the nearby truck explode, a mortar bomb destroyed one of the Tiger IIs, the ammunition of which blew up and dislodged the turret from its ring: one of the rare last models of Tiger had been knocked-out, and would be visited by all the troops in the vicinity.

Since the British saw Tigers and Panthers everywhere, they reported having destroyed many: the claims appearing in the war diaries are thus to be considered with caution, especially in the early campaign, when there were many identification mistakes (several reports state that 88-mm Ferdinand SPGs were present, but these vehicles never fought on the Normandy front). However, when the British were in control of the ground, the enemy knocked-out AFVs

**The famous Tiger II (early production model with Porsche turret) from sPzAbt.503, which has been destroyed by a 2 inch mortar of 5th Duke of Cornwall's Light Infantry, on 7 August in Le Plessis Grimoult, is examined by helmeted British tank men. The inner explosion has dislodged the turret from its ring, and the driver's hatch has been torn apart. (RR)**

# Dangerous "Friends"

The tactical air support, one of the reasons of the success of the Normandy campaign, was not trouble-free: I have already mentioned the problem of bombarding by strategic heavy bombers, the precision of which left a lot to be desired.

But the British armoured units had at their disposal a much more efficient direct support, provided by the Typhoons of 2nd Tactical Air Force. A peculiar tactic, called the Cab Rank, was developed to provide immediate support on request for the ground forces: a group of rocket-equipped fighter-bombers, usually four, circled above a definite area, waiting for a call. A Forward Observation Officer belonging to the RAF was posted in a tank moving up with the armoured units. When strong opposition was met, he was radioed the codename *Limejuice*, and was then able to pass on the exact map location of the target to the nearest aircraft. The intervention of Typhoons with rockets and 20-mm guns did not knock out as many Panzers as is often believed, but the psychological effect was crucial and most often caused the Germans to withdraw.

Unfortunately, when the front became more fluid from early August onwards, the shooting mistakes became more and more frequent. On the one hand, units were often entangled and difficult to make out, and on the other hand, the signals and markings (flares, smoke shells or grenades, bright-coloured panels) proved insufficient. The cases of Friendly Fire increased from 18 August onwards, at the end of *Bluecoat*, since the Spitfire Squadrons which were used as pure fighters before were now directed against ground targets, and their pilots were less experienced in ground identification.

Moreover, the British were fighting on the boundary with the American sector, and the pilots of Lightning and Thunderbolt pilots turned out to be quite trigger-happy...

Thus, on 20 August, the East Riding Yeomanry heading towards Lisieux, and particularly the 152nd Inf.Brig. they were supporting, were attacked by Lightnings despite the splendid and cloudless weather: the tank crews were little affected, but several members of the infantry brigade staff were killed.

should have been easier to count, but combat reports often referred only to the tank commanders' observations: one declared he had shot at a Tiger, another said he had destroyed one, still another one had noticed the presence of a Panther wreck, and despite this information, it could have been one and the same tank.

But as opposed to a certain habit en vogue with some authors, it is not possible to trust the German war diaries to determine the respective losses either: if the British exaggerated their results, they reported their losses quite exactly, unlike the Germans. It happened that exacerbated pride sometimes led a German crew to declare having self-destroyed its Tiger, even though the tank had been hit several times, the tracks were broken, the turret did not rotate anymore, the gun could not fire, and the engine had broken down! Talking about self-destruction in these circumstances was excessive, to say the least!

The British actually made a very accurate and subtle nuance between a destroyed tank, and a knocked-out tank, the latter rather meaning "out of action": and those they thought to be out of action sometimes went on fighting again, after recovery and repair. In the same way, photographs show the obvious destruction of German tanks, although the war diaries of the corresponding units did not mention their loss, or reported it only later. It is actually fully understandable, owing to the fighting conditions in Normandy, that the war diary was not a priority for the German officers who were responsible for drafting it.

**One of the most dangerous adversaries of the Allied tanks, and the parade improvised by the British: on the Argentan – Falaise road, on 22 August, a Panther Ausf.G abandoned in the middle of the causeway is bypassed by a Firefly Ic (see the 17 pounder muzzle brake, and the angular and cut-out rear of the hull of a Sherman M4) from an unidentified unit.** *(RR)*

# Markings, insignia and code numbers

Guards Armoured
Division, 2nd Grenadier Guards
« B » Squadron

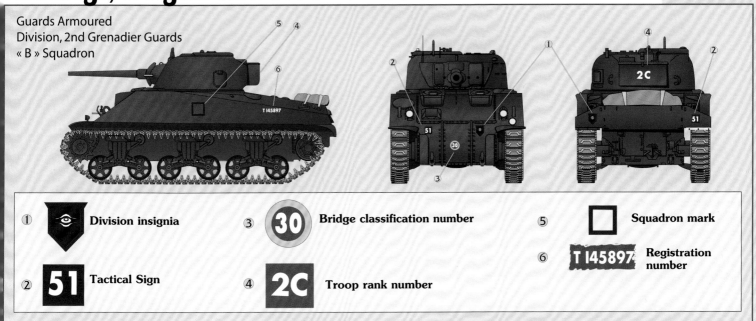

| | | | | |
|---|---|---|---|---|
| ① ◆ **Division insignia** | ③ **30** **Bridge classification number** | ⑤ ☐ **Squadron mark** | | |
| ② **51** **Tactical Sign** | ④ **2C** **Troop rank number** | ⑥ T 145897 **Registration number** | | |

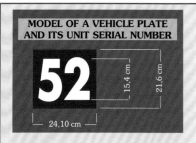

**MODEL OF A VEHICLE PLATE AND ITS UNIT SERIAL NUMBER**

**52**

15,4 cm
21,6 cm
24,10 cm

1.

Army Troops
2nd British Army,
1st Canadian Army

Great Headquarters,
Garrison and Area Troops

Army Group Troops
21st Army Group

Corps Troops

**UNIT SERIAL NUMBERS**

The position of the white stripe indicated that the unit belonged to a higher command than the division

**156** 107th RAC
34th Tank
Brigade

Example 1.

**THE MAIN TYPES OF IDENTIFICATION STARS**

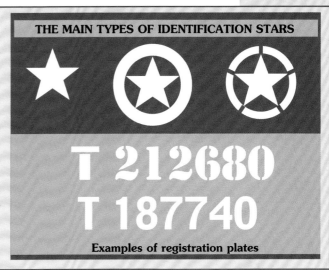

**T 212680**

**T 187740**

Examples of registration plates

**BRITISH ARMOURED DIVISION SQUADRON MARKINGS**

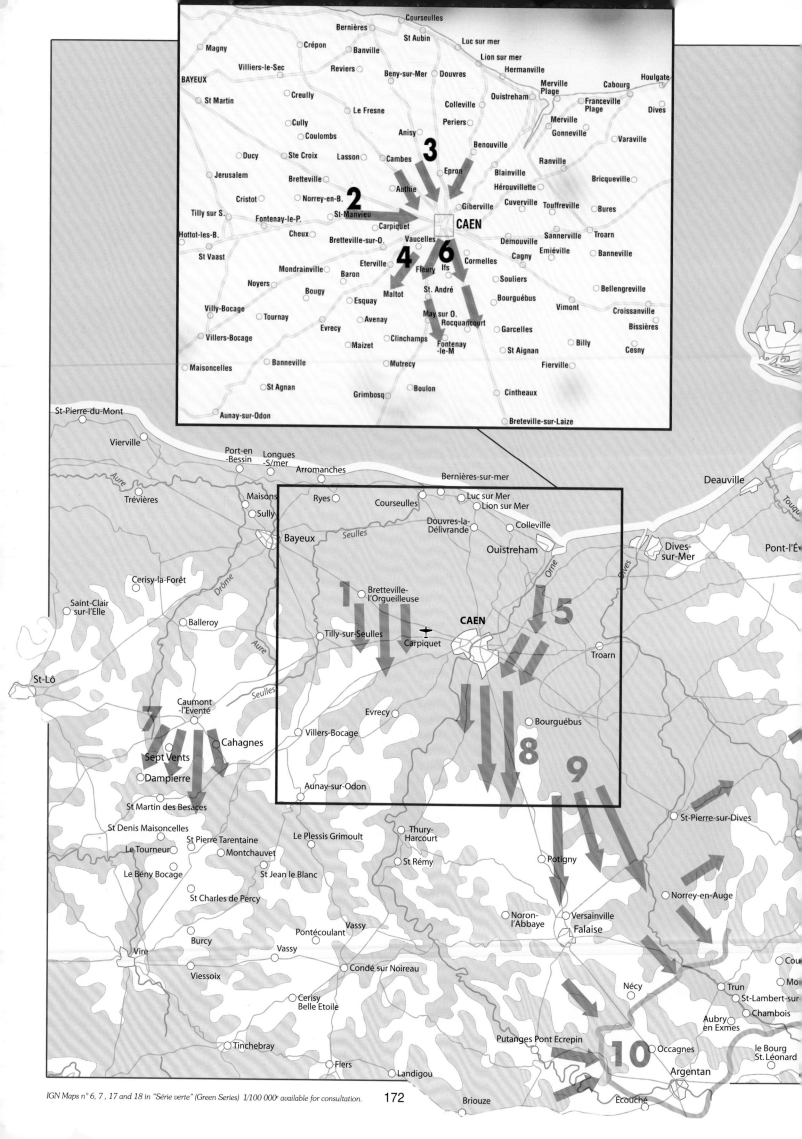

**Inset map (top):**

Courseulles
Bernières
St Aubin
Luc sur mer
Magny
Crépon
Banville
Lion sur mer
Villiers-le-Sec
Reviers
Beny-sur-Mer
Douvres
Hermanville
Merville Plage
Cabourg
Houlgate
BAYEUX
St Martin
Creully
Le Fresne
Colleville
Ouistreham
Merville
Franceville Plage
Dives
Cully
Periers
Gonneville
Varaville
Coulombs
Anisy
Benouville
Ducy
Ste Croix
Lasson
Cambes
**3**
Ranville
Bricqueville
Jerusalem
Bretteville
Norrey-en-B.
Authie
Epron
Blainville
Hérouvillette
Touffreville
Bures
Cristot
**2**
St-Manvieu
Giberville
Cuverville
Tilly sur S.
Fontenay-le-P.
CAEN
Sannerville
Troarn
Hottot-les-B.
Cheux
Bretteville-sur-O.
Vaucelles
Demouville
Banneville
St Vaast
Eterville
**4**
Fleury
**6** Ifs
Cormelles
Cagny
Emiéville
Mondrainville
Baron
St. André
Souliers
Bellengreville
Noyers
Bougy
Esquay
Avenay
May sur O.
Rocquancourt
Bourguébus
Vimont
Croissanville
Villy-Bocage
Tournay
Evrecy
Clinchamps
Garcelles
Bissières
Villers-Bocage
Maizet
Mutrecy
Fontenay-le-M
St Aignan
Billy
Cesny
Maisoncelles
Banneville
St Agnan
Grimbosq
Boulon
Cintheaux
Fierville
Aunay-sur-Odon
Breteville-sur-Laize

**Main map:**

St-Pierre-du-Mont
Vierville
Port-en-Bessin
Longues-S/mer
Arromanches
Bernières-sur-mer
Deauville
Trévières
Maisons
Ryes
Courseulles
Luc sur Mer
Lion sur Mer
Sully
Douvres-la-Délivrande
Colleville
Dives-sur-Mer
Pont-l'É
Bayeux
Seulles
Ouistreham
Cerisy-la-Forêt
**1**
Bretteville-l'Orgueilleuse
CAEN
**5**
Saint-Clair sur-l'Elle
Balleroy
Drôme
Tilly-sur-Seulles
Carpiquet
Troarn
St-Lô
Aure
Seulles
Evrecy
Bourguébus
Caumont-l'Eventé
**8**
**9**
St-Pierre-sur-Dives
**7**
Cahagnes
Villers-Bocage
Sept Vents
Aunay-sur-Odon
Dampierre
St Martin des Besaces
St Denis Maisoncelles
Le Plessis Grimoult
Thury-Harcourt
Norrey-en-Auge
Le Tourneur
St Pierre Tarentaine
Montchauvet
St Rémy
Le Bény Bocage
St Jean le Blanc
Potigny
Versainville
St Charles de Percy
Noron-l'Abbaye
Falaise
Vassy
Pontécoulant
Burcy
Vassy
Nécy
Trun
St-Lambert-sur
Viré
Viessoix
Condé sur Noireau
Putanges Pont Ecrepin
**10**
Occagnes
Aubry en Exmes
Chambois
Cerisy Belle Etoile
le Bourg St. Léonard
Tinchebray
Flers
Landigou
Argentan
Briouze
Ecouché

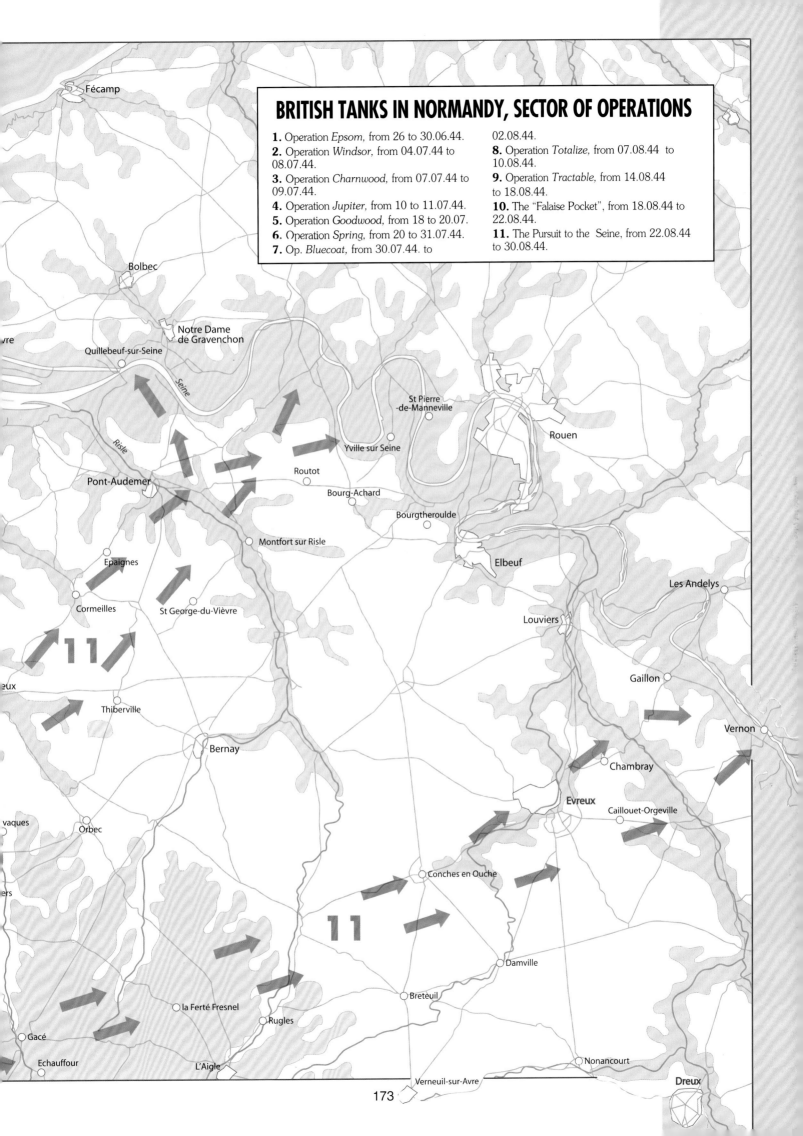

# BRITISH TANKS IN NORMANDY, SECTOR OF OPERATIONS

**1.** Operation *Epsom,* from 26 to 30.06.44.
**2.** Operation *Windsor,* from 04.07.44 to 08.07.44.
**3.** Operation *Charnwood,* from 07.07.44 to 09.07.44.
**4.** Operation *Jupiter,* from 10 to 11.07.44.
**5.** Operation *Goodwood,* from 18 to 20.07.
**6.** Operation *Spring,* from 20 to 31.07.44.
**7.** Op. *Bluecoat,* from 30.07.44. to 02.08.44.
**8.** Operation *Totalize,* from 07.08.44 to 10.08.44.
**9.** Operation *Tractable,* from 14.08.44 to 18.08.44.
**10.** The "Falaise Pocket", from 18.08.44 to 22.08.44.
**11.** The Pursuit to the Seine, from 22.08.44 to 30.08.44.

# Bibliography

**ANONYME** — Taurus Pursuant, a History of 11th Armoured Division *(1945)*

**ANONYME** — The Story of 79th Armoured Division *(1945)*

**BAKER** Anthony — The genealogy of the Regiments of the British Army vol.1 (The Guards and Infantry),
— The genealogy of the Regiments of the British Army, vol.2 (The Cavalry)
— The genealogy of the Regiments of the British Army,vol.3 (The Yeomanry)

**BEALE** Peter — Tank Tracks, 9 RTR at War 1940-45.
*Sutton Publishing*

**BENAMOU** Jean-Pierre — Normandie 1944, guide du champ de bataille.
*Heimdal*
— Album mémorial Bataille de Caen
*Heimdal*

**BOSCAWEN** Robert — Armoured Guardsmen
*Pen & Sword Books*

**BOUCHERY** Jean — Le Tommy de la Libération, tomes I et II
*Histoire & Collections*
— Articles in *Militaria Magazine,*
n° 5, 78, 80,82, 93.
*Histoire & Collections*

**BRISSET** Jean — The Charge of the Bull.
*Bates Books*

**BUFFETAUT** Yves — Les blindés alliés en Normandie
*Militaria HS n°2. Histoire & Collections*
— 6 juin 1944, la première vague
*Militaria HS n°12. Histoire & Collections*
— La bataille du bocage
*Militaria HS n°13. Histoire & Collections*
— Opération Goodwood
*Militaria HS n°26. Histoire & Collections*

**CHAPPELL** Mike — British Battle Insignia (2): 1939-45
*Osprey Men-at-Arms n°187*

**CLOSE** Bill, Major — A View from the Turret.
*Dell & Bredon*

**DELAFORCE** Patrick — The Black Bull.
*Alan Sutton Publishing*
— Monty's Marauders, Black Rat & Red Fox
*Tom Donovan Publishing*
— Churchill's Desert Rats.
*Alan Sutton Publishing*
— Churchill's Secret Weapons. *Robert Hale*
— Taming the Panzers, 3 RTR at War.
*Alan Sutton Publishing*

**DELAFORCE** Patrick — Battles with Panzers, 1st & 5 RTR at War
*Alan Sutton Publishing*

**DAGLISH** Ian — Operation Bluecoat - Battleground Europe.
*Pen & Sword*

**DUNPHIE** Christopher & **JOHNSON** Garry — Gold Beach - Battleground Europe,
*Pen & Sword*

**DYSON** Stephen W. — Tank Twins.
*Leo Cooper*

**ELLIS** Chris — The Churchill Tank
*A&AP, Tanks Illustrated n°25*

**ELLIS** L.F. — Victory in the West tome I
*The Battery Press*

**ERSKINE** David — The Scots Guards 1919-1955
*The Naval and Military Press*

**FITZGERALD** Desmond — A History of the Irish Guards in the Second World War.
*The Irish Guards*

**FLETCHER** David — British Tanks of WWII, France & Belgium 1944.
*Concord*
— Cromwell Tank, Vehicle History and Specification
*HMSO*
Churchill Tank, Vehicle History and Specification
*HMSO*
— Vanguard of Victory, the 79th Arm. Div.
*HMSO*
— British Armour in the Second World War: The Great Tank Scandal
— British Armour in WW II: The Universal Tank
*HMSO*
— Mr Churchill's Tank
*Schiffer Military Books*

**FLETCHER** David & **ARSON** David — Crusader Cruiser Tank 1939-1945
*Osprey New Vanguard n°14*

**FORBES** Patrick — 6th Guards Tank Brigade
*Sampson Low, Marston & Co.*

**FORTY** George — British Army Handbook 1939-1945
*Sutton Publishing*
— A Pictorial History, Royal Tank Regt.
*Guild Publishing*

**FUTTER** Geoffrey W. — The Funnies
*Bellona Books*

**HAMMERTON** Ian C. — Achtung Minen!
*The Book Guild*

**HAYWARD** Mark — Sherman Firefly
*Barbarossa Books*

**HILL E.R,** Colonel & The Earl

# Bibliography

of **ROSSE,** Captain — The Story of the Guards Arm. Div. 1941-45
*Geoffrey Bles*

**HODGES** Peter
**& TAYLOR** Michael D. – British Military Markings 1939-1945
*Cannon Publications*

**HUNNICUTT** R.P. — Sherman, a History of the American
Medium Tank
*Presidio Press*
— Stuart, a History of the American Light Tank
*Presidio Press*

**HUNT** Eric — Mont Pinçon – Battleground Europe
*Pen & Sword*

**KEEGAN** John — Churchill's Generals
*Grove Weidenfeld*

**KILVERT-JONES** Tim — Sword Beach - Battleground Europe
*Pen & Sword*

**MACE** Paul — Forrard, the Story of the East Riding Yeomanry
*Pen & Sword*

**MACKSEY** Kenneth — Armoured Crusader
*Grub Street*

**MCKEE** Alexander — Caen, Anvil of Victory
*Pan Books*

**G. BERNAGE** — Album Mémorial Normandie
*Heimdal*
— Album Mémorial Overlord
*Heimdal*
— Album Mémorial Bataille de Normandie
*Heimdal*

**PERRETT** Bryan
**& CHAPPELL** Mike — The Churchill Tank
Osprey Vanguard n° 13
— Allied Tank Destroyers
*Osprey Vanguard n° 10*

**SANDARS** John — British Guards Armoured Div. 1941-45
*Osprey Vanguard n°9*

**SANDARS** John,
**ROFFE** Michael
**& CHAPPELL** Mike — The Sherman Tank in British Service 1942-
45
Osprey Vanguard n°15

**SAUNDERS** Tim — Hill 112 - Battleground Europe,
Pen & Sword

**TAYLOR** Daniel — Villers-Bocage through the Lens
After the Battle

**TOUT** Ken — Tanks, Advance
*Robert Hale*
— To Hell with Tanks
*Robert Hale*

**TOUT** Ken — A Fine Night for Tanks
*Sutton Publishing*
— The Bloody Battle for Tilly
*Sutton Publishing*

**VERNEY** G.L.,Major-General
— The Desert Rats, the 7th Arm. Div. in WW II
*Greenhill Books*

**WHITE** Brian Terence — British Tank Markings and Names
Arms & Armour Press

**WILLIS** Leonard — None Had Lances, the Story of the 24th
Lancers
*24th Lancers Old Comrades Association*

**WILSON** Andrew — Flame-Thrower
*William Kimber*

**WILSON** Edward — Press on Regardless, the Story
of the Fifth Royal Tank Regiment in WWII
*Spellmount*

**WISE** Terence — D-Day to Berlin
*Arms & Armour Press*

**ZALOGA** Steven J.
**& BALIN** George — D-Day Tank Warfare
*Concord*

**Tanks Units' War Diaries
in Normandy,**

— WO 171/623
*(27th Arm. Brig. HQ War Diary)*
— WO 171/633
*(31st Tk. Brig. HQ War Diary)*
— WO 171/640
*(33rd Arm.Brig. HQ War Diary)*
— WO 171/643
*(34th Tk.Brig. HQ War Diary)*
— WO 171/845
*(13/18th Hussars War Diary)*
— WO 171/859
*(1st Northamptonshire Yeomanry War Diary)*
— WO 171/862
*(East Riding Yeomanry War Diary)*
— WO 171/868
*(7th RTR War Diary)*
— WO 171/876
*(107th RAC War Diary)*
— WO 171/878
*(144th RAC War Diary)*
— WO 171/879
*(147th RAC War Diary)*
— WO 171/881
*(153rd RAC War Diary)*
**Public Record Office**, London

(IWM 2513)

# Aknowledgements

I am keen to thank Jean-Marie MONGIN (who offered me the opportunity to publish this work), Denis GANDILHON
and Yann-Erwin ROBERT for the care they took in the realization of this book, as well as all the collaborators of *Histoire & Collections* who took part in its making.
My most heartfelt thanks to David FLETCHER, curator of the Tank Museum of Bovington (Great-Britain): his work has made a great contribution to develop my passion for World War II British Armour, and his knowledge, his books, his kindness and his availability have been of invaluable help. Thanks too to the whole staff of the Imperial War Museum in London, and of the Public Record Office, for their professionalism and efficiency.
A great thank you to Jean BOUCHERY, who has established himself as one of the French specialists of the British Army in the Second World War, for his advice and his support.
My sincere thanks to Mr Robert BOSCAWEN, M.C., former Lieutenant of the Guards Armoured Division, for his kindness, his availability and his patience.
Thanks too to Russell HADLER from Barbarossa Books, Derek HAYLES from Military Books, and Gillian from The Military History Bookshop, who allowed me to complete my private library with rare or ancient books which were indispensable for my work.
Thanks at last to Philippe CHARBONNIER, Christophe CAMILOTTE and Raymond GIULIANI for their support and their friendship.
My special thanks to Alan McKAY for his thorough correction of the English edition, and for his patience when I asked him so many questions about the translation.

*(Cover photograph © IWM, insignia photographs © Histoire & Collections and profiles by Nicolas Gohin)*

Supervision and Lay-out by Yann-Erwin Robert, Antoine Poggioli, Jean-Marie Mongin and Denis Gandilhon, © *Histoire & Collections 2012*.

ISBN: 978-2-35250-204-3
Publisher's number: 35250
First Print © *Histoire & Collections 2005*
Second Print © *Histoire & Collections 2012*

a book from
*HISTOIRE & COLLECTIONS*

5, avenue de la République
F-75541 Paris Cedex 11 France
Telephone: +33 (0) 1 40 21 18 20
Fax: +33 (0) 1 47 00 51 11

www.histoireetcollections.com

This book has been designed, typed, laid-out and processed by 'Le studio graphique Armes & Collections' on fully integrated computer equipment.

Printed by
Printworks International Ltd
China in August 2012